The Listener's Companion
Gregg Akkerman, Series Editor

Titles in **The Listener's Companion: A Scarecrow Press Music Series** provide readers with a deeper understanding of key musical genres and the work of major artists and composers. Aimed at nonspecialists, each volume explains in clear and accessible language how to listen to works from particular artists, composers, and genres. Looking at both the context in which the music first appeared and has since been heard, authors explore with readers the environments in which key musical works were written and performed.

Experiencing Stravinsky: A Listener's Companion, by Robin Maconie, 2013
Experiencing Mozart: A Listener's Companion, by David Schroeder, 2013
Experiencing Jazz: A Listener's Companion, by Michael Stephans, 2013
Experiencing Verdi: A Listener's Companion, by Donald Sanders, 2014

EXPERIENCING VERDI

A Listener's Companion

Donald Sanders

THE SCARECROW PRESS, INC.
Lanham • Boulder • New York • Toronto • Plymouth, UK
2014

Published by Scarecrow Press, Inc.
A wholly owned subsidiary of Rowman & Littlefield
4501 Forbes Boulevard, Suite 200, Lanham, Maryland 20706
www.rowman.com

10 Thornbury Road, Plymouth PL6 7PP, United Kingdom

British Library Cataloguing in Publication Information Available

Library of Congress Cataloging-in-Publication Data
Sanders, Donald C., 1949–
Experiencing Verdi : a listener's companion / Donald Sanders.
pages cm. — (The listener's companion)
Includes bibliographical references and index.
ISBN 978-0-8108-8467-0 (cloth : alk. paper) — ISBN 978-0-8108-8468-7 (electronic)
1. Verdi, Giuseppe, 1813–1901—Criticism and interpretation. 2. Verdi, Giuseppe, 1813–1901. Operas. 3. Opera—Italy—19th century. I. Title.
ML410.V4S34 2014
782.1092—dc23
2013034436

Printed in the United States of America

In memory of J. Bunker Clark
Scholar, mentor, friend

CONTENTS

SERIES EDITOR'S FOREWORD

The goal of the *Listener's Companion* series is to give readers a deeper understanding of pivotal musical genres and the creative work of their iconic practitioners. This is accomplished in an inclusive manner that does not require extensive music training or elitist shoulder rubbing. Series contributors recreate specific listening experiences so readers can grasp the influence of historical context on the compositional character and social milieu in which the music emerged. By situating readers in the various environments in which composers generated and audiences listened to the music in question, *Listener's Companion* authors deepen for readers their enjoyment and appreciation of this remarkable art form. Often drawing on their expertise as performers and scholars, contributors expand our understanding of major musical genres and the achievements of artists within those genres, emphasizing throughout music as a *lived* listening experience.

A master of Romantic-era Italian opera, Giuseppe Verdi is one of those rare composers of opera whose name and music is well known and instantly recognizable. His masterful career and unique personal history exemplify and illuminate the challenges to tradition that raged around opera as a musical art form in the late nineteenth century. Under the influence of Verdi's dogged efforts—he lived to the ripe old age of eighty-seven at a time when the average lifespan was less than fifty—Italian opera came into full bloom, setting the benchmark for contemporary opera composition and production.

A rising musician from the village of Busseto, Verdi came face to face with the most terrible of tragedies when, at the age of twenty-seven, he suffered the loss of two children and his first wife. When his wife died during the composition of his second opera, which flopped, Verdi angrily swore never to write music again—a promise he would fortunately break as his considerable gifts as musician burst forth with the composition of some of his greatest operatic works, from *Nabucco* to *Rigoletto* to *Aida*. Seeking to establish his own voice in the wake of his great predecessor Rossini, and often linked by contrast of style to the German music dramas of Wagner, Verdi would compose a body of work that transcended his own century, establishing him as one of the greatest opera composers today.

To some, these achievements more than suffice to justify his eminence. But Verdi was not a reclusive maker of music. He stood as a figurehead within Italian politics, throwing his support behind the reunification movement of his homeland. For other composers, such activism would offer little recompense and, if anything, induce a chilling effect on their careers. Not so for Verdi, whose involvement at so substantial a level sets him apart from his contemporaries.

Given such singular accomplishments in the musical and social achievements of the Romantic era, an accurate and worthy *Listener's Companion* contribution on Giuseppe Verdi requires an exceptional author, performer, and scholar. Dr. Donald Sanders, professor of music at Samford University, rises to the challenge of making Verdi's music understandable to and appreciable by those unfamiliar with it and even those who know it well. In *Experiencing Verdi: A Listener's Companion*, Sanders deftly combines his background as an established scholar of Italian music with his own insights as a performer as he guides the listener through Verdi's greatest works.

Gregg Akkerman
Series Editor

INTRODUCTION

During his last years Giuseppe Verdi was generally recognized as the greatest living opera composer. More than a century later, his stature continues to grow. At least ten of his twenty-six operas are central works of the modern repertoire. In his remarkably long and rich career his art continued to evolve and mature even into his eightieth year. Of the composers whose reputation is almost entirely based on opera or music drama only he and his contemporary Richard Wagner are mentioned alongside the masters of symphonic, keyboard, and chamber music.

In addition to his musical achievements Verdi was both a philanthropist and a patriot. Rare is the Italian city without a street, square, theatre, or institution that bears his name.

Verdi's long life began shortly after the defeated Napoleon Bonaparte had lost control of the Italian peninsula, soon to be replaced in the north by Austrian occupiers. He lived through the long, often frustrating struggle for independence that was known as the *Risorgimento*. Eventually he played a role in the foundation of the Kingdom of Italy in 1861 and witnessed the realization of the dream of unification when Italian troops entered Rome in 1870. In European musical history his life encompassed an era that extended from the late works of Beethoven to Debussy's *Prelude to the Afternoon of a Faun* and Schönberg's *Transfigured Night*.

The popular image of Verdi is that of a noble and heroic figure. As with many great artists, however, his character was complex and often contradictory. He could be stubborn and irascible, particularly concerning the performance of his works. He often harassed his librettists, singers, and instrumentalists in order to achieve his artistic vision.

Having grown up relatively poor, he became a shrewd and sometimes uncompromising businessman whose dealings with publishers and impresarios were sometimes adversarial. Despite his artistic idealism he was obsessively aware of each of his works' financial potential.

Regardless of his human frailties, Verdi was a man of unassailable principle. Despite his innate frugality, his was a generous spirit, and he continually came to the aid of friends and colleagues who were in difficulty. In his later years he also became a major public philanthropist, most notably by building and endowing the Casa di Riposo, a retirement home for destitute musicians in Milan.

Verdi's reputation as one of the fathers of the modern Italian state is perhaps disproportionate to his actual contributions. During much of the early phase of the Risorgimento he was consumed with composing and preparing the performances of at least one opera per year in the period he called his "years in the galleys." But later he gave freely of his time to serve in the Senate of the newly formed Italian kingdom, and there is no doubt that his "Risorgimento operas" from the 1840s, with their patriotic overtones, provided inspiration to the movement.

This guide provides a biography of Verdi that includes historical background for all of his twenty-six operas. In addition, twelve of the most popular and significant of them and the Manzoni Requiem are analyzed in detail. Each of these thirteen works is listed beneath the title of the chapter in which it is discussed.

Every effort has been made to avoid technical musical terminology. Terms that might be unfamiliar to the musical amateur are defined briefly in the glossary. Each item included in the glossary is printed in bold type the first time it appears in a chapter.

Verdi scholarship has flourished in recent years, and the available literature is both broad and deep. The works in the selected reading section offer an understanding of Verdi's life in relation to the changing musical and political scene in Italy and Europe during the better part of a century and enhance the pleasure of experiencing his magnificent music.

The selected listening section offers a chronological list of Verdi's major works with suggested audio and video recordings for each. The intent was to provide a mixture of distinguished recent performances with classic ones that feature notable singers and conductors of the past who were important exponents of Verdi's music.

TIMELINE

Year	Verdi's Life	Other Events
1813	Born in Le Roncole	Richard Wagner born
1814		Napoleon abdicates and is exiled
1815		Napoleon defeated at Waterloo
		Lombardy and Veneto ceded to Austria
1816		Rossini, *Barber of Seville*
1821		Napoleon dies
1822	Moves to Busseto	
1825	Begins study with Ferdinando Provesi	Manzoni, *I promessi sposi* (1825–1827)
1827		Beethoven dies
1828		Schubert dies
1829		Rossini, *William Tell*
1831	Moves to home of Antonio Barezzi	Bellini, *Norma*
1832	Denied admission to Milan Conservatory	

1835		Donizetti, *Lucia di Lammermoor*
		Bellini dies
1836	Marries Margherita Barezzi	Meyerbeer, *Les Huguenots*
	Becomes municipal music master in Busseto	
1837	Birth of daughter Virginia	
1838	Publishes *Six Romances* for voice and piano	
	Birth of son Icilio Romano	
	Virginia dies	
	Resigns from Busseto position	
1839	Moves to Milan	
	Icilio Romano dies	
	Oberto premieres at La Scala, Milan	
1840	Margherita dies	
	Un giorno di regno premieres at La Scala	
1842	*Nabucco* premieres at La Scala	Arrigo Boito born
1843		Wagner, *The Flying Dutchman*
1847	*Macbeth* premieres at La Pergola, Florence	*Il Risorgimento* journal founded
	Lives in Paris with Giuseppina Strepponi	
	Jérusalem premiers at Opéra, Paris	
1848	Buys Sant'Agata estate	Cinque Giornate uprising
		Austrians leave Milan
		Donizetti dies

1849	Moves to Busseto with Strepponi	Rome declared a republic
	Luisa Miller premieres at San Carlo, Naples	Garibaldi's troops enter Rome
		France restores pope in Rome
1851	*Rigoletto* premieres at La Fenice, Venice	
1853	*Il trovatore* premieres at Teatro Apollo, Rome	
	La traviata premieres at La Fenice	
1855		Piedmont enters Crimean War
1858		Attempt on life of Napoleon III
		Giacomo Puccini born
1859	*Un ballo in maschera* premieres at Rome	Austria invades Piedmont
	Marries Giuseppina Strepponi	Darwin, *The Origin of Species*
	Elected representative to Parma assembly	
1861	Attends opening of Italian Parliament	Kingdom of Italy founded
1862	*La forza del destino* premieres at Saint Petersburg	
1863		Pietro Mascagni born
		Boito reads "Ode to Italian Art"
1865	Revised *Macbeth* premieres at Paris	Wagner, *Tristan and Isolde*
1866		Veneto transferred to Italy

1867	Carlo Verdi and Antonio Barezzi die	Toscanini born
	Don Carlos premieres at Opéra, Paris	
1868		Rossini dies
		Boito, *Mefistofele*
1869		Tolstoy, *War and Peace*
1870		Rome becomes capital of Italy
		Franco-Prussian War
1871	Attends Wagner's *Lohengrin* at Bologna	
	Aida premieres at Cairo	
1872	European premiere of *Aida* at La Scala	
1873		Manzoni dies
1874	*Requiem* premieres at church of San Marco, Milan	
1875	Conducts *Requiem* at Paris, London, and Vienna	
1876		Bell invents telephone
1877		Edison invents phonograph
1879	Agrees to work with Boito on *Otello*	
1882		Stravinsky born
1883		Wagner dies
1884	Revised, Italian *Don Carlo* premieres at La Scala	
1887	*Otello* premieres at La Scala	
1890		Mascagni, *Cavalleria rusticana*

1892		Leoncavallo, *Pagliacci*
		Debussy, *Prelude to the Afternoon of a Faun*
1893	*Falstaff* premieres at La Scala	Puccini, *Manon Lescaut*
1896		Puccini, *La Bohème*
1897	Giuseppina Strepponi dies	Brahms dies
1898	*Quattro pezzi sacri* published	
1899	Foundation of Casa di Riposo	
1900		Puccini, *Tosca*
1901	Dies at Grand Hotel, Milan	

I

ITALIAN OPERA BEFORE VERDI

The use of music in dramatic productions was probably a feature of Greek theater from at least the fifth century BCE. It was interest on the part of Renaissance humanists in classical drama, poetry, and philosophy that led to the birth of opera in late sixteenth-century Florence. Beginning in the 1580s, members of the wealthy and urbane intellectual circle around the Medici court, known historically as the Camerata, began to discuss the possibility of authentically recreating classical Greek theater by using music. They envisioned a simple style of musical recitation that would enhance the narrative without competing with it or making the words unintelligible.

Their theories became reality in the late 1590s when two gifted singer-composers, Jacopo Peri (1561–1633) and Giulio Caccini (1551–1618), began to set poetry to music in a style they referred to as monody (*monodia*). This was solo song with freely structured rhythm that imitated the natural flow of speech. It was accompanied by **basso continuo**, another new practice in which the composer wrote a bass line under the vocal part with numbers underneath the notes that implied chords to be played on a lute or keyboard instrument. Basso continuo came to be used for virtually all vocal and instrumental music throughout the seventeenth century and for much of the eighteenth. It was emblematic of the new concept of melody accompanied by chords (**homophony**) that was replacing the Renaissance paradigm, which was based on the convergence of several independent melodic lines (**counterpoint**). Although the old contrapuntal style continued to appear in church music and in various instrumental genres, homophony was to remain the predominant musical language of Italian opera.

Monody was the perfect vehicle for musical recitation and made it feasible for an entire dramatic work to be sung. This "reciting style" (*stile recitando*), the immediate ancestor of what came to be called **recitative** (*recitativo*) in later opera, had precedents in earlier musical practice. Much of the chant repertoire in the liturgy of the church was similarly flexible in rhythm. Beginning in the fifteenth century the improvised singing of poetry with the accompaniment of a lute or other string instrument had become popular in northern Italian courts. Also, in the second half of the sixteenth century numerous composers of **madrigals**, the courtly art songs of Renaissance Italy, had turned away from strict, complex contrapuntal settings toward a simpler, more chordal, speech-like style.

In about 1594 Peri collaborated with the poet Ottavio Rinuccini to produce *Dafne*, based on the myth of Daphne and Apollo. Performed in Florence in 1597, it is generally recognized to be the earliest opera. Because Apollo was associated with music and with intellectual pursuits, this was a particularly appropriate subject for musical drama conceived for Florentine nobility. In addition, the divinity of the two main characters gave some dramatic plausibility to the fact that they sang their dialogue. For the theorists and poets of early opera, it was considered feasible for both gods and heroes to sing.

Shortly after the performance of *Dafne*, Peri and Rinuccini were called upon to provide a similar entertainment for the celebration of the wedding of Marie de' Medici, daughter of the grand duke of Tuscany, and King Henry IV of France, which was to occur in Florence in October of 1600. They chose the Greek myth of the musician Orpheus and his bride Eurydice, taking her name as the title. The story, whose central message is the persuasive power of music like that of Daphne and Apollo, provided a fitting theme for musical theater.

In Peri's preface to the printed score, he explained his intention in *Euridice*.

> Having seen that dramatic poetry was being utilized and that it was therefore necessary to imitate speech in song, (and undoubtedly no one ever spoke by singing), I considered that the ancient Greeks and Romans, who in the opinion of many, sang their tragedies throughout on the stage had used a harmony surpassing that of ordinary

speech but falling so far below the melody of song so as to take an intermediate form.

What the composer was describing was a musical substitute for speech that was a virtually perfect manifestation of the theories of the Camerata. On the stage it depended upon the convention that the characters themselves would have heard the monody as speech and not as singing.

Even in this nascent stage Peri faced what was to become the principal dilemma for the opera composer for centuries: the intrinsic tension between the speech-like freedom of the recitative as he had described it and the more regularly metered, more melodic, and, consequently, more musically appealing passages that came to be called **arias**. Rinuccini's libretto made this dichotomy virtually inevitable, with most of the dialogue in lines of irregular length, but with soliloquies and passages of implied song set in regularly metered poetry. As the most prominent proponent and one of the inventors of the new musical recitation, Peri scrupulously avoided jarring contrast between the two styles. His "arias" are simple and almost free from the highly ornamented vocal display that became typical of later opera. Most of the music in *Euridice* perfectly exemplifies the "intermediate form" to which he refers in the preface.

Present at the wedding festivities in Florence was Vincenzo Gonzaga (1562–1612), the pleasure-loving duke of Mantua, whose wife was the bride's sister. He was accompanied by the brilliant Mantuan nobleman and court functionary Alessandro Striggio (ca. 1573–1630). There has long been conjecture that his chief court musician (*maestro di cappella*), Claudio Monteverdi (1567–1643), was also at the wedding, but there is no documentation of his presence.

Six years later, however, Duke Vincenzo's son Francesco, who was president of the prestigious group of Mantuan aristocrats known as the Accademia degli Invaghiti (Academy of the Infatuated Ones), arranged for a new work, *La favola d'Orfeo* (*The Fable of Orpheus*), based on the same myth as *Euridice*, to be performed for the group's members during Carnival in February 1607. This *favola in musica* was another adaptation of the Orpheus and Eurydice myth, with text by Striggio, who as a nobleman was a member of the academy, and music by Monteverdi, who was not. The first performance took place in Mantua on February 24, 1607.

Monteverdi, who had been employed at the Gonzaga court since about 1590, had established himself as the leading madrigal composer of the day. He was recognized for his dramatic use of **chromaticism** (pitches outside the prevailing key) and rich and sometimes unorthodox harmonies to enhance the meaning of a text.

Monteverdi had no misgivings about utilizing all the vocal and instrumental resources at his command and he drew inspiration from all of the prevailing genres of the day: the madrigal, the lavish musical pageant known as the *intermedio*, and, naturally, the monodic style of Peri. Unlike *Euridice*, which had been accompanied by a small string ensemble, *Orfeo* called for an orchestra of more than forty instruments of all kinds. Passages of dialogue were interspersed with orchestral interludes, dances, and choruses in the style of the madrigal.

As the greatest musician of Greek mythology, it was natural and dramatically justifiable that Orpheus not only should sing, but indeed should perform lavishly embellished arias. "Possente spirto" ("Mighty Spirit"), his **virtuosic** entreaty to the boatman Charon to ferry him across the River Styx, is the centerpiece of the entire work and opera's first great aria.

Monteverdi realized that the success of the new genre would hinge upon a complementary relationship between drama and music rather than one in which music was subservient, as envisioned by Mei and Galilei. Thus, he moved slightly away from the theories of the Camerata about musical recitation and also beyond what H. C. Robbins Landon and John Julius Norwich termed "Peri's elegantly monotonous music."[1]

When the extravagant Duke Vincenzo died in 1612, at the age of forty-nine, the duchy of Mantua was in serious debt and Francesco, the new duke, was forced to drastically reduce the size of the court. One of the casualties was Monteverdi, who had been in the employ of the Gonzagas for twenty-two years. The following year he was appointed *maestro di cappella* at the basilica of San Marco in Venice where, among others, Andrea Gabrieli (ca. 1532–1585) and his nephew Giovanni (ca. 1555–1612) had composed church music for various combinations of choirs, soloists, and instruments that was famous throughout much of Europe. In addition to providing new liturgical music for San Marco, Monteverdi eventually composed three operas for Venice.

Despite its wealth and the brilliance of its visual art and church music, Venice had not become a center of opera production by the time Monteverdi arrived there in 1613. But in 1637 the city's musical life and the history of opera changed drastically when the Teatro San Cassiano opened as the first theater designed for that purpose. Until then opera had been performed in the palaces of nobility like the Medicis and Gonzagas.

The immediate success of San Cassiano prompted the opening of three more opera houses in Venice within five years. Not surprisingly, the Venetians, who existed in a visual environment that resembled a stage set and who celebrated every conceivable event with pageantry, were quickly drawn to opera. The change of venue from princely palaces and learned academies to one in which paying subscribers financed the productions precipitated a shift away from the high classical ideals of the Florentine intellectuals who had brought about the birth of the genre to decidedly more popular tastes. The style and structure of Venetian opera that began to evolve in the middle of the seventeenth century was to remain the standard in Italy until the time of Verdi.

For the new paying public, librettists, composers, and impresarios began to introduce more visual spectacle to their productions. They also began to shift the emphasis away from the drama and toward the music. Early Florentine and Mantuan opera had been dominated by recitative with aria interspersed, but that was now reversed. This adjustment was made for two reasons. The paying audiences were better entertained by the tunefulness and rhythmic vitality of arias than by the more static extended passages of recitative. Also, because impresarios faced the need to produce a profit, orchestras were reduced in size and chorus became more rare, thus producing a musical theater that came to be dominated by star soloists.

In order to exploit the abilities of virtuoso singers, elaborate arias proliferated and began to take on set forms that further distanced them from the free-flowing recitative. The most common of these was the three-part aria in which both music and text of the first section were repeated after the second. This simple structure can be represented as ABA or ABA' when the repeat of A is varied musically. During the latter decades of the seventeenth century, arias in ternary form rapidly came to dominate Venetian opera. Such an emphasis on musically satisfying form represented a continuing shift away from the original Florentine ideal of the singing of text as a form of enhanced speech.

In another concession to the taste of the new operatic public, irrelevant comic scenes, often involving stock characters, began to appear in Venetian operas. The comic figures were often based on those of the improvised theater known as *commedia dell'arte* that had been popular in Italy since the sixteenth century. These included the aged, wealthy merchant; the pedantic *dottore* (a doctor, medical or otherwise); and various wily servants.

Venice maintained her position as a vibrant center of the composition and performance of opera well into the nineteenth century, and Venetian works were performed in many parts of northern Europe. But by the end of the seventeenth century her preeminence was challenged by the southern port city of Naples. As a part of the Spanish empire since the early sixteenth century, Naples had suffered politically and financially, but had flourished artistically. Her four conservatories produced some of Italy's finest singers and the city's first opera house, the Teatro di San Bartolomeo, opened in 1654, producing mainly Venetian opera.

By the last decades of the century Naples had established a native operatic tradition. The extremely prolific Alessandro Scarlatti (1660–1725) and his successors emphasized the musical appeal of the aria. The three-part structure became standardized into the **da capo aria**, in which an extended section (A) was followed by a shorter, contrasting one (B), usually in another key, at the end of which the words *da capo* (from the beginning) indicated a repeat of section A. This plan saved time and labor for the composer and allowed a virtuoso singer to improvise elaborate embellishments for the repeated section. The symmetry of the da capo aria was musically satisfying, but such repetition of text was dramatically unnatural. Its popularity represented an almost total shift away from the ideals of opera's creators.

As arias became more numerous and stereotyped, the role of the recitative also changed. The expressive, semimelodic monody of Peri and Monteverdi evolved into a rapid, conversational style with many repeated notes that allowed the singers to move quickly through the dialogue. This was actually much closer to speech than the earlier, more melodic style, but the stark contrast between it and the florid arias compromised the natural flow that had characterized early opera.

Most of the recitative was accompanied only by the basso continuo, which by this time normally consisted of a harpsichord playing chords and a cello, double bass, or bassoon doubling the bass line. This eventually came to be called "dry recitative" (**recitativo secco**) as opposed to accompanied recitative (accompagnato), in which the other instruments, usually strings, joined with the *continuo*. This latter type was used sparingly to set off passages of special importance or to create a solemn or poignant effect.

Around the end of the first century of its existence, there was a strong feeling in some circles that opera had strayed too far from its origins and that there was a need for reform. This movement aimed to restore the purity and integrity of operatic plots that had existed before the decline that had begun in the public theaters of Venice after 1637. Most prominent in this effort was the librettist Pietro Antonio Trapassi, called Metastasio (1698–1782), who had begun his career in Naples.

Metastasio wrote about sixty librettos that were set to music by most of the important composers of Italian opera throughout Europe until the early nineteenth century. Although he used the term *dramma per musica* for these works, Metastasio was the most important figure in the creation of what came to be called *opera seria*. This genre, as its name implies, eliminated the irrelevant comic scenes that had proliferated in the late seventeenth century and emphasized serious, often historical plots. There was typically a happy ending that resulted from a magnanimous gesture by a ruler or other authority figure. This was an affirmation of political status quo at a time when European autocracy was beginning to feel threatened.

Although opera seria represented a significant literary reform, it also served to codify most of the musical practices that had already developed at Venice and Naples. The three acts of the opera were divided into scenes that consisted of long passages of recitative during which the action progressed, followed by arias in which it halted while the characters reflected. The aria, usually in da capo form, was addressed to the audience, not to the other characters onstage. Other vocal pieces were limited to the occasional duet and a larger, more grandiose ensemble at the end of the final act. This succession of contrasting set pieces, later referred to as "numbers," was to characterize Italian opera until well into the nineteenth century.

Even before the reforms of Zeno and Metastasio purged serious opera of comic scenes, some independent comic works were being produced. Around the beginning of the eighteenth century, comic **intermezzos** began to be performed during the two intermissions of serious operas. Sometimes the pair of intermezzos constituted a complete two-part comic opera interspersed between the traditional three acts of an *opera seria*. Their plots were simple, usually including only two or three characters, often based on the commedia dell'arte. Eventually these began to be produced as independent works, and the resulting genre came to be called **opera buffa** (comic opera).

In opera buffa the stock character of the comic older man was normally portrayed by a bass (*basso buffo*), a voice type that was uncommon in serious opera. The presence of the bass, in combination with the traditional higher male and female voices, encouraged the inclusion of trios and quartets. Opera seria, which featured high voice types, had typically been limited to solo arias and duets. Consequently, the larger ensemble, in which three or more characters each reacted to a situation with a different viewpoint, was one of the most significant contributions of opera buffa. In the hands of a skillful librettist and composer, the buffa ensemble could produce a theatrical effect that was unobtainable in spoken drama, transforming dramatic chaos into musical harmony. Such pieces, often divided into several distinct sections, became standard as the finales at the end of acts. The ensemble eventually became a feature of serious works as well and was one of the glories of nineteenth-century opera. By the late eighteenth century, however, opera seria had moved away from its comic counterpart by eliminating extended passages of dry recitative in favor of the accompanied type.

Two of the most successful and influential Italian composers of opera buffa during the late eighteenth century were the Neapolitans Domenico Cimarosa (1749–1801) and Giovanni Paisiello (1740–1811). Both enjoyed international reputations. Cimarosa's *Il matrimonio segreto* (*The Secret Marriage*), composed for Vienna in 1792, is one of the rare works by an Italian composer of that period that remains in the repertoire. Paisiello's *Il barbiere di Siviglia* (*The Barber of Seville*), whose libretto was based on the play by the French diplomat, musician, and inventor Pierre-Augustin Caron de Beaumarchais, was produced for the court at Saint Petersburg in 1782. It became so popular that when the opera of the same name by Gioachino Rossini (1792–1868) appeared in 1816, it was compared unfavorably to its predecessor.

The history of opera was to be strongly influenced for many generations by the construction of new theaters in several Italian cities during the eighteenth century to replace older buildings that had grown outdated or had been destroyed by fire. The first of these was the Teatro San Carlo in Naples. Completed in 1737, its capacity of over three thousand far exceeded that of any other venue of the time. San Carlo's enormous size demanded principal singers with large voices that gradually became a standard for important artists. The Teatro alla Scala in Milan, inaugurated in 1778, was only slightly smaller. In Venice, the Teatro La Fenice, which opened in 1792, was about one-third of the size of the other two, but was still grand and highly ornate. All three houses were to be the venues for notable premieres throughout much of the nineteenth century and into the twentieth.

Ironically, the greatest eighteenth-century composer of Italian opera was the Austrian Wolfgang Amadeus Mozart (1756–1791). He composed two operas of the seria type in his maturity: *Idomeneo, rè di Creta* (*Idomeneo, King of Crete*) (1780) for Munich and an adaptation of Metastasio's *La clemenza di Tito* (*The Clemency of Titus*) (1791) for the coronation of Emperor Leopold II as king of Bohemia in Prague. His operatic genius was manifested most brilliantly, however, in his comedies. In the three great works with librettos by Lorenzo da Ponte (1749–1838), *Le nozze di Figaro* (*The Marriage of Figaro*) (Vienna, 1786), *Don Giovanni* (*Don Juan*) (Prague, 1787), and *Così fan tutte* (*Thus Do They All*) (Vienna, 1790), he brought the musical conventions of comic opera that had evolved in the works of composers such as Cimarosa and Paisiello to a state of classical perfection.

Mozart realized the full potential of the buffa ensemble. In *Figaro* he constructed each act to culminate musically and dramatically in a multisectional ensemble finale, which often proceeded with a musical logic not unlike the movements of a symphony.

Like some of his Italian contemporaries, Mozart challenged the preeminence of the da capo aria. Numerous musical structures had begun to evolve that were more compatible with a natural progression of the drama than the predictable ABA design. One type that was to become important in the early nineteenth century was a two-part aria in which an expressive section in a slow tempo was followed by a faster, virtuosic one. Mozart's sublime "Dove sono" ("Where Are the Beautiful Moments?"), sung by the countess in Act Three of *The Marriage of Figaro*, begins with a beautiful andante in a modified three-part form in which the return of the opening material is abbreviated. This is followed by a fast section (allegro) that features some moderately **virtuosic** passages and a brilliant orchestral ending that accompanies the countess's exit.

With the death of both Paisiello and Cimarosa in the early nineteenth century, opera buffa seemed to be in decline, and the Italian stage lacked a composer of international stature. Soon, however, Gioachino Rossini, a composer of immense talent, arrived on the scene and restored the fortunes of opera buffa and of Italian music in general. By the 1820s Rossini was the most financially successful opera composer who had ever lived, and he rivaled Beethoven as Europe's most famous musician.

A native of Pesaro on the Adriatic coast, Rossini and his family moved to the university city of Bologna when he was very young. There he was educated at the Liceo Musicale, a conservative institution where, as a pupil of the director, Padre Stanislao Mattei (1750–1825), he received a thorough education in Renaissance and Baroque compositional styles.

Comparisons with Mozart are inevitable. Although Rossini was not quite the "child prodigy" that the young Wolfgang had been, he composed his first opera at the age of fourteen and six years later fulfilled a commission from the Teatro San Moisè in Venice with the opera buffa *La cambiale di matrimonio* (*The Marriage Contract*). At twenty-one he produced both the serious *Tancredi* (*Tancred*) and the opera buffa *L'Italiana in Algeri* (*The Italian Girl in Algiers*). Three years later, he produced the comic masterpiece *Il barbiere di Siviglia* (*The Barber of Seville*). Similar to Mozart, he composed very quickly; *The Barber*, like several of his other works, was written in about one month. He also was the successor who most nearly matched Mozart's melodic gifts, his skill at musical characterization, and his genius for creating effervescent buffa ensembles.

The similarities were not coincidental. Rossini studied the vocal and instrumental works of Haydn and Mozart assiduously and called the latter his "idol and master." Like the Austrians, he exploited the woodwind instruments to brilliant effect, making the orchestration in his operas richer and more colorful than that of his Italian predecessors.

Rossini's overtures were so melodically appealing and rhythmically exciting that several of them are regularly performed separately on concert programs. Their endings almost always feature a "Rossini **crescendo**" in which instruments are added gradually, and the rhythmic motion accelerates to a rousing climax.

In terms of both popularity and critical acclaim, *The Barber of Seville* occupies, with the da Ponte settings of Mozart, the summit of the comic opera repertoire. The end of *The Barber*'s first scene, a duet between the count and Figaro, showcases many of Rossini's strongest attributes. In a long passage of recitative the count, a tenor, who is smitten with the beautiful young Rosina, offers the wily barber Figaro, a baritone, a financial reward to arrange a meeting with her. Figaro expresses his enthusiasm for the plot, singing a rapid and ornamented passage that the count repeats at a higher pitch. As Figaro plans the ruse and the count agrees to it, Rossini moves easily from recitative to florid melody and from solo passages to duets in which the two characters sing together in identical rhythms and in close harmony. This is all tied together by melody that recurs regularly in the orchestra in various keys.

When the two men begin to describe Figaro's place of business, they sing in alternating **parlante** (speaking) phrases on a single note while the orchestra plays the melody. In typical Rossini fashion, the accompaniment intensifies in both volume and rhythmic activity as the duet moves toward its end. The infectious rhythm that is so apparent in his overtures also propels Rossini's ensembles.

Rosina's **cavatina** (entrance aria), "Una voce poco fa" ("A Voice Has Just Resounded in My Heart"), which opens the second scene, is, like Mozart's "Dove sono," a two-part (slow-fast) composition. The first section alternates gracefully between expressive melody and accompanied recitative and, at one point, moves to parlante style accompanied by a melody from the orchestral introduction. After a short vocal **cadenza** (a passage in the style of an improvisation), an interlude featuring woodwind solos introduces a faster section in which Rosina, in the tradition of the commedia dell'arte, describes how she uses her quick wit to control every situation. The text is repeated, giving the singer the opportunity to further embellish her already florid melody. Although improvised ornamentation by singers declined during the next generation, Rossini permitted and even encouraged the practice.[2]

In the nineteenth century the opening slow section of a sectional aria like "Una voce poco fa" was usually called a **cantabile** and the lively passage that followed, filled with rapid, highly ornamented passages referred to as **coloratura**, was a **cabaletta**. Various versions of this "two-movement" aria became standard in Italian opera during the first half of the century. Sometimes the two principal sections are separated by a passage called a *tempo di mezzo* (middle movement) in which a sudden turn of events becomes the catalyst for the abrupt change of mood and tempo. The rousing end of the typical cabaletta, often with an even faster coda, called a **stretta**, ensured enthusiastic audience response. A passage of dialogue in recitative often preceded the aria and could also be interspersed between its sections. The resulting composite structure comprised a complete **scena** (scene). Ensembles generally followed the same pattern, although the tempo order sometimes varied.

The spectacular popularity of *The Barber of Seville* ensured Rossini's fame as a composer of comic opera, but he also achieved considerable success with serious works. *Elisabetta, regina d'Inghilterra (Elizabeth, Queen of England)* (1815) and *Otello (Othello)* (1816), both composed for Naples, were the products of the same amazingly productive period as *The Barber*. After his move to Paris in 1824, Rossini composed several operas on French librettos and adapted some of his Italian works for French production. His last work for the stage, *Guillaume Tell (William Tell)* (1829), with its famous overture, became one of the models for the French **grand opera** that dominated the Parisian stage during the next two decades.

In 1858, after his retirement, Rossini purportedly complained "Alas for us, we have lost our **bel canto** [beautiful singing]." Although he was certainly not the first to apply this rather generic term to an Italian tradition in which beauty and elegance of vocal line was the singer's ultimate goal, his comment prompted the association of the term with his own operatic style and that of his younger contemporaries Gaetano Donizetti (1797–1848) and Vincenzo Bellini (1801–1835).

Certainly the sheer beauty of the voice had been an important aspect of Italian opera at least since its emergence as a public entertainment in seventeenth-century Venice, and some variant of the term bel canto had occasionally been applied to the rarified tradition of virtuoso singing in opera seria. Although Rossini's statement referred to what he perceived as a decline in modern vocal performance, the usual modern understanding of the term pertains to the musical style itself, whose elegance demands great refinement from its performers. There is also a nationalistic implication in that nineteenth-century Italian opera preserved an emphasis on vocal beauty in contrast to the more dramatic German romantic opera that forced the singers to compete in sheer volume with dense orchestration.

Rossini's younger contemporary Gaetano Donizetti was born in the small but historically important city of Bergamo, northeast of Milan. He was fortunate that the *maestro di cappella* at the city's cathedral was the distinguished composer and pedagogue Simon Mayr (1763–1845). During his long life Mayr, a native of Bavaria, composed more than fifty symphonies and nearly seventy operas. He remained a mentor, friend, and supporter of Donizetti until the end of his life.

Between 1815 and 1817 Donizetti studied in Bologna with Padre Mattei, who had taught Rossini a decade earlier. After he completed these studies, he received a commission to compose an opera, *Enrico di Borgogna* (*Henri of Burgundy*), for the Teatro di San Luca, one of the minor houses in Venice. After several more works for the smaller Venetian theaters, Donizetti composed *Zoraida di Granata* (*Zoraide of Granada*) for production at Rome's Teatro Argentina in 1821 and *La zingara* (*The Gypsy Girl*) for the Teatro Nuovo in Naples in 1822.

For the decade between 1828 and 1838 Donizetti held the position of director of the royal theaters of Naples and supplied several new works for San Carlo. The major turning point in his career, however, came with the production of his *Anna Bolena* (*Anne Boleyn*) in 1830 at the Teatro Carcano in Milan. This was the composer's first collaboration with Felice Romani (1788–1865), one of Italy's most renowned librettists, who had provided the text for Rossini's *Il turco in Italia* (*The Turk in Italy*). *Anna Bolena* was soon repeated in Paris, London, and, in 1839, New Orleans.

The immediate success of *Anna Bolena* owed much to the glittering cast at its premiere, led by the prima donna Giuditta Pasta (1797–1865) and the great tenor Giovanni Battista Rubini (1794–1854). The role of Anne Boleyn was the first of Donizetti's great bel canto soprano roles, and in recent years it has served as an important vehicle for Maria Callas (1923–1977), Joan Sutherland (1926–2010), Beverly Sills (1929–2007), and Anna Netrebko (b. 1971).

After 1830 Donizetti's work was in enormous demand, and he composed at a breathtaking pace. Among the best known of his more than eighty operas are *L'elisir d'amore* (*The Elixer of Love*) (Teatro della Canobbiana, Milan, 1832), *Lucrezia Borgia* (La Scala, 1833), *Maria Stuarda* (*Mary Stuart*) (La Scala, 1835), *Lucia di Lammermoor* (San Carlo, 1835), and *Don Pasquale* (Théâtre-Italien, Paris, 1843). Like Rossini, Donizetti enjoyed considerable popularity in Paris and in addition to French adaptations of some of the Italian works (including *La favorite* of 1840) he composed the French comic opera *La fille du regiment* (*The Daughter of the Regiment*) (Opéra-Comique, Paris) and the grand opera *Dom Sébastien* (*Don Sebastian*) (Opéra, Paris, 1843).

The most celebrated of Donizetti's operas is *Lucia di Lammermoor*, on a libretto of Salvadore (Salvatore) Cammerano (1801–1852), based on Sir Walter Scott's 1819 novel *The Bride of Lammermoor*. The role of Lucy is one of the most spectacular vehicles for bel canto soprano and has been central in the repertoires of such legendary performers as Nellie Melba (1861–1931), Amelita Galli-Curci (1882–1963), Lily Pons (1898–1976), and Joan Sutherland.

The plot is typical of the gothic melodrama that replaced the classical themes of opera seria and came to dominate Italian opera throughout much of the century. Lucy's noble family, the Ashtons, are facing financial ruin, and her cruel brother Henry has betrothed her to the wealthy Lord Arthur Bucklaw, hoping that the match will restore the Ashtons' fortunes. Lucy, however, is secretly in love with Henry's mortal enemy, Edgar of Ravenswood.

In the second scene of Act Two a large company is assembled for the wedding of Lucy and Arthur. Just as Lucy signs the contract under duress, Edgar enters, fully armed. Realizing what is happening, he believes he has been betrayed by Lucy, but still loves her. Edgar, Henry, Lucy, and Arthur are joined by the chaplain, Bidebent, and Lucy's confidante, Alice, in the famous sextet "Chi mi frena?" ("What Restrains Me?"). Edgar and Henry begin the ensemble, singing one of Donizetti's most memorable melodies, which is then repeated by Lucy and Bidebent. Eventually all six characters sing together and are joined by the chorus, the lower voices all providing a foundation for Lucy's soaring coloratura. This sextet demonstrates that an ensemble can function as powerfully to heighten the drama in serious opera as it can serve to propel the comedy in opera buffa.

In the celebrated third-act "mad scene," in which Lucy appears, disheveled and demented, after having murdered her husband on their wedding night, Donizetti skillfully combined several of the procedures that were common in the operas of his predecessors. The extended scene is essentially a variation of the two-part cantabile-cabaletta structure with an even faster coda. Within this familiar form Donizetti interpolated a variety of recitative passages, both for Lucy and other characters, and interjections by the chorus, including the scene-setting introductory choral statement at the first sight of the mad Lucy: "Oh righteous heaven, like issuing from the grave!"

Lucy's soliloquy begins in accompanied recitative, with the orchestra playing the principal melody, and moves through **arioso** passages, unaccompanied declamation, and virtuosic cadenzas. When she begins to hallucinate about her wedding to Edgar, whom she had loved, two flutes announce the theme of the cantabile, which she then repeats. The chorus enters and she sings a florid passage above them. After more recitative for Lucy, her brother Edward, and Bidebent, the cabaletta is sung twice and followed by a **coda** for the three characters and chorus that grows increasingly intense in the tradition of the "Rossini crescendo."

The third important bel canto composer, Vincenzo Bellini, was born in Catania, on the east coast of Sicily, into a musical family. His grandfather, Vincenzo Tobia Bellini (1744–1829), an organist, composer, and conductor of local distinction, provided early instruction for his grandson, whose musical precociousness became legendary in the city. In 1819 the young Vincenzo was admitted to the Conservatorio di San Sebastiano in Naples, where he progressed well and eventually was accepted as a pupil of the conservatory's director Nicoló Zingarelli (1752–1837). Zingarelli, a notable composer of opera and church music, was a disciplined and conservative pedagogue who strove to uphold the distinguished Neapolitan tradition.

Of the earlier Neapolitans, Bellini particularly admired the melodic gifts of Giovanni Battista Pergolesi (1710–1736). Of his contemporaries, he was initially drawn to Donizetti. But after hearing a performance of Rossini's *Semiramide* at San Carlo in 1824 he commented, "After hearing *Semiramide*, it's futile for us to try to achieve anything."[3]

Despite being humbled by the genius of Rossini, Bellini began to work on an opera of his own only a few months later. The result was

Adelson e Salvini, on a libretto by Andrea Tottola (d. 1831), who had
provided the text for Donizetti's *La zingara.* This work, termed an
"opera semiseria," contained comic elements, including a role for a
basso buffo. Donizetti attended the premiere and was lavish in his
praise.[4]

Due to the success of this student work and through Zingarelli's
influence, the twenty-five-year-old composer was commissioned to produce a work for San Carlo the following year. This two-act opera seria,
Bianca e Fernando, premiered in May of 1826 in the presence of the
royal family and was extremely well received. Bellini's success at San
Carlo led to the request for a new work for La Scala for the 1827
season.

For this opera he collaborated with Felice Romani (1788–1865),
already a renowned librettist whose texts had been set by Rossini, Donizetti, and numerous other composers. Romani became an important
friend and adviser to Bellini and provided the librettos for all but one of
his operas for the rest of his life.

The result of Bellini's first collaboration with Romani was *Il pirata*
(*The Pirate*), based on a melodramatic Irish play. The opera was performed at La Scala by a stellar cast and was repeated more than a dozen
times to enthusiastic audiences. The following year it was produced in
Vienna. From this triumph until his premature death in 1835, Bellini
produced almost one opera every year. These included *La straniera*
(*The Stranger*) (La Scala, 1829), *I Capuleti e I Montecchi* (*The Capulets
and the Montagues*) (La Fenice, 1830), *La sonnambula* (*The Sleepwalk-
er*) (Teatro Carcano, Milan, 1831), *Norma* (La Scala, 1831), and *I puritani* (*The Puritans*) (Théâtre-Italien, Paris, 1835).

The "sleepwalking scene" in *La sonnambula* and the "mad scene" in
I puritani, like their famous counterpart in Donizetti's *Lucia di Lammermoor,* provide both dramatic and vocal challenges for the prima
donna. Such melodramatic moments became emblematic of the highly
charged atmosphere of romantic Italian opera.

Although the title character of *Norma,* which preceded *Lucia* by
four years, suffers no similar lapse of consciousness, the role is perhaps
best known for its immense musical and dramatic challenges. Norma is
high priestess of the Druids in Roman-occupied Gaul. She is secretly in
love with the despised Roman proconsul, Pollione, and has borne him
two children, breaking her sacred vow of chastity. Pollione has, howev-

er, fallen in love with Adalgisa, a young novice in the temple. Adalgisa is devoted to Norma, and neither woman knows of the other's relationship with Pollione. The Druids want to go to war to drive the Romans out of Gaul, but in an attempt to protect Pollione, Norma urges them to wait.

Norma's scena in Act One that includes the cavatina "Casta diva" ("Chaste Goddess") is the most famous section of the opera and one of the greatest moments in the bel canto literature. After a long passage of recitative in which the priestess reprimands her people for their eagerness to go to war, the principal melody of the cantabile is introduced by the solo flute, accompanied by broken chords in the strings and then repeated by Norma in her prayer to the moon goddess. Elegant, expressive melodies with carefully placed, poignant **chromatic** tones were Bellini's greatest strength and that of "Casta diva" is among his most beautiful.

Norma's father, Oroveso, and the chorus join in to accompany Norma's florid embroidery on the repetition of the words "senza vel" ("unveiled"). The opening music returns for the second stanza of text, in which Norma is joined by the chorus halfway through. This is followed by a passage of martial music by the onstage wind band (**banda**). The tradition of the banda had begun with Rossini and its presence became something of a cliché in the works of his successors.

The banda interlude leads to the tempo di mezzo in which Norma realizes that she possesses the power to call for Pollione's death, but that her heart will not allow it. The orchestra then introduces the rousing cabaletta for Norma, "Ah! Bello a me ritorno" ("Ah! Beautiful One, Return to Me"), accompanied by the chorus, in which she declares her love for the proconsul and her hope for his return.

Two years after *Norma*'s premiere Bellini, expecting to obtain a commission from the Opéra, arrived in Paris, where he soon became acquainted with Frédéric Chopin (1810–1849). The younger composer was fond of Italian opera and the similarity of many of his melodies to those of Bellini's cantabiles like "Casta diva" is striking. It has often been pointed out that many of the same qualities required of bel canto singers, such as beautiful sound and elegant phrasing, are also necessary for the performance of Chopin's piano works.

By the time of Bellini's death in 1835, he and Donizetti had both achieved international fame. Although Rossini was to live for more than thirty years, enjoying his wealth and enormous celebrity, he had ended his career as an opera composer. Building on Rossini's models, Bellini and Donizetti, although never approaching the radical experimentation with harmony and orchestration that characterized German romanticism, had moved toward an operatic style in which music and text were more closely allied.

Unlike Rossini, whose brilliant but generic overtures could be interchanged between serious and comic opera, they began to favor orchestral preludes that created the appropriate atmosphere for the drama that followed. Also, they both attempted to smooth the transition between recitative and aria. They experimented with the insertion of recitative passages within the arias and ensembles and with the use of the more melodic arioso style for particularly dramatic declamation.

As the term bel canto implies, however, Italian opera of the 1830s was still "singers' opera" in which composers were obliged to tailor their music to the whims of the star performers. Unlike in French and German works of the period, melody continued to reign supreme. Although this style is generally associated with elaborate melodic ornamentation, coloratura passages in Donizetti and Bellini were typically more restrained than in the arias of Rossini. Bellini, in particular, conceived his melodies to elicit strong emotional reaction from the listener rather than purely to display vocal virtuosity. He wrote: "The music drama must make people weep, shudder, die by means of singing."[5]

Although all three composers provided more opportunities for the orchestra, especially the woodwinds, to share in the melodic material, the role of the instruments was still primarily to support and enhance the voices. Also, despite the desire for a more seamless flow, the bel canto repertoire is still "number opera," in which recitatives, arias, and ensembles are conceived as separate musical entities and are listed (and often numbered) as such in an index at the beginning of the score.

In the year of Bellini's death, a twenty-two-year-old music student in Milan attended a performance of *Norma* at La Scala. The Milanese musical elite could not have guessed at the time that the young, provincial Giuseppe Verdi would take up the mantle of bel canto and, during an astounding career of nearly fifty-five years, would completely transform that style into something new and vital; that his fame and fortune would surpass even that of the great Rossini; and that he would almost single-handedly uphold the Italian lyrical tradition in the face of the ascendancy of German music drama.

2

THE EARLY YEARS

Oberto

It is difficult to imagine a less auspicious setting for the birthplace of a great artist than the Po Valley village of Le Roncole, about twenty miles from Parma, where Giuseppe Verdi was born on October 9 or 10, 1813. The flat farmland around the hamlet was fertile and today it lies in one of modern Italy's more prosperous regions, but political unrest made life there in the early nineteenth century difficult and unpredictable.

In the years just before Giuseppe's birth Napoleon Bonaparte had united much of the Italian peninsula, but his empire ended with the Treaty of Vienna in 1815. Vast territories in the south central region reverted to the Papal States. The kingdom of Sardinia, ruled by the Savoy dynasty, controlled Piedmont, Savoy, and the former republic of Genoa. Much of northern Italy, including most of Lombardy and the Veneto, reverted to Austrian control. The province of Parma was placed under the rule of Napoleon's second wife, the Austrian princess Marie Louise (1791–1847), who was installed as duchess. In Verdi's youth the lingering influence of Bonaparte's incursion into the region was a hotly debated subject.

Italy was not a political entity, but a cultural and nationalistic concept that was held largely by an intellectual elite in the north. Many Italians had fared well under foreign domination and had little interest in challenging the status quo. The city of Milan had especially thrived under Austrian rule, and the international prominence of the Teatro alla Scala attested to the positive cultural impact of the northern occupiers.

Under the leadership of the journalist and activist Giuseppe Mazzini (1805–1872), who founded the group known as Giovine Italia in the early 1830s, and the politician Camillo Benso, Count of Cavour (1810–1861), a movement to expel foreign rulers and unify the Italian peninsula became known as the Risorgimento (Resurgence). During his long life Verdi would witness the slow, halting progress of this movement and its eventual fulfillment in the establishment of the Kingdom of Italy. Although he was not fundamentally political, he eventually came to be regarded with Mazzini, Cavour, and others as a hero of the movement.

Giuseppe's parents, Carlo (1785–1867) and Luigia (1787–1851), operated a small tavern and general store whose upper floor served as the family's living quarters. Although in later life Verdi liked to emphasize the poverty of his upbringing, his family's circumstances were better than those of many of their neighbors.

Like many villages in the region, the only real edifice in Le Roncole was the parish church of San Michele Arcangelo, and it was the church that provided the young Verdi's first exposure to music. Most biographies relate the story of the young Giuseppe who, while serving as an altar boy at San Michele, became distracted by the music and neglected his duties. The angry priest struck the boy, who reportedly shouted "May you die by lightning!" Later in life Verdi claimed that several years after the incident the priest was indeed struck and killed by lightning as he celebrated mass at another church. This incident is often cited as the root of the mature Verdi's anticlericalism.[1]

At about the same time Giuseppe apparently made an effort to play the church's organ and was encouraged and probably instructed by the organist, Pietro Baistrocchi. Upon Baistrocchi's recommendation, Carlo Verdi bought his seven-year-old son a dilapidated spinet that he kept for the rest of his life.[2] Although Carlo's relationship with his son became strained in later years, he deserves credit for encouraging his musical interests and ensuring that he received a decent education.

Baistrocchi died when Giuseppe was about nine and the boy was appointed to succeed him as parish organist. Shortly afterward, Carlo sent his son to the *ginnasio* (high school) in the nearby market town of Busseto, where he boarded with a local tradesman. On Sundays and feast days he walked about three miles home to Le Roncole to play for mass. Verdi never attended a university, so the instruction he received at the *ginnasio* was his only general education.

Busseto was a relatively prosperous city and boasted an active, albeit unsophisticated musical life. The town's philharmonic society, a motley collection of amateur instrumentalists that more resembled a band than an orchestra, presented regular concerts. The founder and president of the society, who also played flute in the ensemble, was a wealthy merchant named Antonio Barezzi (1787–1867), from whom Carlo Verdi bought provisions for his store. He was an enthusiastic and discerning musical amateur who recognized Giuseppe's talent and quickly became his devoted patron and advocate.

As Verdi would soon discover, Busseto was rife with political factionalism, with Barezzi as a leader of the liberal, anticlerical group. Like several of the more prosperous citizens in the area, Barezzi's business interests had thrived under the French occupation and the resulting sales of church property to private entrepreneurs. He was an admirer of Napoleon and of the original ideals of the French Revolution. A much more sophisticated man than Carlo Verdi, he became a father figure to Giuseppe and was perhaps the most important influence on the young man's political and philosophical views.

Verdi began to study with Busseto's leading musician, Ferdinando Provesi, the organist at the principal church, San Bartolomeo, and director of the town's secular music. The young man quickly became active in the local musical life, providing arrangements and original compositions for the performances of the philharmonic society. In 1831 he moved into the Barezzi home and within the year had fallen in love with his patron's daughter Margherita. At this point he decided that in order to support a family as a musician he would need training beyond what Provesi could provide. The loyal Barezzi offered to provide the funds for his education at the Milan Conservatory and, accompanied by his father and Provesi, Verdi traveled to the city to take to the entrance examinations.

Much to the surprise of his supporters in Busseto, Verdi was not admitted to the conservatory. The professors found him talented, but lacking in solid keyboard technique and in compositional discipline. The irony was not lost on Verdi later in life when the same institution decided to take the name Giuseppe Verdi Conservatory. There is little doubt, however, that the young man's training in Le Roncole and Busseto had not been up to the standards expected by a major conservatory. In addition, Verdi, at eighteen, was over the age limit, and his admission would have required a special dispensation.

The faculty suggested that Verdi remain in Milan to study privately and referred him to Vincenzo Lavigna (1776–1836), a former pupil of Paisiello in Naples who had been a keyboard player and vocal coach at La Scala. This was a fortunate match, for Lavigna was the kind of thorough and disciplined teacher that the young man had lacked in the provinces. The lessons were dominated by work with counterpoint exercises in the venerable Renaissance style of Palestrina (1525–1594) and study of Italian Baroque music like that of Arcangelo Corelli (1653–1713). Lavigna's fees and all of Verdi's other expenses were funded by the generous Barezzi.

Lavigna was pleased with his young pupil's progress and introduced him to Pietro Massini, director of the Filodrammatici, the highly regarded Milanese philharmonic society. Like Barezzi's organization in Busseto, it was an amateur group, but it operated on a much more ambitious artistic level. In the spring of 1834 Verdi attended a rehearsal of the society for a performance of Haydn's *Creation* at which the three assistant conductors, who shared the responsibility of playing the keyboard part, failed to appear. Massini asked Verdi to fill in, and he performed so successfully at sight that the maestro asked him to play for the performance. The members of the Filodrammatici were among the most elite families of Milanese aristocracy, so this performance exposed the young man to a wealthy and influential public. He was asked to conduct rehearsals for other performances, providing him with the important opportunity to work with a competent orchestra. He also coconducted an amateur performance of Rossini's *Cenerentola*.

By this time Provesi had died in Busseto and Barezzi assumed that Verdi would be the obvious choice to succeed him. He and other supporters were confident that Giuseppe would easily prevail in the traditional examination of candidates for the position. Church authorities, however, were suspicious of the headstrong young man who was associated with Barezzi and Provesi, both of whom had been openly critical of the ecclesiastical establishment. Consequently, they appointed Giovanni Ferrari, another of Provesi's pupils, to the San Bartolomeo position without administering the examination. The incident further divided Busseto into opposing camps, and Verdi himself sought the intervention of government authorities in Parma, including even that of Duchess Marie Louise.

In February of 1836, after months of negotiation, Verdi went to Parma for an examination by that city's maestro di cappella, who pronounced him more than qualified to assume the secular portion of Provesi's position: conducting the philharmonic society, teaching in the local music school, and composing incidental pieces for civic occasions. In April he was named the town's *maestro di musica* with a nine-year contract that was renewable every three years. Because Ferrari remained in charge of church music, Verdi was forced to accept a meager salary. Two weeks after the appointment he and Margherita were married, and the following year she gave birth to a daughter, Virginia.

There is little doubt that Verdi already had more ambitious goals than the role of music master in a provincial town. The salary was meager and he had virtually no exposure to performance on a professional level. But in order to begin his married life and start a family, he obviously believed that he needed the security that Busseto, the Barezzi family, and a steady income could provide.

During this period Verdi maintained a correspondence with Massini in Milan about various projects, most important of which was an opera libretto titled *Rocester* by the Milanese journalist Antonio Piazza that Verdi was already setting to music. The original plan was that the work would be performed by the amateurs of the Filodrammatici. Negotiations dragged on with no certainty of a production in Milan, and the possibility of a premiere in Parma also came to nothing. The frustration of being outside a musical center was exacerbated by continuing factional squabbles in Busseto.

1838 brought both a minor success and great sorrow to the young family. Verdi's first publication, six songs for voice and piano, including two settings of Italian translations of texts from Goethe's *Faust*, was printed in Milan with the title *Six Romances*. A son, named Icilio Romano, was born in July, but his sister Virginia died suddenly one month later. This tragedy was the catalyst that convinced Verdi that they had to leave Busseto. Within a few weeks he had requested a loan from his father-in-law to support them temporarily in Milan, had resigned from his position as maestro, and the family had left Busseto.

Due to the efforts of Massini and others in his circle, a single benefit performance of Verdi's opera was scheduled for the spring of 1839 at La Scala. The cast was to be a stellar one with the prima donna soprano Giuseppina Strepponi (1815–1897), the tenor Napoleone Moriani (1808–1878), the baritone Giorgio Ronconi (1810–1890), and the bass Ignazio Marini (1811–1873). Verdi's ill fortune continued, however, when Moriani became seriously ill just after rehearsals had begun and the entire project had to be cancelled.

During this time Massini recommended Verdi to Bartolomeo Merelli (1795–1879), who had been impresario at La Scala since 1836. Analogous to both the general manager of a modern opera company and the producer of a play or motion picture, an impresario in the eighteenth and nineteenth century made both business and artistic decisions at an opera house. He also assumed some financial risk for the productions. Consequently, because La Scala was now Italy's most prominent company, Merelli possessed the power to promote a young composer's career or to discourage it. Largely because of the endorsements of the opera from both Strepponi and Ronconi, Merelli agreed to produce it during the regular fall season of La Scala.

By this time, the work in question was no longer *Rocester*, but *Oberto, Conte di San Bonifacio* (*Oberto, Count of Saint Boniface*). Although there is disagreement about the relationship between the two operas, the consensus is that the work that had its premiere at La Scala in November of 1839 as *Oberto* was a thorough reworking of text and music of the older opera by the house librettist, Temistocle Solera (1815–1878), and Verdi. The possibility that an unpublished, unperformed first opera might still exist has tantalized scholars and Verdi devotees for many years, but *Rocester* has never been found.

During the period when he was composing *Oberto*, Verdi also produced numerous instrumental and vocal works, mostly for performance in Busseto. One composition from this period was a setting of *Il cinque maggio* (*The Fifth of May*), an ode to Napoleon commemorating his death on May 5, 1821, by the Milanese poet Alessandro Manzoni (1785–1873). Manzoni's most famous work was his novel *I promessi sposi* (*The Betrothed*), which he originally completed in 1823, but extensively revised and republished in 1840. In addition to its undisputed position as the great Italian novel, its adoption of the Tuscan dialect almost single-handedly established the modern Italian language. Such a standardization was a crucial step toward national unification. This, along with the novel's essential patriotism and empathy for the common citizenry, made Manzoni the literary icon of the Risorgimento. Like most Italian students, Verdi had read the original version of *I promessi sposi* as a teenager and revered it as one of the greatest of all literary works.

Less than four weeks before *Oberto* was scheduled to open, the Verdi family faced another loss when Icilio Romano died at the age of one year. While he and Margherita were mourning the loss of both children, however, Verdi's professional outlook improved substantially. *Oberto* had its premiere at La Scala on November 17, 1839, and was generally well received. Although Marini was the only member of the cast of the cancelled production to appear in the new one, he was joined by the excellent tenor Luigi Salvi (1810–1879) as Riccardo. The devoted Antonio Barezzi came from Busseto for the occasion.

OBERTO: SYNOPSIS

Like so many nineteenth-century Italian librettos, that of *Oberto* is melodramatic and somewhat contrived. The plot concerns the struggles between rival families in the Veneto region in the early thirteenth century. The historical figure of Ezzelino da Romano (1194–1259), who was the despot of Verona for about thirty years, does not appear, but before the action begins he and his ally, Riccardo, the Count of Salinguerra, have defeated Oberto, driving him into exile in Mantua. Riccardo has seduced Oberto's daughter Leonora, but soon afterward has been betrothed to Cuniza, the sister of Ezzelino. Leonora is still in love with Riccardo and is torn between hope to win him back and desire for revenge. Her father, having returned temporarily from exile, rebukes her for falling in love with his bitter enemy and commands her to go to Ezzelino's castle, where the wedding festivities for Riccardo and Cuniza are being prepared, and denounce him publicly for his infidelity.

When Leonora visits Cuniza and tells her the truth about her fiancé, she is sympathetic and agrees to confront him. When she does, Riccardo responds by falsely accusing Leonora of unfaithfulness and Oberto, appearing dramatically from his nearby hiding place, challenges him to a duel.

Oberto waits in a remote place near the castle for his rival. Riccardo arrives, but is reluctant to fight an older man. Finally angered by Oberto's taunts, he draws his sword, but the action is halted by the arrival of Leonora and Cuniza. The princess convinces Riccardo that he must marry Leonora. He consents to this, but Oberto still insists on defending his honor and arranges to continue the duel later. This eventually transpires, and Riccardo kills Oberto with Leonora looking on. Seized with regret, he leaves the country and the heartbroken Leonora, who has lost both father and lover, vows to become a recluse.

OBERTO: THE MUSIC

Oberto is a bel canto opera with both positive and negative features of the genre. There are numerous beautiful arias for all four vocal types represented by the principal characters. Verdi's melodies are strong and straightforward, avoiding florid passages except where they enhance the poetry. The presence of the singers Marini and Salvi inspired Verdi to particularly powerful writing for bass and tenor. The two- and three-movement forms for arias and ensembles, already something of a cliché by 1839, are still present, but there is variety in the ordering of the sections and in the connections between them.

The overture is in two parts: a brief slow section followed a longer, more complex fast one. The first is songlike, in triple meter, using the theme of the first-act chorus that celebrates the upcoming wedding of Cuniza and Riccardo. The second begins with a dramatic passage in a minor key suggesting the music that accompanies the duel in the second act. The overture ends with a martial passage with a final Rossini-like buildup. Both here and in the orchestral passages within the opera Verdi tends to overindulge in the march-like and fanfare passages that were common in the **banda** music of the bel canto repertoire. Such writing also reflects the influence of the music that Verdi had composed for the band of the philharmonic society of Busseto.

In Act One Riccardo, greeted by a chorus of knights, ladies, and vassals, arrives in the countryside near Ezzelino's castle to await his wedding to Cuniza. After his two-part **cavatina**, partially accompanied by chorus, Leonora enters, expressing anguish at her father's defeat and outrage at Riccardo's duplicity while still maintaining her love for him.

After an expressive orchestral passage, whose dramatic effect is heightened by off-beat accents and rich **chromatic** harmonies, Oberto, who has secretly returned from his exile, appears. The following scene begins with a powerful passage, "Oh patria terra, alfine io ti rivedo" ("Oh fatherland, at last I see you again"), that moves fluidly between unaccompanied declamation, accompanied recitative, and **arioso**. Leonora returns to the scene and recognizes her father, who denounces her for her relationship with the despised Riccardo.

Here as in his later works, Verdi was stirred by human conflict, particularly between parent and child. This scene of confrontation and reconciliation is one of the emotional and musical high points of the opera. Set in the traditional three-part bel canto structure, the **scena** begins with the **cantabile** "Non ti bastò il periglio d'un padre sventurato" ("The peril of an unfortunate father was not enough for you"), with father and daughter singing alternate statements. In the second section, "Del tuo favor soccorrimi" ("With your favor succor me"), Leonora prays for heaven's favor and Oberto responds with his own prayer for more tangible aid: "Del braccio tuo soccorrimi" ("With your arm succor me"). The sound of trumpets from the castle introduces the final section of the duet, "Odi! In quell' alte torri" ("Hated one! In these high towers"). Oberto commands his daughter to go to the castle and confront Riccardo. She agrees unquestioningly, and the two unite musically for the first time, singing the same melody.

In the finale of Act One, Verdi again exploits a dramatic confrontation scene to produce a powerful ensemble. With Oberto hiding in an adjoining room in the castle, both women face Riccardo, who rashly accuses Leonora of lying about their past. She responds angrily in a florid passage, at which point her father bursts into the room. The principals are joined by Imelda, Cuniza's confidante, and the chorus, singing in unison "A quell' aspetto un fremito perogni fibra io sento" ("At that appearance I feel a shudder in every fiber"). The frenetic activity comes to a halt as Riccardo, Leonora. Cuniza, and finally Oberto repeat that text, entering one at a time with the same melody in **canon**. *Oberto*, like all Italian opera of its era, is dominated by melody with chordal accompaniment, so such a drastic change to **contrapuntal** texture amid this highly charged scene provides an arresting contrast.

There is no doubt that Verdi was well equipped to employ the venerable technique of the canon; such exercises in counterpoint had been the foundation of his studies in Milan with Lavigna. His decision to utilize it so dramatically at this point, however, anticipates the seasoned master of late works such as the *Requiem* and *Falstaff*.

Oberto then vows to take up the sword against Riccardo: "Una spada so cingere ancor!" ("I can clasp the sword again"). The chorus reenters, reacting to this pivotal turn of events, and the excitement level increases to the end in a Rossini-like **stretta** marked *prestissimo* (the fastest of the standard **tempo** designations).

The success of Act Two also relies on the strength of its ensembles. In the scene for the four principal characters, "Eccolo! È desso! Or son tranquillo" ("Here he is! He is desolate. Now I am calm."), the impending duel is interrupted by the arrival of Cuniza and Leonora. Verdi's treatment of the conflicting emotions in this passage hints at the powerful ensemble writing of later works such as the great *Rigoletto* quartet: Oberto stubbornly seeks vengeance; Riccardo is reluctant to take advantage of a weaker opponent; Cuniza nobly offers to step aside in favor of her rival; and Leonora still expresses love for Riccardo. In Leonora's arioso "La vergogna ed il dispetto ahi combattono il mio seno" ("Alas, shame and spite battle in my breast"), the pulsating rhythm of the orchestra brilliantly portrays his inner conflict. The scene moves with admirable suppleness from declamatory to melodic vocal styles and from solo passages to various combinations of the four voices. Predictably, the tempo accelerates toward the end.

In the final scene of the opera Leonora has witnessed her father's death in the duel and expresses her despair in the moving recitative "Tutto ho perduto" ("I have lost everything"). The chorus offers comfort, leading to the aria "Sciagurata! A questo lido ricercai l'amante infido" ("Unfortunate one! On this shore I searched for the unfaithful lover"). This cantabile, in a minor key, has a poignancy and elegance that is reminiscent of Bellini. Cuniza, Imelda, and the chorus all join in words of comfort.

Leonora is inconsolable, and as she grows more agitated, singing "Qui lo sguardo, oh Dio" ("Here I glance at him, oh God"), her line is broken into short, breathless motives separated by rests. The end of Leonora's aria is followed by a fanfare that announces the delivery of a message informing Cuniza that Riccardo has left Italy to go into exile. After a striking short aria by Cuniza, Leonora sings a final cantabile-

cabaletta sequence, joined for the rousing final stretta by the other two women and the chorus.

The music of *Oberto* was derivative in numerous ways, with obvious influences from the styles of Verdi's older contemporaries. But Rossini had retired, Bellini was dead, and Donizetti had almost abandoned Italy for the greater financial rewards of Paris. Consequently, this somewhat unpolished first work was enough to mark Verdi as the obvious heir to the great Italian lyric tradition. Although *Oberto* probably possessed no individual aria or ensemble that could rival the best work of the other three, it had a dramatic flow and forward thrust that was soon to become Verdi's hallmark. From the beginning, as Georges Bizet was to write twenty years later, "Verdi was never boring."

As with Mozart, Rossini, and all great composers for the theater, a significant aspect of Verdi's genius was his instinct for keeping the listeners engaged throughout a performance. The Italian audiences of the 1830s were very different from those at the end of his career fifty years later. The boxes that encircled La Scala and other theaters typically opened into anterooms where the wealthy, aristocratic patrons could eat, drink, and converse. If the onstage momentum slowed, the boxholders often took advantage of the opportunity to leave their seats to socialize. The ubiquitous "crescendos" at the ends of Rossini's overtures, arias, and ensembles had been designed in part to regain the attention of distracted audience members. Beginning with *Oberto*, Verdi successfully avoided dramatic and musical stasis by eschewing long passages of recitative, by providing memorable melodies and vigorous rhythms, and by emphasizing basic human conflict.

Those in attendance at the premiere of *Oberto* were in general agreement that the performance was successful, and it was repeated thirteen times that season. The publisher Giovanni Ricordi purchased the rights to the score, initiating a long and productive relationship between Verdi and the prestigious house of Ricordi. In addition, Merelli immediately contracted with Verdi to compose three more operas for La Scala.

The first of these works was originally to be another serious opera, but Merelli decided that the upcoming season needed a new comedy. They turned to a two-decade-old libretto, *Un giorno di* regno (*A Day's Reign* or *A One-Day Reign*), a *melodrama giocoso* (humorous melodrama) by Felice Romani, who had supplied so many librettos for Bellini.

The young Verdi was considered by many acquaintances to be serious and dour, and the period when he began to work on the new opera was one of the darkest times of his life. Undoubtedly, a comic opera was an unpropitious project for him at that moment. But more loss was in store. In June of 1840, while Verdi was working on the new score, Margherita died of an undiagnosed illness at the age of twenty-six.[3] He asked to be released from the contract for the new opera, but Merelli refused his request. Verdi stayed in Busseto for two months after his wife's burial, but then returned to Milan to fulfill his contract.

Like *Oberto*, *Un giorno di regno* is loosely based on an historical figure who never appears on the stage. Stanislav Lescinski (1677–1766) was king of Poland from 1705 until he was deposed in 1709. In 1725 his daughter Maria married King Louis XV of France, after which he lived at the Château of Chambord until his restoration to the Polish throne in 1733. Romani's libretto begins after Stanislav's return to Poland when, to keep his whereabouts unknown to his enemies, he has traveled in disguise and appointed the Cavalier Belfiore to impersonate him in France. In typical buffa style, Belfiore, disguised as the king, stymies an arranged betrothal in order to bring young lovers together and, after revealing his true identity, claims a love of his own.

The premiere of *Un giorno di regno* was to be the single unmitigated disaster of Verdi's career. The audience, typical of La Scala, noisily registered their disapproval. Romani's libretto, based on a play by Alexandre Vincent Pineu-Duval and originally conceived as *Il finto Stanislao* (*The False Stanislas*) for an 1818 performance in Vienna, was well written, but opera buffa was no longer in style in Milan in 1840. The conventions of the genre, including the use of dry recitative, seemed quaint and old-fashioned, and the resulting disjunction between recitative and aria kept Verdi from achieving the natural flow that had existed in *Oberto*.

In the composer's defense there was almost universal agreement that the performance was a poor one. As he wrote to the publisher Tito Ricordi nearly twenty years later: "Certainly the music was to some extent to blame, but then so too was the performance."[4] The opera was revived in other theaters in later years and achieved some success, especially in Venice.

Such a public failure at La Scala, coming just as his career had seemed to be blossoming and in the wake of such an overwhelming personal loss, threw Verdi into a deep depression. He initially asserted that he would compose no more opera. Such a decision by a man who had suffered so much loss and disappointment in such a short period of time is understandable, but it was not to be permanent. The remaining scheduled performances of *Un giorno di regno* in the autumn of 1840 were replaced by *Oberto*, and Verdi made some revisions to accommodate different voices in the cast. Soon Merelli was to present him with another libretto that he found appealing, and his career was about to enter a new era.

3

CHANGE OF FORTUNE AND "YEARS IN THE GALLEYS"

Nabucco, Ernani, Macbeth

The libretto that Merelli brought to the despondent Verdi in the winter of 1840–1841 was *Nabucodonosor* (*Nebuchadnezzar*), Temistocle Solera's adaptation of the Old Testament account of the Hebrews in Babylonian captivity during the sixth century BCE.[1] The German composer Otto Nicolai (1810–1814) had been contracted to set the libretto for La Scala, but had rejected it, leaving Merelli in immediate need of a replacement. Verdi quickly offered him *Il proscritto* by Gaetano Rossi (1774–1855), which he was originally to have composed after *Oberto*.[2] In turn, Merelli virtually forced him to take Solera's libretto. Nicolai's *Il proscritto* had its premiere in Milan the following spring and was as great a failure as *Un giorno di regno* had been.

Many years later Verdi provided two slightly different accounts of why Solera's text persuaded him to compose again.[3] The story that is most often quoted originated in a conversation with his publisher and friend Giulio Ricordi in 1879. In this reminiscence of an event nearly forty years in the past he described how, with total disdain for the prospect of setting a new libretto, he hurled the bundle of pages that Merelli had given him down on a table. His eyes were immediately drawn to the line: "Va pensiero, sull'ali dorate" ("Go, thought, on golden wings"), Solera's loose paraphrase of Psalm 137 that expresses the longing of the exiled Jewish people for their homeland ("How can we sing the Lord's song in a strange land?").

After being moved by this text, Verdi still resisted, but as he related to Ricordi, he read the entire libretto several times and gradually began to set it to music. By the fall of 1841 he had finished the opera and presented the score to Merelli.

Several biographers have suspected that Verdi edited this story in his old age to enhance the image that he had acquired by that time. His setting of the "Va pensiero" ("Go thoughts") text as a stirring chorus of Hebrews longing for freedom from foreign captors had, during the intervening years, become an iconic anthem of the Risorgimento, and Verdi had achieved a place in the pantheon of Italian unification along with Mazzini, Cavour, and Manzoni. By the 1870s, after the Kingdom of Italy had finally been established, the chorus was viewed as an obvious metaphor for the Italians' dream of ridding the peninsula of foreign domination. Even in twenty-first-century Italy "Va pensiero" still retains strong patriotic significance.

When Verdi presented Merelli with the completed score, he reminded him of his original offer to present it the following spring. By this time, however, he had already committed to produce three new operas at La Scala during the season and believed a fourth would be excessive. Displaying the strong will and business acumen for which he later came to be known, Verdi angrily asserted that any delay would be unacceptable. Although his standing had been weakened by the failure of *Un giorno di regno*, he prevailed and Merelli reluctantly agreed to produce *Nabucco* in the spring.

The premiere was scheduled for March 9, 1842. Part of the reason for the composer's insistence on that time was the availability of a stellar cast: baritone Giorgio Ronconi (1810–1890) as Nabucco, bass Prosper Dérivis (1808–1880) as the high priest Zaccaria, and Giuseppina Strepponi as the slave Abigaille. There is some evidence that, as in the case of *Oberto*, Strepponi used her considerable influence with Merelli to convince him to accept Verdi's terms.[4]

As Merelli had warned, the expense of so many new productions left him short of funds; consequently, rather shabby costumes and scenery had to be recycled from a ballet on the same subject that had been presented four years earlier. As was her habit, Strepponi fit the *Nabucco* performance into an impossibly demanding schedule and was in terrible voice at the premiere. Despite it all, the production was a spectacular success.

Solera's libretto was based on the ballet that had in turn been adapted from an 1836 drama, *Nabucodonosor*, by the French playwrights Auguste Anicet-Bourgeois and Francis Cornue. It is a fictional account of the conquest of Judah by the Assyrian king Nebuchadnezzar in the sixth century BCE and the Babylonian captivity of the Jews that followed. Biblical references to this event are in the books of Jeremiah, Second Kings, Second Chronicles, Ezra, and Psalms, but none of the characters in the opera are biblical except Nabucco (Nebuchadnezzar) himself.

Such a great religious pageant had several precedents, the most important of which was Rossini's *Mosè in Egitto* (*Moses in Egypt*), which had premiered at San Carlo in 1818, and its 1827 adaptation for the Paris Opéra, *Moïse et Pharaon* (*Moses and Pharoah*). The French version was enlarged from three acts to four, with an added ballet scene and extensive use of the chorus, as Parisian taste demanded.

NABUCCO: SYNOPSIS

Like *Moïse*, *Nabucco* is divided into four acts (called "parts" by Solera), titled "Jerusalem," "The Ungodly One," "The Prophecy," and "The Broken Idol." The first is set in Solomon's temple and the other three in the precincts of Nabucco's palace in Babylon.

At the beginning of the opera Nabucco and the Assyrian army have defeated the Hebrew forces and are advancing on Jerusalem. The Jewish high priest and prophet Zaccaria attempts to calm his terrified people, pointing out that they are holding Nabucco's daughter Fenema hostage. He puts her in the care of Ismaele, a military officer and son of the king of Jerusalem. Ismaele had previously served as ambassador in Babylon, where both Fenema and Abigaille, also believed to be the king's daughter, had fallen in love with him. He had been imprisoned there and Fenema had helped him to escape.

Abigaille arrives, sword in hand, to announce that the Assyrians have captured the temple. Finding Fenema and Ismaele expressing their love for each other, she tells him that if he reciprocates her own love, she will save him and his people. Ismaele refuses and Fenema prays to the God of Israel to protect him.

Nabucco enters the temple in triumph, but is denounced by Zaccaria for defiling a holy place. In his anger he lifts his sword to kill Fenema, but Ismaele saves her and surrenders her to her father. This angers the Jewish people, and they pronounce him a traitor. Nabucco orders that the temple be destroyed.

At the beginning of Part Two the Jews have been taken to Babylon as prisoners. Nabucco has left to lead another military campaign, appointing Fenema as regent in his absence. In the palace Abigaille has found a document that indicates that she is not the daughter of the king, but of slaves.[5] This only strengthens her resentment for both Fenema and Nabucco.

The high priest of Baal enters to report that Fenema intends to free the Jewish slaves. He and the other priests have started a false rumor that Nabucco has been killed in battle. At his urging Abigaille decides to seize the throne.

Zaccaria converts Fenema to Judaism, and Ismaele is forgiven because the life that he saved is now that of a fellow Hebrew. Fenema is told that her father is dead and that her life is in danger. The high priest of Baal arrives, proclaims Abigaille ruler, and invokes a death sentence on the Jewish captives. Abigaille demands that Fenema give her the crown, but she refuses.

Suddenly Nabucco enters, furiously telling his people that their god has caused them to betray him and that he has defeated the God of the Hebrews. He takes the crown from Fenema and puts it on his head, proclaiming that now he alone is God. Zaccaria condemns him for blasphemy, and at the sound of a great thunderbolt the crown falls from his head onto the ground and he becomes insane. Abigaille seizes the crown.

Now seated on the throne, Abigaille is about to sign the death warrant for Fenema and the Hebrews. The demented Nabucco enters and Abigaille goads him into signing the warrant. At this point he realizes that he has condemned his own daughter. He also remembers the document that proves that he is not Abigaille's father and begins to search for it. Triumphantly she produces it and tears it to shreds. Defeated, he begs her to spare Fenema, but she refuses.

In the most celebrated scene of the opera, the Hebrew slaves are on the banks of the Euphrates. They think of their homeland and lament their exile. Zaccaria enters and delivers his prophecy that God will deliver them and punish Babylon.

Nabucco, now a prisoner in his own room, looks out the window to see Fenema being led to her execution. Helpless to intervene, he kneels and prays to the Hebrew God, promising to convert to the Jewish faith and rebuild the temple in Jerusalem. Immediately his mind clears, his guards release him, and he rallies his former followers.

In the Hanging Gardens the condemned Jews are about to be put to death. Nabucco enters dramatically and orders that the idol of Baal be destroyed. Just as the king's crown had been miraculously removed from him in Part Two, the idol now mysteriously shatters. Nabucco releases the Jews from their captivity.

Abigaille, who has taken poison, enters and confesses her deception. As she dies she gives her blessing to Fenema and Ismaele and prays for pardon. She falls dead and Zaccaria blesses the newly converted Nabucco: "Serving Jehovah, you will be king of kings."

Nabucco was unusual for an Italian opera of its time in that the central issue is not the love story, but national, religious, and familial conflict. In the original libretto the finale of Part Three was a love duet for Fenema and Ismaele, but Verdi convinced Solera to omit it and substitute Zaccaria's prophecy that the Lion of Judah would destroy Babylon. The emphasis on religion and conversion to the true God seems incompatible with Verdi's generally negative view of organized religion, but similar themes are not uncommon in his later work, and they often inspired heartfelt music.

NABUCCO: THE MUSIC

The overture, like that of *Oberto*, is a medley of tunes rather than an integrated whole. It begins strongly with a solemn, slow introduction that creates the appropriate atmosphere for the seriousness of the drama. After this, several themes from choral sections of the work are presented. The first is the melody of the chorus in which the Hebrews pronounce a curse ("Il maledetto") on Ismaele for freeing Fenema and returning her to her father. This passage, with its memorable rhythm, recurs twice, serving as a unifying factor. Its first two appearances frame a statement of the tune from the great third-act chorus "Va pensiero."

Part One begins with a commanding orchestral passage that introduces the first chorus. The harmony is strikingly **chromatic**, moving through several keys. The tonal instability dramatically depicts the terror of the Hebrews as the conquering Assyrians approach the temple. The chorus begins and ends with massive chords written in seven vocal parts. The heaviness is relieved by a passage for the priests (Levites) in unison and a three-voice chorus of virgins accompanied by harp and woodwinds.

Both the overture and opening chorus are predictable, somewhat heavy-handed early Verdi, but with the entrance of Zaccaria everything changes. The presence in the libretto of the prophet and high priest gave Verdi the opportunity to compose a great basso role for the magnificent French bass Dérivis. Zaccaria's stentorian accompanied **recitative** is marked by large leaps that emphasize his power and authority. In the first section of the aria, "D'Egitto là sui lidi" ("From Egypt There on the Shores") marked "Andante maestoso," the chorus provides occasional accompaniment or commentary.

This section demonstrates one of Verdi's signature rhythmic characteristics. In the accompaniment, each beat is subdivided into three (triplets) while the vocal line maintains a duple division with an occasional triplet. This kind of rhythmic conflict, which was also common in German romanticism, creates a tension that enhances the drama of the text.

Zaccaria's **cantabile** and **cabaletta** are separated by the entrance of Ismaele, who announces the approach of the Assyrian army, thus providing impetus for the more aggressive allegro. This occupies the position of the tempo di mezzo, the middle movement in the traditional tripartite aria. Donizetti and Bellini had used the same procedure, but as Verdi's skills developed, he constantly looked for more natural ways to bridge the divide between recitative and aria and between the aria's sections.

The cabaletta is accompanied by the "long-short-short-long-long" rhythm that is characteristic of the Spanish bolero and the Polish polonaise. This was one of several stereotypical rhythmic patterns of **bel canto** opera that Verdi continued to utilize in most of his early works, but abandoned later. As in the cantabile, the chorus joins Zaccaria, sometimes in unison with his vocal line, suggesting its unwavering support of his pronouncements.

In the scene that follows, Fenema and Ismaele are fondly recalling their first meeting in Babylon when they are interrupted by the arrival of Abigaille. Her opening recitative matches that of Zaccaria in power and authority with its large leaps, frequent key changes, and dramatic **cadenza** on the words "di mia vendetta il fulmine su voi sospeso" ("my revenge, like lightning hanging over you"). In the strength of the music for Abigaille and Zaccaria, Verdi emphasizes their position as polar opposites, united by their steadfastness of purpose.

In the ensuing trio this classic love triangle is cleverly depicted by the music. Abigaille confesses that she still loves Ismaele. He responds negatively to her advances, but repeats her melody. Fenema enters with a different melody with the surprising statement: "Ah! Già t'invoco, già ti sento, Dio verace d'Israello" ("Ah! Already I invoke you, already I hear you, true God of Israel."). As the trio ends, the vocal lines of the two lovers become more synchronized, with Abigaille singing almost hysterically above them.

In the finale of Part One Nabucco leads the Assyrian forces into the temple, accompanied by a rather simplistic march for orchestra and banda. In his confrontation with Zaccaria, the king's sinuous lines contrast with the angular melodies of the righteous, resolute prophet.

This is followed by a grand ensemble in which Zaccaria's sister Anna joins the other five principals. As in the sextet from *Lucia di Lammermoor*, Abigaille's voice soars above the others. The tempo accelerates from andante to allegro to presto with the six characters and full chorus.

Part Two opens with an extended **scena** for Abigaille during which she finds the document that reveals her parentage. The long declamatory passage moves from accompanied recitative to **arioso**. Swelling with anger toward Nabucco and calling him a false father, she ends the passage with the words "O fatal sdegno" ("Oh fatal disdain") on a short, unaccompanied cadenza that steps up to a high C and leaps down two full octaves. A solo flute plays a variation on this passage and leads to the tender cantabile in which she thinks of her love for Ismaele. This is followed by martial music that signals the entrance of the high priest of Baal with the news that Fenema is freeing the Jewish captives. This provokes such outrage from Abigaille that the vocal fireworks in her cabaletta, "Salgo già del trono aurato" ("Once I mount the golden throne"), rival any in the bel canto repertoire.

That evening Zaccaria prays that God will give him the power to turn the hearts of the Assyrians. His prayer, "Tu sul labbro de' veggènte fulminasti, o sommo Iddio!" ("From the lips of prophets you dumb-founded, oh supreme God!"), is accompanied delicately by a small string ensemble that anticipates the sensitive instrumental writing of Verdi's later works. William Ashbrook has commented that "the chamber orchestration of Zaccaria's prayer gives the lie to the charge that all early Verdi is noisy and obstreperous."[6]

The remainder of Part Two is densely packed with melodrama. After Nabucco enters, shocking those who believed him to be dead, and places the crown on his head, he begins a great ensemble in which Abigaille, Ismaele, Fenema, and finally the chorus, in unison, all imitate him, with each voice entering twelve measures after the prior one. All sing the same words: "S'appressan gl'istanti d'un ira fatale" ("The instant of a fatal wrath approaches").

The supernatural occurrence that follows, in which a thunderbolt lifts the crown from Nabucco's head and causes him to lose his senses, gave Verdi the opportunity to compose one of the staples of bel canto: a "mad scene." Unlike in famous ones for soprano, the king's derangement is not expressed by dazzling vocal pyrotechnics, but by rhythmic irregularity, breathless silences, and unorthodox shifts of tempo from allegro to adagio. Verdi has boldly heightened the sense of realism by avoiding the traditional cabaletta.

Nabucco's rantings are interrupted by Zaccaria, who proclaims "Il cielo ha punito il vantator" ("Heaven has punished the boaster"), and then by Abigaille, who cries: "Ma del popolo di Belo fia spento lo splendor" ("But the people of Baal have not exhausted their splendor!"). The act ends without chorus or ensemble, but with these two lines of recitative followed by a concluding fanfare.

Part Three begins with Abigaille seated on the throne in the Hanging Gardens. The musical high point of this act and one of the most effective moments of the opera is the duet between her and Nabucco. In the extended passage of recitative, Abigaille shames him into signing the death warrant for the Jews, but he immediately realizes that he has condemned his daughter. Verdi moves easily from **parlante** to arioso. The music, perfectly aligned with the text, depicts Abigaille as totally in control, with the large melodic leaps and florid passages that have characterized her from the beginning. When she destroys the document that disproves her royal birth, she sings a dazzling cadenza on the line "Tale ti rendo, o misero, il foglio menzogner" ("So I give you, oh wretched one, the lying page").

When the cantabile begins, Nabucco sings in the same minor key that had represented his madness in the prior act, but when he joins with Abigaille, he submissively moves into her key. A trumpet fanfare introduces the cabaletta that follows the traditional pattern of steadily increasing excitement.

The second scene is set on the banks of the Euphrates with the enslaved Jews lamenting their plight and reflecting on their homeland in the chorus "Va pensiero." This stirring passage is familiar to many who know nothing else of the opera. The flowing sextuple division of the beat in the accompaniment suggests the "golden wings" of the text. As with Zaccaria's first-act aria, the rhythm of the vocal line conflicts with the accompaniment with its mainly duple divisions.

Most of "Va pensiero" is for chorus in unison. As Rossini accurately suggested, it is a "grand aria" for chorus. At the words "Arpa d'or dei fatidici vati" ("Golden harp of our prophets"), Verdi shifts dramatically to six-voice harmony. The key of F-sharp major, with six sharps, was still fairly unusual in 1842, and for the perceptive listener it further sets this chorus apart from any other part of the opera. Composers at least as early as Mozart associated certain keys with specific character types or emotions. As his career progressed and his tonal vocabulary grew richer, Verdi increasingly relied on such key symbolism.

Verdi indicated that the first stanza of "Va pensiero" and the first half of the second were to be sung **sotto voce** ("under voice," especially soft). Leading into the memorable phrase "Oh mia patria si bella e perduta!" (Oh my homeland so beautiful and lost!"), he designated a crescendo (growing louder).

The finale of Part Three is Zaccaria's prophecy that the Lion of Judah will destroy Babylon. The chorus responds joyfully to the prophet's message of deliverance. This is another great tour de force for bass. The tempo increases twice as the fervor intensifies. The vocal range extends through two full octaves, and at the climax Zaccaria sustains an F-sharp, a spectacularly high pitch for a bass, for almost a full measure.

Part Four begins with a grand scena for Nabucco. As the curtain rises, he is seated in his room in "deep lethargy" while the orchestra plays a long prelude. Several themes from prior scenes are heard, beginning with that of the king's "mad scene" from Part Two. Nabucco muses about his helplessness while an offstage banda plays a funeral march to accompany Fenema to her execution. The recitative climaxes with the king's plea for forgiveness that he addresses to the Hebrew God. A duet for flute and cello ending with a flute cadenza leads to the cantabile "Dio di Giuda" ("God of Judah"), providing a moment of touching humility, with this once-powerful man on his knees.

The tempo accelerates, Nabucco demands to be released, and his loyal guards, seeing his return to sanity, accede to his wishes. This leads to a rousing and enthusiastic cabaletta, begun by the chorus of guards and continued by Nabucco.

The final scene of the opera is again in the Hanging Gardens, where the funeral march for Fenema has resumed. She sings a prayer, "Oh dischiuso è il firmamento" ("Oh, the firmament is revealed"), which describes her vision of heaven. It shares its key, accompaniment style, and certain rhythmic figures with her father's prayer.

The finale is a momentous ensemble in which Nabucco returns to set everything aright. After the statue of Baal crumbles and the king frees the Jews, all the principals and the chorus join in an unaccompanied hymn of praise, "Immenso Jeovha, chi non ti sente?" ("Great Jehovah, who does not hear you?").

In subsequent performances the dying Abigaille's entrance was often omitted, apparently with Verdi's approval. The triumphant chorus that precedes it would have been a typical vehicle for the ending, but Verdi's brief scena for the repentant villainess is not musically disappointing. The delicate accompaniment that features English horn and harp provides a striking contrast with the massive sonorities that precede it. As she exhorts the people to raise their afflictions to God, the key changes from minor to major and the chorus of Hebrews joins her. This is the same brilliant key in which the opera's opening chorus had concluded. Another bit of theatrical symmetry is that Zaccaria, the first of the principals to be heard, is also the last. With the same majestic declamatory style of his first statement, he proclaims to Nabucco that if he serves Jehovah, he will be king of kings.

Although *Nabucco* shares a number of qualities with Verdi's earlier works, such as occasional heavy-handed instrumental writing and reliance on clichéd accompaniment figures, the boldness and power of a more mature Verdi is apparent in much of the score. Although his orchestration does not yet match the subtlety of some of his French and German contemporaries, Verdi has equaled their dramatic exploitation of the chorus.

The musical depiction of the characters and situations is also considerably more sophisticated than in the preceding operas. For Zaccaria and Nabucco, Verdi created two great roles for low male voices that prefigure the commanding bass and baritone roles in *Rigoletto, Simon Boccanegra, Don Carlos,* and several other works. The contrast between the angular melodic lines of the prophet and the supple ones of the king strikingly represent the steadfastness of one and the mercurial nature of the other. The strength of Zaccaria's music is matched only by that of Abigaille, who until the final scene is just as resolute as he.

Verdi displays an increasing interest in musical unity throughout the opera. Certain keys represent specific ideas and accompaniment patterns and rhythmic and melodic motives recur throughout the work. Individual numbers move beyond old formal stereotypes and exhibit more elasticity in their movement between vocal styles.

❃ ❃ ❃

The opening night audience was wildly enthusiastic. Although the Austrian authorities had outlawed encores for fear that they could provoke political fervor, legend has it that a repetition of "Va pensiero" was demanded and granted. In 1969 Charles Osborne repeated the orthodox view of this occurrence: "It was easy for the Milanese, governed by Austrians, to see themselves as Jews suffering under the Babylonian yoke; they made the connection and made it vociferously. With this one chorus in an opera on a biblical subject, Verdi immediately and inadvertently became the composer of the Risorgimento."[7] Osborne was probably correct that such a political statement was inadvertent on Verdi's part. Although he was certainly a believer in the cause of Italian unification, he was essentially apolitical at this stage of his life.

If the story is true, the audience's reaction probably resulted from more than one stimulus. There is no doubt that in Solera's text for "Va pensiero," particularly the line "Oh my homeland so beautiful and lost," many of those present would have inferred a metaphor for their own experience. A significant number of the La Scala patrons, however, were prosperous and content under Austrian rule and would not have identified with the longing of the Hebrew slaves. If they joined in the fervent response, it was more likely a reaction to the power of the music. Some evidence actually suggests that the repeated chorus was not "Va pensiero" at all, but the choral finale to Part Four, "Immenso Jeovha."[8]

Nevertheless, whatever transpired in March of 1842, "Va pensiero" eventually attained iconic status as an unofficial national anthem of a unified Italy. Its continuing potential to stir strong political feelings was demonstrated in recent times during a performance of *Nabucco* at the Teatro dell'Opera of Rome on March 18, 2011. At the end of "Va pensiero" Maestro Riccardo Muti interrupted the performance, turned to the audience, passionately denounced the drastic cuts to arts funding by the government of Prime Minister Silvio Berlusconi, and asked the audience to join in a repetition of the chorus.

Nabucco was performed more than seventy times at La Scala during 1842 and was soon heard in most of Italy's major theaters, in Vienna, and, in 1845, in Paris. Years later Verdi wrote, "With *Nabucco* my career can be said to have begun." He also commented that this marked the beginning of his sixteen "years in the galleys," during which he produced at least one opera each year. Although such incessant work was not exceptional for an Italian opera composer of the time, his responsibilities did not end with the preparation of the score. He was also expected to conduct the first rehearsals of a new production from the piano. This often involved dealing with singers who were poorly prepared or those who wanted changes in their arias that were more flattering to their voices. Verdi normally waited until these piano rehearsals to complete the orchestration, a procedure he found practical, but one that added to the stress of a premiere. On numerous occasions during his "galley years" he suffered with minor ailments that were probably the result of overwork.

In addition to international fame and a significantly improved financial situation, Verdi soon became a favorite of Milan's aristocracy. He became especially close to the poet Andrea Maffei (1798–1885) and his wife, Countess Clara Maffei (1814–1886), whose salon attracted members of the intellectual elite, both Italian and foreign. The countess was a fervent supporter of the Risorgimento, and Alessandro Manzoni was an occasional guest.

The Maffeis separated in 1846, but Verdi remained a close friend of both of them for the rest of their lives. At the time that he began to frequent the Maffei salon he was still an unpolished young man, so the discussions of literature, art, music, and politics that he experienced there comprised an important part of his education. Also, his ongoing correspondence with the Maffeis provides important biographical information about a man who was famously private regarding his personal life.

After the overwhelming success of *Nabucco*, Merelli was eager to move ahead with another Verdi opera for the following year. It was decided that this would be *I Lombardi alla Prima Crociata* (*The Lombards at the First Crusade*), with Solera as librettist, based on a popular epic poem by Tommaso Grossi (1791–1853). Grossi was a friend of Manzoni and *I Lombardi* is mentioned in *I promessi sposi*. Several of Grossi's works were considered to be politically incendiary by the Austrian authorities.

Verdi turned to Giuseppina Strepponi for advice on the appropriate fee to ask of Merelli for the new work. She suggested that he request the same fee that Bellini had been paid for *Norma* in 1831, and the impresario agreed without question.

I Lombardi takes place at the end of the eleventh century and, like *Nabucco*, places fictional characters within a historical event. Arvino, a Milanese nobleman, has been appointed to lead a crusade to the Holy Land. He and his brother Pagano have been rivals for the love of Viclinda, whom Arvino has eventually married. Years later Pagano's jealousy is rekindled and he tries unsuccessfully to kill his brother. For this he is banished from Milan.

The crusaders arrive at Antioch and lay siege to the city. Arvino's daughter Giselda has been captured and held in the harem of Acciano, the sultan of Antioch. Oronte, Acciano's son, has fallen in love with her and has converted to Christianity.

Arvino's forces, aided by a mysterious hermit, storm the palace and kill Acciano. Giselda, thinking that Oronte has also been killed, wanders into the wilderness, where she finds him alive, but wounded. The hermit appears and baptizes Oronte just before he dies.

Giselda, reunited with her father in the desert outside Jerusalem, tells him of her dream in which Oronte has told her that the crusaders will be able to capture the city. The hermit, now wounded and dying, appears and reveals himself to be Pagano. The brothers embrace and Pagano dies as they see Jerusalem in the distance in the hands of the crusaders.

Before the premiere of *I Lombardi*, Verdi experienced the first of what was to be a long series of episodes of censorship. Because the Milanese audience would be seeing their own ancestors engaged in a struggle with foreigners, this plot was potentially more politically provocative than that of *Nabucco*. Ironically, however, it was not the Austrians who objected, but the church. The archbishop of Milan had heard that Oronte would be baptized on stage and that Giselda's prayer in the first act began with the words "Ave Maria," both of which he considered to be sacrilegious when used in the theater. Verdi refused to answer the criticisms, but Merelli and Solera made some trivial adjustments, including changing "Ave Maria" to "Salve Maria." The performance was allowed to proceed on February 11, 1843, and was another great success.

In the second scene of the last act, Solera and Verdi attempted to duplicate the choral phenomenon of *Nabucco*. The Lombard forces outside Jerusalem have been frustrated in their efforts to take the city. They pray for divine aid in the chorus "Signore, dal tetto natio" ("Lord, from our Native Land"), which is reminiscent of "Va pensiero" in its melodic and rhythmic structure as well as its predominantly unison setting. The public received it with comparable enthusiasm, but it never achieved the lasting renown of its predecessor.

When the score was published by Ricordi, Verdi chose to dedicate it to his sovereign, Marie Louise, Duchess of Parma. Although there is some irony in the dedication of this Italian nationalistic work to an Austrian princess, "Maria Luigia" was almost universally admired by her Parmesan subjects, and her government had been sympathetic to the composer during his Busseto years.

There are some inspired moments in *I Lombardi*. Giselda's "Salve Regina," with its chamber-like accompaniment and ravishing chromatic harmony, is a masterpiece. The extended composition for solo violin and orchestra that precedes Oronte's baptism in the third act testifies to Verdi's growing command of orchestral writing. There are also some distinguished ensemble passages. The opera as a whole, however, was not so strong as *Nabucco* and was never consistently successful outside Milan. It was, however, the first of Verdi's works to be performed in New York.

In 1847 Verdi extensively revised *I Lombardi* with a French libretto for its debut at the Paris Opéra. This opera, titled *Jérusalem*, which transformed the Lombard crusaders into Franks, was later retranslated into Italian as *Gerusalemme* and premiered at La Scala in 1850. *Jérusalem* was successful in Paris, but probably because the 1850 version no longer had Italian nationalistic implications, it was never so popular in Italy as the original.

At about the time that *I Lombardi* was introduced at Milan, *Nabucco* had a successful premiere at La Fenice in Venice, and Verdi began to correspond with that theater's director, Count Carlo Mocenigo, about productions for the following spring. Mocenigo proposed a performance of *I Lombardi* to open the season, followed by a new opera from Verdi. Although his dealings with Merelli had been profitable, Verdi feared that a fourth new work for La Scala in hardly more than four years might cause the Milanese audience to tire of him. Consequently, after some negotiation about the terms of Mocenigo's offer, he signed a contract on May 28, 1843.

At this point the discussion turned to finding the right libretto. Although the composer was interested in Shakespeare's *King Lear* and Byron's *The Corsair*, he believed they would not be effective without a low male voice comparable to that of Giorgio Ronconi, and such an artist was not available at La Fenice. Verdi expressed interest in Byron's *The Two Foscari*, a Venetian topic that he thought was "full of passion." But Mocenigo rejected it on the grounds that descendents of the patrician Foscari family might find the story offensive.

By June the officials at La Fenice had put Verdi in touch with the Venetian poet Francesco Maria Piave (1810–1876). At that point he had only written one libretto, and the composer was concerned about his inexperience. Piave wrote that he was working on a libretto called *Allan Cameron* that was based on Sir Walter Scott's novel *Woodstock*. Verdi was interested and they continued their correspondence about its progress. By late summer the title had been changed to *Cromwell*, but both Verdi and Mocenigo, while expressing approval of Piave's work, were dissatisfied with the basic plot. They began to discuss Victor

Hugo's 1830 drama *Ernani*, set during the reign of Spanish king Charles I (later Emperor Charles V) during the sixteenth century. Verdi immediately seized on this and suggested that Piave be compensated for his work on *Cromwell* and that he begin to adapt *Ernani*. The poet was naturally upset at the thought of this radical change of plans, but with a flexibility that Verdi was to value in later years, he deferred to the stronger personality.

Hugo's original contained some material that would never have been approved by the censors, and considerable negotiation was necessary to produce a libretto that could actually be performed. There were also disagreements about the singers. Since the success of *Nabucco*, however, Verdi had gained the confidence to fight for his artistic vision, and in most instances he prevailed.

Amazingly, considering the multiple setbacks that the project suffered, *Ernani* opened on March 9, 1844, less than six months after Piave began to work on the libretto. Before the premiere, those involved began to predict that it would be a triumph, and they were not disappointed. Despite the fact that several of the leads were not in good voice, the audience was enthusiastic. After the La Fenice season ended, the Teatro San Benedetto, also in Venice, mounted its own production to even more acclaim.

ERNANI: SYNOPSIS

Similar to many opera plots of the era, *Ernani* involves a love story played out against political conflict. The nobleman Don Juan of Aragon has become a bandit and taken the name Ernani after having his title and domain taken away by the father of Don Carlo (Charles I), king of Spain, and he is determined to exact revenge. He is in love with Elvira, but she has been betrothed, against her will, to her aged uncle, Don Ruy Gomez de Silva.

Like both *Nabucco* and *I Lombardi*, the libretto of *Ernani* provides a title for each of the four parts or acts: "The Bandit," "The Guest," "The Pardon," and "The Mask." The action begins in 1519 in the mountains of Aragon, where Ernani and his fellow bandits are plotting to rescue Elvira from Silva's castle. Scene Two shifts to the castle. As the reluctant bride longs for Ernani, she is visited by the king, disguised as a peasant. He declares that he too is in love with her, but she recognizes him and tells him that she is in love with his rival. As he tries to abduct her, Ernani arrives and a fight ensues.

At this moment Silva enters and, not recognizing the king, challenges both him and Ernani to a duel. Carlo's equerry arrives, making his master's identity apparent, and Silva asks for his forgiveness. The king grants this and explains that he has come to ask for Silva's support in the upcoming election of a new Holy Roman Emperor. Carlo allows Ernani to go, but he secretly tells Elvira to prepare to escape.

Ernani, disguised as a pilgrim, returns to Silva's castle, where preparations for the wedding are proceeding. According to the code of nobility, Silva offers him hospitality, but finding him in an embrace with Elvira, he vows vengeance. When the king arrives, he suspects that Ernani is there, but because of his vow of hospitality Silva hides him. Carlo leaves, taking Elvira with him.

Silva challenges Ernani to a duel, but when he tells him that the king has abducted Elvira, Ernani convinces him that they must unite against him. To seal their agreement he gives the older man his hunting horn as a guarantee of his good faith. If Silva sounds the horn, Ernani will take his own life.

At the tomb of Charlemagne at Aix-la-Chapelle, where the plot to kill the king will be devised, Carlo enters and reflects on the glory that will be his if he is elected emperor. Silva, Ernani, and their fellow conspirators arrive to plan the murder, and Ernani is selected to do the deed. All of this is overheard by Carlo, who is hidden inside the tomb. A cannon shot is heard, announcing the king's election as emperor. When he is crowned, he condemns the conspirators to death. Ernani reveals his true identity, and Elvira begs for Carlo's mercy. Magnanimously, he forgives Ernani, restores his property, and agrees to his marriage to Elvira.

At Ernani's palace at Saragossa the wedding is about to take place. Amid the festivities a mysterious masked stranger is present. As the bridal couple celebrates, the sound of a horn is heard, and the masked man reveals himself to be Silva. He insists that Ernani fulfill his vow and hands him a dagger. He plunges it into his breast and dies in Elvira's arms.

ERNANI: THE MUSIC

Verdi chose to begin *Ernani* with a short prelude in which he skillfully combined the mystical passage that accompanies the fateful offering of the horn to Silva with an affecting melody that represents the love between hero and heroine. Each is heard once in full, and then both are repeated in abbreviated form and with strikingly different orchestration.

After a rousing drinking chorus sung by the bandits that begins Act One, Ernani takes the stage to sing of his love for Elvira in one of Verdi's first important showpieces for tenor, "Come rugiada al cespite d'un appassito fiore" ("Like dew on a withered flower"). After the cantabile his companions encourage him, and he apostrophizes his beloved in the **virtuosic** cabaletta, "O tu che l'alma adora" ("Oh you, beloved soul"). Although this scene is a natural crowd-pleaser, it looks back toward the entertaining but static arias of Verdi's predecessors rather than toward the powerful dramatic momentum that he had achieved in portions of *Nabucco*.

Scene Two begins with Elvira's cavatina, in which she expresses her disdain for her imminent marriage to Silva and her love for Ernani. The cantabile, "Ernani, Ernani, involami" ("Ernani, Ernani, Carry Me Away") has a graciousness and subtlety that were absent in Ernani's scena. The touches of chromaticism are reminiscent of the best of Bellini. In what had become almost standard procedure for Verdi, a women's chorus follows the cantabile, separates the two statements of the cabaletta, and joins with Elvira to punctuate the ending.

King Carlo enters in disguise and sends for Elvira, who recognizes him immediately. Their tense dialogue lies somewhere between accompanied recitative and arioso, with the woodwinds and brass alternating, sometimes in unison with the vocal parts and sometimes in harmony. Carlo begins the andantino that follows, revealing his soul in a tender plea for Elvira's love in a major key. His final note is interrupted by her first one with a stunning change to the minor and increased agitation in the accompaniment. Proudly referring to her Aragonese blood, she boldly renounces his crown and his love in a melody that is almost a mockery of the one that he has just sung.

Facing rejection in favor of one he believes to be a common bandit, Carlo, one of the most powerful men in Europe, begins to lose patience and to exert his authority, joining Elvira in the minor key, but soon forcing her back to the major. They eventually sing together, in harmony at the sweet-sounding intervals of thirds and tenths that for generations had been the musical manifestation of unity of purpose, friendship, or most often, love.[9] Here Verdi is resorting to blatant musical irony, since Carlo's love is decidedly unrequited.

Just as Elvira seizes a dagger from the king's belt, threatening to end both their lives, Ernani appears. After Carlo warns him to flee from his wrath, the two lovers sing together against the counterpoint of the king's interjected warning. This all moves at breakneck speed and Verdi increases the excitement by constantly shifting the place of the accents within the measure. The finale of Part One begins with the arrival of Silva who, finding his fiancée being pursued by two younger men, sings an affecting andante about his unfortunate situation. Carlo's equerry arrives and reveals his master's identity to Silva and his household. This evokes an enormous mass of sound from the entire company, followed by a complex ensemble for the four principals and three servants at an appropriately majestic adagio tempo. The final **stretta** is filled with energy with all seven characters and the chorus participating, accompanied by pulsating triplets in the brass instruments.

Act Two, set at Silva's castle, features a multisectional ensemble with alternating trios and duets. As the curtain rises, the orchestra and banda play festive music. Ernani finds Elvira preparing to marry Silva, so their scene begins in conflict with his accusing her of infidelity. But he soon has a change of heart, and they sing a tender andantino, sotto voce, accompanied by solo woodwinds, low strings, and harp.

Silva returns and finds them in an embrace. His outburst begins with a range of only three pitches, but expands with his increasing fury to end with an ascending line that covers more than a full octave. The two lovers join forces against him, singing together just as they had in the first-act trio with the king.

Carlo enters, suspicious of Silva because he has fortified his castle and is sheltering a "pilgrim" who is suspected to be Ernani. Their confrontation duet cleverly contrasts their characters. Now Carlo exudes power and impulsiveness with widely spaced intervals, while the older man moves cautiously within a narrow range. The king turns to Elvira and launches into a fervent cabaletta with choral accompaniment.

The act ends with an extended duet for Ernani and Silva. Their progression from antagonists to co-conspirators against Carlo is brilliantly depicted in the music, which moves seamlessly between keys, vocal styles, and varieties of orchestration. Everything comes to a dramatic halt, however, when Ernani offers Silva the horn that will eventually lead to his demise. Bassoon, trombone, and cello play the dark passage that began the prelude.

This rather unlikely symbol of goodwill satisfies Silva and the two men join together in unison and in obligatory thirds. This leads to a stretta for the two, joined by male chorus.

Act Three begins with a slow, ominous prelude played by solo bass clarinet with woodwind accompaniment as the curtain rises on the underground tomb of Emperor Charlemagne. Carlo enters and reflects on life and power in a grand scene that looks ahead to the magnificent soliloquy of his son, Philip II, in *Don Carlos*. At the outset of his aria he is accompanied delicately by low strings, but the full orchestra joins at the emotional high point: "e vincitor de'secoli li nome mio farò" ("and conqueror of centuries my name will be").

The conspirators enter and Ernani wins the right to assassinate the king. The members of the league now sing a rousing chorus, ""Si ridesti il Leon di Castiglia" ("May the Lion of Castile Awaken"), in which Verdi returns to the spirit of "Va pensiero." The underlying rhythmic structure is the same, and the men sing in unison almost throughout. At the beginning of the chorus the key shifts from the darkness of B minor to the brilliance of the major.

Three cannon shots are heard, and Carlo emerges from the tomb. The terrified league cries "Emperor Charlemagne!" and Carlo responds "Charles V, oh traitors." He condemns the commoners among the conspirators to prison and the nobles to death. Ernani then reveals his true identity and offers himself for execution. Elvira kneels at the feet of the emperor and summons all the powers of the prima donna as she begs him for mercy. Her last phrase descends more than two octaves in a span of four measures. Carlo turns and addresses Charlemagne's tomb in one of the most beautiful moments of the opera, "O sommo Carlo" ("Oh Supreme Charles"), in which he vows to match his predecessor's virtues. He grants a general amnesty and blesses the union of Elvira and Ernani.

The chorus joins in a massive song of praise for the emperor, supported by the full orchestra with percussion. The choral outbursts become interwoven with repetitions of fragments of Carlo's aria as the act comes to a triumphant end. This mass of sound almost obliterates, however, the character who has just lost his bride. In the background Silva vows never to forgive.

Act Four opens at Ernani's castle with banda and chorus celebrating his wedding to Elvira. The couple appears and Ernani serenades his bride with the melody that was heard as the second component of the opera's prelude. Elvira recalls her longing for him during her engagement to Silva, and the two express their joy together. Just as they reach the musical climax the dreaded sound of the horn is heard in the distance.

For a time Ernani believes that he is hallucinating, but Silva appears, removes his mask, and shows him the horn, singing the motive that was heard at the instrument's first appearance and in the prelude. An extended trio follows in which both Ernani and Elvira plead unsuccessfully for Silva's mercy. At the end Silva repeats his command that Ernani must die, and the horn motive is heard for a final time. Ernani stabs himself and he and Elvira sing their final farewell.

In *Ernani* Verdi continued to polish his craft. The ensemble writing is more dramatically cohesive and the melodies, though still owing a debt to Donizetti and Bellini, are consistently appealing. This is the earliest of Verdi's operas from which scenes and arias have regularly been excerpted for concert performance. Although the celebratory music in Acts Two and Four still contain vestiges of the crude banda style, there are many orchestral passages of great delicacy. Also, though it was not an entirely new concept in 1844, Verdi's use of the "horn motive" in the prelude and in two acts provides a measure of unity.

❀ ❀ ❀

With the unqualified success of *Ernani* at Venice, Verdi had conquered both of the great opera centers of northern Italy, and the demand for new works from him became almost insatiable. Within two years four more new Verdi operas had been produced: *I due Foscari* (*The Two Foscari*) (Teatro Argentina, Rome, November 3, 1844), *Giovanna d'Arco (Joan of Arc)* (La Scala, February 5, 1845), *Alzira* (San Carlo, August 12, 1845), and *Attila* (La Fenice, March 17, 1846).

For Rome, Verdi returned to Byron's *The Two Foscari*, which he had proposed and outlined for Venice the year before. Now without the danger of offending the sensibilities of Venetian aristocracy, he and Piave could proceed with their adaptation. Byron's story of intrigue and rivalry between two of Venice's patrician families was less suitable for an opera libretto than Verdi had originally thought, and the public reaction was less positive than it had been for *Nabucco* and *Ernani*. But Verdi continued to refine his craft by utilizing recurring melodies to represent characters.

After having ignored La Scala in 1844, Verdi contracted with Merelli for a new opera for the following year with a libretto to be provided by Solera. This work, *Giovanna d'Arco*, was loosely based on the 1801 drama *Die Jungfrau von Orleans (The Maid of Orleans)* by Friedrich Schiller. As with *Nabucco* and *I Lombardi*, the historical and religious references appealed to Solera.

In Solera's adaptation, Charles, the dauphin of France, falls in love with Joan, and her father is convinced that her vision of leading the French army against the English is the result of demonic possession. Following Schiller, Joan dies in battle rather than at the stake.

Merelli also chose to open his season in December with a production of *I Lombardi*. Verdi began to rehearse it while he was still composing the new opera and found that the artistic standards at La Scala had declined since he had last worked there. He was dismayed not only with the soloists, but with the orchestra and chorus as well.

Unfortunately, the same conditions prevailed for *Giovanna d'Arco*. The principal singers were weak, with the exception of Erminia Frezzolini (1818–1884), who sang the role of Joan. Frezzolini was a distinguished coloratura who had sung *Lucia di Lammermoor* and had created the role of Giselda in *I Lombardi*. Her presence prompted Verdi to compose one of the strongest soprano roles among his early works.

By now Verdi's public image as the great figure of Italian opera was ensured, and the La Scala audience received the new work with great enthusiasm. The Milanese critics were less kind, however, suggesting that Verdi was repeating himself and condemning the banalities they perceived in some of the choruses and banda passages. Of the production itself, the only high praise was reserved for the performance of

Frezzolini. The composer was especially offended that even the house journal of his publisher Ricordi printed an ambivalent review.

Because of his disappointment at the performances of his works that season and a disagreement with Merelli about publication, Verdi swore never to work for the company again. Like his vow to quit composing entirely after *Il giorno di regno*, this was not to be a permanent decision, but in this instance he stayed away from La Scala for almost twenty-five years.

By this time Verdi was already in negotiation with Vincenzo Flauto, the impresario of San Carlo, about a new opera for Naples. Of the three principal Italian theaters, San Carlo was the oldest, and the Neapolitan tradition was a glorious one. In addition to its venerable history, San Carlo's principal librettist, Salvatore Cammarano, had established a stellar reputation with the texts that he had supplied to Donizetti, including *Lucia di Lammermoor*. Cammarano suggested *Alzira*, an adaptation of Voltaire's *Alzire ou les Américains* (*Alzira* or *The Americans*), for the new work and Verdi agreed immediately. This story of Spanish conquistadors and the Incas in Peru contained all the elements that he favored for a libretto. Like *Nabucco* and *I Lombardi*, it presented a love story set against the clash between opposing cultures and religions.

In the original drama Voltaire had expressed his cynicism about organized Christianity, but for the conservative Neapolitan censors Cammarano carefully removed that element and focused on the love triangle between Alzira, daughter of an Inca chieftain; Gusmano, the Spanish governor of Peru; and Zamoro, a native warrior. Verdi was pleased with the libretto and wrote to Andrea Maffei that the composition had gone very easily. [10]

Despite the composer's confidence, the premiere on August 12, 1845, was not a great success, and subsequent performances at Rome and Milan received negative reviews. The failure of *Un giorno di regno* had occurred at an exceedingly vulnerable time for Verdi, but by 1845 his career had attained such momentum that he had little time for self-doubt.

Because of the perceived betrayal by Giovanni Ricordi in the review of *Giovanna d'Arco*, Verdi had begun to communicate with the rival Milanese publisher, Francesco Lucca. Soon he had entered into an agreement with Lucca and La Fenice for the spring season of 1846. Upon the suggestion of Andrea Maffei, Verdi became interested in the

German drama *Attila, König der Hunnen* (*Attila, King of the Huns*) by Zacharias Werner. Because the composer did not read German, Maffei had written a synopsis for him. Now, only three years before a major outbreak of revolution in Italy and elsewhere in 1848, Verdi was carefully considering the public's appetite for political metaphor. This story of Pope Leo the Great's turning back from Rome of Attila and his Germanic horde in 452 and of the founding of Venice by refugees from the Germanic invaders was a perfect vehicle for a premiere at La Fenice.

Verdi originally discussed a libretto with Piave, but quickly concluded that Solera would be more suitable for a story of this scope and intensity. Unfortunately the notoriously lazy Solera procrastinated, and the composer had the awkward task of asking Piave to complete the last act. The compositional process was further delayed by Verdi's debilitating attack of rheumatism that lasted for several months.

As with *Alzira*, time has proved *Attila* to be one of the weaker works in the Verdi canon. The composer was correct, however, in his assessment of audience reaction to the opera's symbolism. The metaphor of the Hebrews longing for their homeland in *Nabucco* and that of the Lombard troops praying for divine aid in capturing Jerusalem in *I Lombardi* were both debatable, but no Italian in 1846 could have misunderstood the implication when the Roman general Ezio, proposing a truce to Attila, sang the great stentorian phrase: "Avrai tu l'universo, resti l'Italia a me" ("You may have the universe, leave Italy to me"). At La Fenice and eventually all over Italy audience members responded by shouting "A noi! Italia a noi!" ("To us! Italy to us."). Now Verdi had unquestionably become the musical voice of the Risorgimento.

After the premiere of *Attila*, Verdi was still ill and exhausted, and his doctor ordered him to rest for six months. Back in Milan he was cared for by his devoted pupil and de facto assistant Emanuele Muzio (1821–1890). He also journeyed to take the waters at Recoaro Terme, near Vicenza, accompanied by Count Maffei. He had another contract to fulfill with Lucca and both Paris and London were clamoring for a new opera, but for a time he was content to concentrate on his convalescence.

In July of 1846 Verdi returned to Milan and was ready to discuss librettos. He respected Maffei's literary judgment, and the time he had spent with him at Recoaro had probably stimulated his interest in new subject matter. Maffei had suggested Schiller's *Die Räber* (*The Robbers*) and volunteered to write the libretto himself. Verdi, always an admirer of Shakespeare, had become interested in *Macbeth*. Eventually he decided to set Maffei's libretto, to be titled *I masnadieri* (*The Highwaymen*), for London and *Macbeth*, with a libretto by Piave, for the Teatro alla Pergola in Florence. Remarkably, they would be performed four months apart in 1847.

His period of recuperation had given Verdi an opportunity to reflect on both the positive and negative aspects of the seven operas that he had produced in a span of less than seven years. At this point he was prepared to break away from some of the rigid molds of the past and to attempt to achieve an integration of drama and music that had proved so elusive to composers since Monteverdi.

The composer's renewed energy and creativity proved to be a trial for the obliging Piave. Verdi bullied him unmercifully about virtually every aspect of the libretto and even sought the aid of Maffei to rewrite passages in which Piave could not please him. The finished libretto was as much a product of Verdi as of the two poets. From the outset it was apparent that this first essay in Shakespeare was especially meaningful to him. When he sent his synopsis of the drama to Piave, he wrote: "This tragedy is one of the greatest creations of humanity. If we can't make something great of it, let us try at least to do something out of the ordinary."[11]

Verdi also had a hand in all of the details of staging and the vocal nuances of the singers. On several occasions he corresponded with the baritone Felice Varesi (1813–1889), who was to sing the title role, always emphasizing that he was to serve the drama more than the music. When he arrived in Florence and the rehearsals began, he mercilessly forced the principals to work for hours on the specific effects he was seeking.

MACBETH: SYNOPSIS

Three groups of witches are gathered on a Scottish heath in the eleventh century. Macbeth and Banco (Banquo), commanders of the Scottish army who have just won a battle, enter and are greeted by the witches. They prophetically hail Macbeth as Thane of Cawdor and future king and address Banco as one whose sons will be kings. Macbeth soon learns that indeed King Duncan has made him Thane of Cawdor.

Shortly afterward Lady Macbeth reads a letter from her husband relating the witches' words and immediately decides that they must attempt to obtain the throne. She is told that King Duncan will be staying with them for the night and determines that they should have him murdered. When Macbeth returns and the king arrives, Lady Macbeth convinces her husband to do the deed. He kills Duncan while he is sleeping, but loses his nerve and flees before he can smear blood on the sleeping guards as they had planned. Disgusted with his lack of courage, Lady Macbeth finishes the gruesome task. Macduff, a nobleman who is in the king's party, discovers the crime, and all those present, including Macbeth and his wife, call for vengeance.

Macbeth is now king, but he worries about the witches' prophecy that Banco will father a royal line. He and Lady Macbeth plot to have both him and his son murdered. Banco is killed, but his son escapes.

At a banquet that night Macbeth receives the news about Banco. When he brazenly goes to sit at the murdered man's seat at the table, he sees his ghost in the chair. He is so horrified at this figure that no one else can see that the guests believe he is mad.

Macbeth goes to the witches' cave and asks them for more prophecies. They produce three apparitions, and each delivers a message: to beware Macduff, that no man born of a woman can harm him, and that he is invincible until Birnam Wood marches toward his castle. He then sees a vision of a procession of Banco's descendents, who are kings of Scotland. When he tells his wife of this, they decide that to secure their throne they will kill Banco's son as well as Macduff and his family.

Later, near the English border, Macduff vows revenge on Macbeth for the murder of his family. He and a band of Scottish refugees are joined by Duncan's son Malcolm and the English army. Malcolm instructs each man to cut a branch from a tree in Birnam Wood and to carry it as they attack Macbeth's forces.

Observed by a doctor and her lady-in-waiting, Lady Macbeth sleepwalks. In her unconscious state she is horrified at what she has done and attempts to clean the bloodstains from her hands.

In the final scene Macbeth is told that his wife has died and that an army is advancing on the castle. Despite this news, he is reassured by the memory of the witches' second and third prophecies. But as he prepares for battle, he learns that Birnam Wood is indeed moving toward the castle. Macduff confronts him and tells him that he was not born naturally, but by Caesarean. He kills Macbeth and proclaims Malcolm king of Scotland, prompting general rejoicing.

MACBETH: THE MUSIC

Verdi revised *Macbeth* for a production at the Théâtre Lyrique in Paris that took place in 1865. This included revisions of preexisting sections and the addition of new ones, including a ballet scene that was de rigueur for Paris. Some of the new music for the French version is stronger than what it replaced, but the eighteen years between the two versions made it inevitable that the whole 1865 opera is, as Verdi expressed it, something of a mosaic. Although it was not well received in Paris, the later version continues to be performed most often.

Like *Ernani*, the opera begins with a short prelude instead of an overture. It is based on music from the witches' scenes and the sleepwalking scene. The pervasive gloom of the tragedy is foreshadowed by the persistence of a single minor key throughout.

Act One opens with the appearance of the witches. Verdi was fascinated by the grotesqueness of the two scenes in which they appear, and he provided them with some of his most colorful music. In the orchestral introduction the fury of the thunderstorm is combined with grace notes and irregular rhythms that suggest both the strangeness and the bizarre humor of the witches.

The second scene introduces Lady Macbeth, who reads a letter from her husband concerning the prophecies he has received from the witches. The tempestuous orchestral music that accompanies her entrance is reminiscent of the witches' music, but without any element of humor. Her opening recitative reveals her character in the space of only two phrases. The first ends with the dissonant descending seventh on "potenza" ("power"), and the second contains a blazing **cadenza** that climbs to the soprano high C on "retrocede" ("retreat").

Lady Macbeth's andantino is not the typical cantabile, but is characterized by martial rhythms. There is no tenderness in this woman. The great leaps in her vocal line are similar to those of Abigaille and other strong characters in the earlier works.

A servant enters to tell her that the king will be spending the night, and she immediately begins to form her fateful plan. Her cabaletta, "Or tutti sorgete, ministri infernale" ("Now Arise, You Ministers of Satan') expresses Shakespeare's line: "Come you spirits that tend on mortal thoughts, unsex me here; and fill me from the crown to the toe, top-full of direst cruelty!" This is one of the most florid of Verdi's arias. By this time he had largely abandoned virtuoso writing for the sake of pure display, but here the vocal fireworks, like those in Mozart's "Queen of the Night" arias, are a perfect vehicle to express fury and defiance. When her husband arrives, she easily convinces him to agree to her plot. When they hear the sound of the approaching king, she bids her husband to come with her to greet him with a precipitous two-octave stepwise descent.

The extended banda passage that announces Duncan's arrival represents a regression for Verdi to the style of the occasional music he had composed for the amateur ensemble in Busseto. Perhaps he thought this naive, rustic march created the appropriate bucolic atmosphere for medieval Scotland.

The juxtaposition of such banality with the power of the following scene is shocking, and perhaps it was such a contrast that Verdi had in mind. The passage begins with Macbeth's vision of a dagger, progresses to his resolve to commit the crime, and reaches a climax with his duet with his wife. Except for a few outbursts the entire scene is to be sung with hushed voices, and the orchestration for delicate woodwinds and muted strings enhances the effect. Throughout the duet Macbeth expresses compassion for the king and regret for what he has done, while his wife taunts him and laughs, repeating the word *follie* (foolishness). The contrast between their characters is clearly reflected in the music. Lady Macbeth's line is jagged and disjunct while his is sinuous. His conscience, a quality that she lacks, is eloquently expressed in the beautiful soaring phrase on "Com'angeli d'ira, vendetta tuo narmi udrò di Duncano le sante virtù" ("Like angels of wrath, telling me of revenge, I will hear of Duncan's godly virtue"). With this single line, Verdi succeeds in arousing compassion for this tragically flawed character.

In the final scene of Act One Macduff asks Banco to wait while he awakens Duncan. Banco sings a very slow (largo) arioso that describes the tempestuous night that has just passed. The pulsating accompaniment elevates the tension and leads toward Macduff's announcement of the king's murder. The response is a massive choral finale with all those present expressing real or feigned horror and outrage at the event.

Through much of the finale Macbeth, Lady Macbeth, and her servant sing with Macduff while Duncan's son Malcolm, Banco, and the chorus form a second group. In their hypocrisy the couple ally themselves musically to the most commanding figure in the room. The most arresting passage occurs on the words "O gran Dio, che ne' cuori penetri" ("Oh great God, who sees into our hearts"), when these two groups sing their petitions in alternation, without accompaniment, and with a *ppp* **dynamic** marking.

The prelude to Act Two features music from the Act One duet in which Macbeth tells his wife about his reaction to committing the murder, setting the scene appropriately for another conversation between the couple. Macbeth announces to her that he will have Banco and his sons killed. At this point Verdi inserted a new aria for Lady Macbeth for the Paris production. "La luce langue" ("The Light Fades") is one of his great soprano arias and one of the most conspicuous improvements in the 1865 revision. The cantabile moves through several foreign keys and from aria to recitative to arioso. The key changes from minor to major as Lady Macbeth revels in her new stature as queen. The cabaletta eschews florid lines, but like most of Lady Macbeth's arias, it covers an enormous range and features large leaps.

Outside the castle assassins lie in wait for Banco and his son. In a short aria Banco expresses his intuition that the night seems like the one when the king was murdered. Verdi highlights that parallel by using similar rhythmic material in the vocal line. The final and highest note of the aria, accompanied by full orchestra, is followed by a sudden drop to a four-measure passage, marked *ppp*, during which Banco discovers that he has walked into a trap. The assassins seize him, but his son escapes.

The finale is the banquet scene. At her husband's request, Lady Macbeth sings a drinking song that is repeated by the chorus. Here Verdi has purposely written trivial music that fits the jovial mood of the moment. After the first stanza Macbeth learns in a whispered conversation that Banco is dead, and he brazenly decides to sit in the murdered man's place at the table. Invisible to all but Macbeth, Banco's ghost appears in the chair. As Macbeth reacts in horror, the banal party music changes abruptly to an agitated passage in the minor. His wife calms him and begins her song again. The ghost reappears, provoking an even more violent reaction from Macbeth. He begins a largo passage that expresses his fear of the ghost and his determination to return for more prophecies from the witches. This leads without a break into a complex ensemble in which Macbeth vows to shed more blood, his wife chides him for being frightened by an hallucination, and Macduff plans to leave his doomed country, all above a choral accompaniment. The defiant Lady Macbeth soars over all.

Act Three begins with another witches' scene, this time in a dark cave. The introductory music is different from that of the first act, but has similar effects that suggest thunder and cackling laughter. The grotesqueness of the scene is emphasized by the fact that the passage avoids the home key until the fifteenth measure. A witches' chorus is followed by a ballet that had to be added for the Parisian audiences. Interesting both rhythmically and harmonically, this is some of the finest instrumental writing that Verdi had produced. After Hecate, the goddess of the night, appears and orders the witches to answer Macbeth's questions, they dance to a very sophisticated waltz with strange off-beat accents. This is far removed from Verdi's earlier "Busseto style."

After the ballet, the scene in which the three apparitions appear before Macbeth was much revised for Paris and marks another musical high point. A man's head, a bloody child, and a crowned child each deliver a prophecy. They all sing from offstage in recitative mostly on single repeated pitches, and all are accompanied by winds. The final vision is of eight kings descended from Banco who appear one at a time. This ghostly procession is accompanied by woodwinds playing under the stage to imitate subterranean bagpipes. The music for each king moves from major to minor, but the home key keeps changing. The tonality becomes the most unstable with the eighth king, who is Banco himself.

When the witches tell Macbeth that Banco's line will survive, he collapses. At this point spirits appear to offer him comfort. In the original 1847 version Verdi insisted on including a short ballet for them. Lanari objected that ballet was not allowed in Florence during Lent, but Verdi prevailed. This was his first use of ballet in an opera, suggesting that he was already beginning to be influenced by the French style.[12]

When Macbeth revives, his wife enters and learns of the visions he has seen. In finely crafted accompanied recitative, they encourage each other in their intentions to kill Macduff and Banco's son. Macbeth begins their triumphant duet, "Ora di morte e di vendetta" ("Hour of Death and Revenge"), and she responds by imitating his melodic lines. The intensity builds to the threefold iteration, sung together, of the word *vendetta* (revenge). This is followed by a stunning shift, by now typical of Verdi, from minor to major and from *ff* to *pppp* on the repetition of "ora di morte." The duet and the act end triumphantly with Lady Macbeth reaching a high C on her fifth frenzied cry of "vendetta."

Act Four begins on the English border with Scottish refugees lamenting the loss of their country. Added in 1865, this passage demonstrates the maturing of Verdi's choral style. Instead of continuous massive blocks of sound, this chorus moves fluidly from solo writing for individual sections of the choir to **contrapuntal** texture to full chords. The harmonies are rich and chromatic.

Macduff and Malcolm agree to unite against Macbeth. With their duet, "La patria tradita" ("The Betrayed Homeland"), Verdi returns to the patriotic style of *Nabucco* and *I Lombardi*, with the two tenors singing in unison and the chorus responding, also in unison and accompanied by a martial rhythmic figure.

The narrative returns to Macbeth's castle for the dramatic high point of the opera with Lady Macbeth's celebrated sleepwalking scene. Although it is in the tradition of the numerous mad scenes in the bel canto literature, Verdi portrays dementia here not with the vocal acrobatics associated with *Lucia di Lammermoor*, but almost entirely with intense chromaticism.

The extended introduction is delicately scored with woodwinds and muted strings. Its central section is the lyrical melody that was introduced in the opera's prelude, the first phrase of which is repeated as accompaniment to the doctor's stunned observation: "Her eyes are wide open!"

In the aria, short, breathless fragments are juxtaposed with long soaring lines. The vocal range encompasses a full two octaves, and at the end Verdi demands a nearly impossible high D above the treble staff sung "a fil di voce" ("on a thread of voice").

Appropriately, the final scene of the opera belongs to the title character. In a recitative he expresses confidence in the prediction that no man born of woman can harm him, but suddenly realizes that death might be near. In the beautiful aria that follows, "Pietà, rispetto, amore, conforto" ("Pity, Respect, Love, Comfort"), Macbeth reflects on the realization that no one will mourn his death. This is his most melodic aria, and once again Verdi's moving music arouses sympathy for the wretched king. The second section moves to a distant key, but returns home for a repetition of the opening melody played by winds and strings.

When Lady Macbeth's lady-in-waiting informs the king that his wife has died, he delivers an abbreviated version of Shakespeare's great "tomorrow and tomorrow and tomorrow" soliloquy. This is interrupted by sounds of the approaching army and the announcement that Birnam Wood is moving.

For the 1865 revision Verdi chose to use an orchestral **fugue**, one of the most complex types of contrapuntal writing, to represent the battle. Because a fugue could be interpreted as one musical line "chasing" another, it was often used in Baroque music to suggest war. Although this one does not follow the strict procedures exemplified in the music of J. S. Bach, it cleverly builds intensity by having each entry of the main theme, or subject, begin a fifth higher than its predecessor. The fugue continues as Macduff orders the troops to strike and as he and Macbeth confront each other. They exit brandishing their swords, and the battle music gradually dies away as a women's chorus prays for mercy.

Macduff reenters to announce that he has killed Macbeth. The chorus of women, soldiers, and bards rejoice in the victory, praising Macduff and Malcolm, the new king. The two tenors sing in unison, sometimes with the chorus and sometimes alone, bringing the opera to a triumphant conclusion.

The audience reaction to the first performance was wildly enthusiastic. The composer was called to the stage more than twenty times. Antonio Barezzi came from Busseto for the opening, and several days later, Verdi wrote to inform him that he was dedicating *Macbeth* to him. In the letter he told his benefactor: "Now here is this *Macbeth*, which I love more than all my other operas and which I think the most worthy to be presented to you."[13]

Although most of the music in the Paris version of *Macbeth* displays a much more mature style, the 1847 original already represented an important advance in Verdi's development as a composer. His reverence for Shakespeare's tragedy inspired him to conceive of this work as something closer to the German concept of music drama than to the typical bel canto opera.

When *Macbeth* was being prepared for a performance at San Carlo in 1848, Verdi wrote to Salvatore Cammarano that the two principal pieces of the work were the first-act duet between husband and wife and the sleepwalking scene. He demanded that these passages were not to be sung. Instead, he wrote: "It is necessary to act them and declaim them with a very hollow and muffled voice."[14] The idea that the dramatic element should dominate the musical was a radical repudiation of the concept of bel canto and a major shift away from the aesthetic that had dominated Italian opera since it became a public entertainment in seventeenth-century Venice.

The music itself reflects this new concept. Although the outline of the Rossinian two-section aria is still present in Macbeth, its ossified structure with the repeat of the cabaletta has disappeared. Also the aria in general has become less central to the whole work. There are fewer extended solos during which the action comes to a halt. Shorter ones tend to exist as components of complex scenes.

Verdi's orchestral writing was continuing to evolve. Although stereotypical accompaniment figures like the notorious triple "oom-pah-pah" still appear, they are less common than in earlier works. There is increased attention to details of orchestration, and instrumental preludes are utilized to achieve appropriate dramatic atmosphere.

Chromaticism, which had been used skillfully, but within specific parameters, by Donizetti and Bellini, is now a pervasive element of the musical language. Virtually every extended passage in *Macbeth* moves through one or more tonal areas that are foreign to the home key. Verdi had effectively brought Italian opera into the mainstream of European romanticism, in which chromatic harmony is the principal means of strong expression.

But the "galley years" had not ended. In the four years between the premieres of *Macbeth* and *Rigoletto* Verdi composed five new operas and completely reworked another, none of which ever enjoyed universal success. But the refinements that he achieved in *Macbeth* laid a solid foundation for the great masterpieces of the 1850s.

4

"SIGNORA VERDI," NEW HOPES FOR ITALY, AND THREE ICONIC OPERAS

Rigoletto, Il trovatore, La traviata

In the summer of 1847, three months after the premiere of *Macbeth*, Verdi, accompanied by Muzio, set out for London to prepare for the July performance of *I masnadieri* at Her Majesty's Theatre. This was his first premiere outside Italy, and London, like Paris, offered both prestige and substantial monetary reward.

Since *Nabucco* Verdi had grown more exacting in his demands for the production of his works, and his dealings with the London impresario Benjamin Lumley proved to be no exception. He had originally planned to have *I masnadieri* performed at Florence instead of *Macbeth*, but had switched the two because Florence could not provide the tenor Gaetano Fraschini (1816–1887). Verdi had created the part of Zamoro in *Alzira* for him and wanted him for the difficult role of Carlo, the central figure of *I masnadieri*. Ironically, Fraschini had not been successful in London, and Lumley convinced Verdi to accept Italo Gardoni (1821–1882), who had received great acclaim there in several major bel canto roles.

Lumley had promised that Jenny Lind (1820–1887), the "Swedish Nightingale," would sing the prima donna role of Amalia, and on this point Verdi was unwilling to compromise. When he heard rumors that Lind was reconsidering learning the new role, he paused in his circuitous journey to London, staying several extra days in Paris while Muzio went ahead to assess the situation. Fortunately, he found that Lind was enthusiastic about *I masnadieri* and eager for Verdi to arrive and begin the rehearsals, so the recalcitrant maestro hurried to London.

Maffei's libretto, based on Schiller, concerns the conflict between two sons of a German count: the idealistic, but rebellious older brother Carlo, who leaves home and becomes associated with a band of robbers, and the devious, ambitious Francesco, who feigns his father's death and steals his brother's inheritance. He also covets Carlo's lover, Amalia, telling her that his brother has died and has willed that she marry Francesco. In the end Carlo is doomed by the vow he has made to devote his life to the robbers' band. To save the faithful Amalia from such a life, he kills her and then gives himself up to the authorities.

This plot contained several of the elements that Verdi found propitious for an opera: familial conflict, a love triangle, and the tragic consequences of an oath. Maffei was still inexperienced as a librettist, however, and his adaptation emphasized the more implausible, melodramatic elements of Schiller's drama. The unity of the whole work also suffered because Verdi had put it down to work on *Macbeth* and then had been forced to finish it very quickly.

The premiere was a glittering occasion. Italian opera had been popular in England since the time of Handel, but *I masnadieri* was to be the first work by a major Italian composer to have its premiere in London. All of the British aristocracy, including Queen Victoria and Prince Albert, were present, and the evening was a brilliant success. Much of the acclaim was directed to the figure of Verdi himself, who had conducted the performance. By this time he was universally recognized as the great figure of Italian opera, and audiences were prepared to react to his celebrity even if they were not entirely pleased with the new work.

Critical reaction was mixed. The queen herself wrote in her diary that the music was "noisy and trivial." Only three more performances were given, and the opera never became popular, even in Italy. Although *I masnadieri*, like each of its predecessors, contains some evidence of Verdi's musical maturation, it lacks the consistency, continuity, and realism of *Macbeth*.

Despite the new opera's failings, Lumley was obviously impressed with Verdi's prowess as both composer and conductor and presented him with the possibility of becoming director of Her Majesty's Theatre. In this position he would be responsible for all the productions, conduct some of them, and compose one new opera per year. The salary was generous and Verdi was interested. Although he had complained bitterly about the London weather, he had been impressed by the vitality and prosperity of the city. He made numerous demands, Lumley delayed, and eventually nothing transpired.[1]

Verdi left for Paris shortly after the London premiere. The French capital had two important attractions for him. The Opéra had expressed interest in a new or adapted work by Verdi, and his friend and supporter Giuseppina Strepponi had moved there in 1846 after her premature retirement from the stage.

Verdi may have initiated a conversation with the Opéra management about a French adaptation of *I Lombardi* during his brief stay in Paris en route to London, but the plan was solidified after his return from England. The Paris Opéra had become the world's leading company in the post–Napoleonic era with the rise of grand opera: great historical dramas, in four or five acts, with huge, elaborate crowd scenes, ballet, and lavish stage effects. The leading figure of French grand opera was the German-born Giacomo Meyerbeer (1791–1864), whose *Les Huguenots* (1836) was perhaps the most celebrated work of the genre. The ever-resourceful Rossini had also made a contribution to the early history of grand opera with *Guillaume Tell* (1829). An equally important figure was the dramatist Eugène Scribe (1791–1861), who provided some of the most successful librettos.

The basic aesthetics of French grand opera were not foreign to Verdi. *I Lombardi*, as well as *Nabucco* and others of his early works, dealt with similar grandiose historical subjects and featured magnificent choral scenes. Indeed, it was just this kind of grandeur that he had valued in the librettos of Solera. He obviously felt confident about the adaptation of *I Lombardi* into the French *Jérusalem*; he signed a contract to have it premiered during the fall season of 1847.

In the great cosmopolitan metropolis of Paris Verdi enjoyed the personal privacy that he could never find in Busseto and that was difficult to maintain even in Milan. This allowed his relationship with Strepponi to evolve into something more than the professional one that had existed intermittently since 1839 when she had helped persuade Merelli to produce *Oberto*. Strepponi had lived a life in the theater that was well outside the bounds of middle-class morality. She had been involved with a number of men and had given birth to four illegitimate children. The three who survived infancy, a boy and two girls, were placed in foster homes. Strepponi provided for her son, but took no financial responsibility for her daughters.

There is no indication of Verdi's attitude toward Strepponi's past. From the time of his stay in Paris in 1847 and 1848 they lived as a couple until she died in 1897. They were not married until 1859, but for several years prior to that she was often called "Signora Verdi" and the composer referred to her as his wife. In late 1847 Verdi invited his father-in-law, Antonio Barezzi, to come to Paris for a visit. He spent time in the company of Strepponi and, upon his return to Busseto, he wrote to Verdi praising the welcome he had received from "Signora Peppina."

On the advice of Scribe, Verdi chose Alphonse Royer and Gustave Vaëz to adapt Solera's original libretto of *I Lombardi*. The subject was still the First Crusade, but the fictional Lombard Arvino was replaced by the historical figure of Raymond, Count of Toulouse. The heroine, Hélène, like the original Giselda, had been imprisoned in a Palestinian harem. This gave Verdi and his librettists the opportunity to add a fifteen-movement ballet set in the harem garden.

Although Verdi was disappointed in the quality of the singers and the orchestra, the premiere in November 1847 was a great success, and soon afterward he was honored by being admitted to the French Legion of Honor. Unlike the Paris revision of *Macbeth*, nearly eighteen years later, *Jérusalem* was a vastly different work from the original *I Lombardi*. Verdi was sufficiently pleased with it that he immediately began to plan for an Italian translation. This opera, titled *Gerusalemme*, was published by Ricordi with a dedication to Giuseppina Strepponi. It was performed at La Scala in December of 1850, having come full circle from Italian to French and back.

Despite *Jérusalem*'s positive reception at the Paris premiere, neither *Jérusalem* nor *Gerusalemme* enjoyed lasting popularity. Nationalistic sentiment may have prejudiced some Italian audiences toward the original *I Lombardi*, in which their countrymen were the crusaders rather than Frenchmen.

By February of 1848 Verdi had finished *Il corsaro*, Piave's libretto based on the poem by Byron about the dashing Greek pirate Conrad and his struggle with the Turks. This story had interested him since 1844, when he had put it aside in favor of *Ernani*. *Il corsaro* was to be the last work that Verdi produced for the publisher Lucca, for whom he had developed a strong dislike. He decided not to go to Trieste, where it had its first performance in October, delegating Muzio to conduct. This was the first premiere in which he was totally uninvolved in the preparation, and his lack of concern was obvious. It was a disastrous failure, and after a few more performances in Italian theaters it virtually left the repertoire.

The failure of *Il corsaro* was also symptomatic of the fact that in order to satisfy the demand for new operas Verdi was again working at a feverish pace. The Trieste premiere was only eleven months after that of *Jérusalem* in Paris, and during the same period he was dealing with the Italian translation of that work.

This all transpired against a backdrop of serious political unrest in much of Europe. In France there had been growing dissatisfaction with the constitutional monarchy of Louis-Philippe (1773–1850) as the conditions of the working class had deteriorated under his rule. In February 1848 a series of protests in Paris led to the army firing on the crowd and killing more than fifty demonstrators. Louis-Philippe chose to abdicate and flee to England, where he lived the rest of his life. His action prevented further bloodshed.

The following month a violent protest against Austrian rule broke out in Milan. During a period from March 18 to March 22, known in Italian history as the Cinque Giornate ("five days"), the Milanese built barricades in the streets and almost miraculously drove thousands of occupying troops from the city. On March 23 King Carlo Alberto of Piedmont, at the urging of the Milanese, declared war on Austria. Finally the concept of Risorgimento was being manifested in aggressive action, and Verdi was jubilant.

Only a few weeks later he was able to celebrate on his home ground. On April 5 the *Gazzetta Musicale* reported: "This morning the celebrated maestro Verdi arrived in Milan."[2] On April 21 he wrote to Piave in Venice that he had found it impossible to remain in Paris when he heard about the events in Italy. He added: "Honor to these brave men! Honor to all Italy, which at this moment is truly great!"[3]

Although Verdi sincerely wanted to share this hopeful moment with his countrymen, his trip had a practical motivation as well. While he was there he negotiated the purchase of a farm at Sant'Agata, a few miles west of Busseto. He had several motivations for this investment. Carlo

Verdi's ancestors had been property owners at Sant'Agata, and Verdi's immediate plan was to move his parents there with his father as manager. He also knew how fertile the Po Valley was and recognized the potential for a profitable farming operation. Finally, despite the obvious professional advantages of Paris, London, or Milan, Verdi was to some extent still a *contadino*, a countryman, who was attached to the land. He had little use for the glittering social life of the city and probably envisioned for his future a quiet, bucolic life with Giuseppina at Sant'Agata.

The revolutionary euphoria in Italy inspired Verdi to consider another opera in a patriotic vein. He wanted Cammarano to write the libretto and to put the work in the hands of Ricordi for both publication and premiere as Lucca had done for *Macbeth*, *I masnadieri*, and *Il corsaro*. Cammarano suggested a historic plot about the twelfth-century Lombard League, a group of city-states of the region that banded together to defeat the occupying German emperor Frederick Barbarossa (ca. 1123–1190). The decisive battle was fought in 1176 near the small town of Legnano, a few miles northwest of Milan. Cammarano's libretto, *La battaglia di Legnano*, would focus on this battle, but fictional elements involving a love triangle would be adapted from a French drama, *La bataille de Toulouse*, by Joseph Méry (1797–1866), which was set during the Napoleonic Wars.

Even though Cammarano was more experienced and less malleable than Piave, Verdi exerted considerable influence on the final version of the libretto. Although *Nabucco*, *I Lombardi*, and *Attila* have traditionally been termed "Risorgimento operas," *La battaglia di Legnano* is the only one of these works that makes a direct political statement. The opening chorus on a Milanese street sings: "Viva Italia! Sacro un patto tutti stringe I figli suoi" ("Long live Italy! A sacred pact binds her sons together."). In Act Three, when the hero, Arrigo, is locked in a castle to prevent him from joining in the decisive battle, he leaps into the moat crying "Viva Italia!" No northern Italian audience could have doubted that this was a celebration of the Cinque Giornate.

By the time the new opera was finished, however, much of the elation that had followed the Cinque Giornate had faded. The problem, as it had been for centuries on the Italian peninsula, was a lack of political unity. The forces of King Carlo Alberto were engaging the Austrian troops in Lombardy and the Veneto, but the Venetians had declared themselves a republic in March, and most of the Milanese, encouraged by Mazzini and Manzoni, wanted to do the same rather than to become part of an expanded Kingdom of Piedmont. Farther south, the progressive Pope Pius IX (1792–1878), whom many liberals had seen as their champion, had disappointed them by refusing to take up the cause against Austria. During the next few years Verdi and many others began to realize that the only hope for Italian independence and unification lay with stable, prosperous, and relatively liberal Piedmont.

Ricordi arranged for the premiere of *La battaglia di Legnano* to take place at the Teatro Argentina in Rome in January of 1849. Shortly before the performance the pope had gone into exile, and Rome was about to declare itself a republic. Many of the leaders of the republican movement had converged on the city to elect an assembly. Patriotic emotion was at a fever pitch. The opera created a sensation. The audience demanded that the final act, which was only fifteen minutes long, be repeated. In the subsequent performances this encore became a tradition. The crowd alternated their cheer of "Viva Italia" with "Viva Verdi."

The reputation of *La battaglia di Legnano* has suffered in other times and locales because it has generally been viewed at best as an "occasional" work and at worst as a "potboiler" by a composer who was also a shrewd businessman. Such stereotyping is unfortunate, for the work, like many of Verdi's less popular operas, has definite strengths. The overture is stirring, with its paraphrase of "La Marseillaise," and Verdi's orchestration had continued to mature. The final act, with its grand ensemble of the principal characters, accompanied by church bells, organ, and choir, anticipates the great *Miserere* scene of *Il trovatore*.

While *La battaglia di Legnano* was still being composed, Verdi had already entered into a discussion of a new opera for Naples. Three years earlier he and Cammarano had contracted to supply work for San Carlo. But Verdi, whose experience at Naples had not been positive, reneged, leaving the librettist in a difficult position. In a letter to the San Carlo impresario, Vincenzo Flauto, in November 1849 Verdi expressed his willingness to compose a new opera as " a small service" for Cammarano. He also explained his doubts about the project, protesting that "great successes are difficult in Naples and especially for me."[4]

After some discussion with Cammarano about a libretto that would not be a target for the censors, they agreed on an adaptation of Schiller's early drama *Kabale und Liebe* (*Intrigue and Love*). Verdi demanded "a short drama of much interest, much movement, of the greatest passion."[5]

The story, set in a Tyrolean village in the early seventeenth century, concerns Count Walter, a member of the minor nobility who wants his son Rodolfo to improve the family's position by marrying a widowed duchess. His son is in love with Luisa Miller, the daughter of a retired soldier, who is also admired by the count's treacherous employee Wurm. Telling Luisa that he will have her father killed for threatening the count, Wurm forces her to write a letter stating that she is actually in love with him and had planned to marry Rodolfo for financial gain. Thinking that Luisa has betrayed him, Rodolfo drinks poison and offers it to Luisa. Before they both die, she tells him the truth about the letter and he manages to fatally wound Wurm.

Luisa Miller represented a change in the middle of Verdi's career from grand historical pageants to more intimate human drama. The final act, generally considered the finest, contains poignant duets for Luisa and her father and Luisa and Rodolfo, and a trio for the three. Here and in works like *Rigoletto* and *La traviata* that soon followed, without the need for great static choral finales, Verdi was able to concentrate more directly on the interaction of the principal characters in duets and other ensembles.

Luisa Miller was well received at San Carlo, but the success was soured by squabbles with the directors of the financially troubled theater. Verdi vowed never to produce another new opera for Naples and, unlike his similar pronouncement concerning La Scala, this was a vow that he kept.

The year 1849 brought an important change in Verdi's domestic life. In the late summer he and Strepponi moved from Paris to Busseto. Four years earlier, before the purchase of the farm at Sant'Agata, he had bought a townhouse known as the Palazzo Dordoni (later known as Palazzo Orlandi) on the town's main street. Verdi had always envisioned returning to country life in the Po Valley, and because his career was now an international one, nothing tied him to a specific city.

The move back to a town of about two thousand inhabitants was, however, an audacious one. Verdi was by far the most celebrated native of Busseto. His fame was a source of pride to staunch supporters like Antonio Barezzi, but some of the town's more traditional residents resented his wealth and interpreted his natural reticence as arrogance. Moreover, he was living in the center of his deceased wife's hometown with a woman to whom he was not married and whose checkered past was well known.

The period at the Palazzo Dordoni was not a happy time for Giuseppina. The townspeople shunned her, not even acknowledging her in church. While Verdi was busy composing and spending time away to rehearse new works, she was isolated in their house with only the servants for company.

The move to Busseto demonstrated Giuseppina's commitment to devote her life to Verdi. The cosmopolitan environment of Paris was much more appealing to her than to him. Subjecting her to the cruelty of small-town gossip and censure seems selfish and insensitive. In his defense, however, Paris was in the midst of a serious cholera epidemic that soon spread to other large, crowded cities. Perhaps both Verdi and Giuseppina believed that the rural life would be safer. Also her son Camillino, the only one of her children with whom she was actively involved, was in Florence, and she would be much closer to him in Busseto than in Paris.

Continuing the work routine that he had followed fairly consistently for ten years, while Verdi composed *Luisa Miller*, he planned his next opera. Originally this was to have been for Naples, with Cammarano once again as librettist. But after his difficulties with the San Carlo management, he offered it to Ricordi, both for publication and for contracting the premiere. Originally, his choice for the plot was Victor Hugo's *Le roi s'amuse* (*The King Amuses Himself*). He then turned again to his long-held dream of adapting *King Lear*, a task about which Cammarano was not enthusiastic.

By this time Ricordi had arranged for a premiere at Trieste in November of 1850, and there was insufficient time to do justice to *King Lear*. Verdi was already involved in discussions with Piave about a new work for La Fenice for the spring of 1851. Among other subjects, Piave suggested *Le Pasteur* or *L'Évangile et le foyer* (*The Pastor* or *The Gospel and the Hearth*) by Émile Souvestre and Eugène Bourgeois. Verdi did not know the play, about the family of a Protestant minister in Austria, but Piave sent him a summary of the plot. Verdi approved and it was decided that *Le Pasteur*, adapted as *Stiffelio*, would be the new work for Trieste and *Le roi s'amuse* would be the basis for the La Fenice opera.

The action of *Stiffelio* takes place around the beginning of the nineteenth century near Salzburg. The title character is an evangelical minister whose wife Lina is seduced by the young nobleman Raffaele. Count Stankar, Lina's father, suspects the affair and seeks to avenge the family's honor. Lina confesses the liaison to her husband and asks for forgiveness, but he demands a divorce. Eventually Stankar kills Raffaele in a duel. The following scene is a church service at which Stiffelio presides, with Lina and Stankar in attendance. Opening the Bible at random, he reads the passage that relates Christ's forgiveness of the woman who had committed adultery and is so moved that he forgives his wife publicly.

Verdi had become relatively sophisticated in his literary taste, but with *Stiffelio* he had chosen a subject that was ill suited for an Italian opera. The original drama was a profound study of the tension between the Christian principles of righteousness and forgiveness. It lacked the action and the forward momentum that he had always asked of his librettists. To make matters worse, the censors, concerned with the implications of the opera's religious themes, demanded drastic revisions. Perhaps the most detrimental was their objection to having the gospel passage concerning Jesus and the adulteress read onstage.[6] In the censored version the gospel reading is omitted, and Stiffelio preaches a sermon on the principle of forgiving one's enemies.

Although *Stiffelio* was politely received at Trieste, it was obvious that in its censored version it would never enjoy sustained success. In 1854 Piave and Verdi transformed it into *Aroldo*, set during the Crusades of the thirteenth century, while maintaining the core of the plot and much of the music. *Stiffelio* has been revived in recent times as a result of interest in performing the entire Verdi canon, but *Aroldo* is largely forgotten.

In addition to the basic unsuitability of the libretto, Verdi composed *Stiffelio* quickly and without the care that he lavished on projects that truly moved him. He had written to Piave to give his approval of the subject on May 8, 1850, and the work had its premiere just over six months later on November 16. The same letter reveals that during that time he was already concentrating on *Le roi s'amuse*, which he called "perhaps the greatest drama of modern times."[7]

Verdi knew that Hugo's drama was controversial and might be an easy target for the censors. The play was banned in Paris after its opening night in 1832 because its plot, loosely based on episodes from the life of King François I (1494–1547), presented the monarch's morals in an unflattering light. The French establishment saw it as a thinly veiled indictment of the reigning king, Louis-Philippe (1773–1850), and thus as a threat to the institution of the monarchy. *Le roi s'amuse* was not performed again in France for fifty years.

Despite this, Verdi and Piave received some assurance from the administration of La Fenice that their adaptation, to be titled *La maledizione* (*The Curse*), could be performed as they had conceived it. But only three months before the projected premiere the censors rejected the entire libretto. Verdi, already a wily negotiator in financial matters, eventually worked out a compromise. The Austrians, like the French, objected to the depiction of an amoral monarch, so Verdi and Piave moved the setting from the French royal court to that of the Duke of Mantua and changed the names of all the other characters. Although the plot revolved around the fulfillment of a curse, the censors considered the use of *La maledizione* as the title to be sacrilegious. Composer and librettist willingly changed the title to the name of the hunchbacked court jester, now called Rigoletto. They also agreed to omit a provocative scene in which the innocent young heroine, now called Gilda, hides in a room in the palace and the duke triumphantly produces the key to what proves to be his bedroom.

Verdi successfully argued to preserve the final scene, in which the body of Gilda appears on the stage in a sack, and to preserve the jester's physical deformity. On the latter point he was adamant, writing: "I find it most beautiful to present this person, extremely deformed and ridiculous, but internally passionate and full of love."[8] By this time Verdi's dramatic instincts were keen and he was willing to fight for his principles. He knew that La Fenice desperately wanted the new work, and he also remembered that he and Piave had been successful in skirting the Venetian censors in their adaptation of Hugo's provocative *Hernani* in 1844.

The choice of Mantua as the setting for *Rigoletto* was intriguing in several respects. The city and former duchy in the northern Po Valley is about eighty miles from Busseto, so the locale and its history would not have been unfamiliar to Verdi. If he and Piave had a historic duke of

Mantua in mind, it was most likely Vincenzo I Gonzaga (1562–1612) who, like François I, was both a great patron of the arts and a libertine. The perfect prototype for an operatic figure, he was personally charismatic and magnanimous and was a talented musical amateur. He was notoriously profligate with the duchy's wealth and virtually bankrupted the treasury. Vincenzo's court was the setting for the premiere of the first great opera, Monteverdi's *Orfeo*, in 1607. A darker coincidence is that Vincenzo's father, Duke Guglielmo (1538–1587), like some earlier Gonzagas, was hunchbacked.

RIGOLETTO: SYNOPSIS

The action begins at a lavish ball at the palace of the Duke of Mantua. The duke confides to the courtier Borsa that he is secretly pursuing a young woman whom he has seen in church. He has followed her to her house and discovered that she is visited every night by a mysterious man. As they observe the revelers, Borsa comments on the beauty of the ladies and the duke singles out the wife of Count Ceprano as the most attractive of all. When Borsa warns him that the count might hear him, he explains that he likes to move from one lovely woman to another and has only scorn for jealous husbands. He dances with the countess and kisses her hand. Her husband's jealousy is aggravated by the taunts of the hunchbacked jester Rigoletto, and he conspires with his friends to exact revenge.

As soon as Rigoletto is out of sight, Marullo, another courtier, laughingly gossips that the jester has a mistress whom he visits nightly. Meanwhile, the duke tells Rigoletto that he would like to get rid of the count and take his wife for himself. Brazenly, the jester suggests prison, exile, or even beheading. As the celebration continues, the old Count Monterone enters to denounce the duke, who has taken advantage of his daughter. The duke has him arrested, to the amusement of Rigoletto, but as Monterone is led away, he turns to the jester and pronounces a curse (*maledizione*) on both him and the duke. Uncharacteristically, Rigoletto trembles with horror.

Rigoletto, returning to his house, is accosted by the professional assassin Sparafucile, who offers his services in eliminating the jester's enemies and gives him information on where he may be found if his services are ever needed. As he continues into the courtyard of his house, he is greeted by his daughter Gilda. Obsessed with her safety, he warns her to remain near the confines of their home. Hearing a sound outside, he walks out onto the street. The duke, who has been waiting, slips into the courtyard and tosses a purse to Gilda's nurse to keep her quiet. When Rigoletto leaves, the duke, disguised as a student, enters the house and declares his love for Gilda. When he leaves, Gilda reflects lovingly on his assumed name.

Near his house Rigoletto encounters a group of masked courtiers who tell him they have come to abduct Countess Ceprano, whose home is nearby, on behalf of the duke. He points out the Ceprano house and agrees to help them. They insist that he must also be masked and trick him into being blindfolded. He mistakenly holds a ladder for them against the wall of his own house instead of that of Ceprano. The courtiers break into Rigoletto's house and carry off Gilda. Hearing her call for help, Rigoletto tears off the blindfold, rushes into the house, and finds her missing. Realizing that he has been tricked, he cries out "Ah! Ah! Ah! The curse!" and then faints.

The duke, back in his palace, is unhappy after having returned to Gilda's house to find her missing. The courtiers enter, laughing at having tricked Rigoletto into assisting with their abduction of his "mistress." Learning that they have brought her to the palace, the duke hurries to her.

Rigoletto enters, suspecting that Gilda is in the palace. The courtiers restrain him, but are shocked to learn that she is his daughter. Gilda emerges from the adjoining room where she has been with the duke and runs to her father's arms. Monterone, being led to the dungeon, passes through the room and, glancing at the duke's portrait, observes that he has suffered no consequences from his curse. Rigoletto then addresses the portrait, vowing to obtain revenge.

The final act is set at Sparafucile's run-down inn near the River Mincio on the outskirts of the city. The duke has been lured there on the pretext of meeting Sparafucile's sister Maddalena. He sings a coarse song in which he cynically accuses all women of the kind of infidelity that he practices himself. Rigoletto arrives with Gilda. He asks her if she still thinks fondly of the duke, and she confesses that she still loves the "student" who followed her from church. Hoping to show her the truth about her lover, Rigoletto leads her toward the inn where, from outside, they can observe the duke flirting with Maddalena.

Rigoletto instructs Gilda to flee to safety in Verona, where he will soon follow.[9] When she leaves, he finds Sparafucile and gives him half of his assassin's fee to murder the duke. They agree that the remainder will be paid when Sparafucile delivers the duke's body to him in a sack. By this time Maddalena has also succumbed to the duke's charms and convinces her brother not to kill him. He agrees to murder the next guest who arrives at the inn and to substitute that body for the duke's. Gilda hears this conversation and realizes that this is her opportunity to save the one she loves. As a fierce storm approaches, she enters the inn and is stabbed by Sparafucile.

Rigoletto returns and Sparafucile gives him the sack. As he gloats over the duke's demise, he hears him inside the inn singing the song from earlier in the evening. The jester tears open the sack and a flash of lightning reveals Gilda, who is still alive. She begs for her father's forgiveness and then dies. As he sobs over her body, he once again cries "Ah! The curse!"

RIGOLETTO: THE MUSIC

Rigoletto begins with a short prelude that is completely based on the arresting repeated-note motive that is associated with Monterone's curse (*maledizione*). The importance of that element in Verdi's mind is made clear in the music from beginning to end of the opera. It is first announced in octaves by trumpets and trombones. The motive is more a rhythmic entity than a melodic one, but it firmly establishes the dark key of C minor. This is reaffirmed at the end of the prelude by five strong **cadences** in that key punctuated by timpani rolls. This leads without pause into Act One, with celebratory music played for a ball at the ducal palace by an offstage **banda**. By this time Verdi was gradually moving away from the use of the banda, which had become an Italian operatic cliché. In this instance, however, its presence serves as a perfect musical embodiment of the banality of the duke's court, where he boasts of his own infidelities and his courtiers deal in trivial gossip. This passage contains at least five separate melodies, the second of which is consistently associated with the duke. This music serves as the unifying factor for the entire scene, with portions of it returning intermittently.

The duke is introduced not by the traditional two- or three-part entrance aria, but in a dialogue with his confidant, Borsa, played out against the dance music. He confides that he is most attracted to Countess Ceprano, and Borsa warns him not to let her husband hear. At Borsa's warning the orchestra takes over from the banda in preparation for the duke's response, in which he laughs off the warning and launches into the *ballata* "Questa o quella" ("This [Woman] or That One"). Historically, a ballata was a light, dance-like fourteenth-century song that was popular in northern Italian courts like Mantua. From the moment that Borsa warns the duke, the orchestra takes over the accompaniment and continues through the ballata. Thus, "Questa o quella" grows organically out of its surroundings. The accompaniment is a trivial dance pattern, but the duke's melody is light and elegant and, despite its simplicity, it is one of the most popular tenor solos in the repertoire. It ends on a low note, without encouraging applause, and the dancing resumes without a pause.

The guests dance a minuet, accompanied by an onstage string ensemble. This very refined and old-fashioned composition has often been compared to the minuet in Mozart's *Don Giovanni*. It serves as the backdrop for a flirtatious conversation between the duke and Countess Ceprano.

Rigoletto enters and, sizing up the situation, begins to taunt the jealous count as the minuet ends and the opening dance music resumes. As with the duke, the title character enters without the fanfare of a *cavatina*. At his exit the dancers begin a French country dance called a *perigordino*, perhaps a subtle reference to the Gallic origins of the story.

The gossiping courtiers enter with the hilarious news that Rigoletto has a mistress. Their dialogue is accompanied by still another repetition of the opening music, this time played by the onstage ensemble. Marullo delivers the news, with response by Borsa and a male chorus.

The duke and Rigoletto enter and glibly discuss what should be done about the jealous Count of Ceprano. The jester goes a bit too far, however, when he suggests that they behead him, arousing Ceprano's fury and drawing a reprimand from his master. Ceprano and the other courtiers begin to plan their vengeance. This leads to the opera's only semblance of a grand choral scene, in which the duke, Rigoletto, the courtiers, and chorus ignore the hostilities that have surfaced and sing a paean to the enjoyment of life.

In one of his most ingenious dramatic strokes, Verdi now turns this scene upside down with the entrance of the vengeful Monterone, whose daughter has been seduced by the duke. Once again, the only operatic parallel is the entrance of the statue into the party scene in the finale of *Don Giovanni*. Monterone pronounces the fateful curse with the repeated-note figure that was heard in the prelude. The duke reacts with characteristic bravado and scorn and the fickle courtiers do the same. Rigoletto, however, is horrified, and his reaction provides a striking counterpoint to that of the others. The music underscores the terror rather than the boldness with its minor key and the *sotto voce* (literally "under voice," extremely soft) in both vocal and instrumental parts. Monterone joins the ensemble, providing a third layer as he repeats his cry to Rigoletto: "You serpent who laughs at a father's sorrow, be cursed!"

It is not surprising that some of the Venetian critics found this scene perplexing. Nothing in Italian opera had ever been quite like it. Influenced by the French style, it is almost entirely comprised of dance music performed alternately by orchestra and the two smaller ensembles. Layered above this is virtually continuous dialogue between various combinations of seven characters with nothing that, in the strictest sense, is either recitative or aria. Verdi wrote later that he had conceived *Rigoletto* "without arias, without finales, with an interminable series of duets." [10]

Scene Two, which follows, is often performed as a separate act, resulting in a four-act opera. It takes place on the street outside Rigoletto's house and in its courtyard. The palace of Ceprano is also visible nearby. The contrast with the brilliant festivities of the first scene is stark. Now all is dark and ominous as Rigoletto worries about the curse. His first utterance is a version of the "maledizione" motive. He is approached by the assassin Sparafucile, who offers his services to eliminate an enemy. They converse above a serpentine melody played by muted cello and bass that aptly suggests Sparafucile's deviousness.

When Sparafucile exits, Rigoletto compares himself to the hired murderer in his powerful accompanied recitative "Pari siamo" ("We Are Alike"). He declares that while Sparafucile kills with the dagger, he does so with his tongue. He bemoans his fate in life and expresses resentment for the duke, who has put him in such a position.

He enters his courtyard and Gilda, accompanied by lighthearted music, throws herself in his arms. Gilda inspires a transformation in Rigoletto, who in Scene One has been presented as vile and scornful. Now, with the one thing he values ("my universe is in you"), he is tender and loving. Their opening dialogue, like the preceding ones, is carried out above continuous melody in the orchestra. When Gilda probes too deeply about his identity and that of her dead mother, the musical style changes abruptly to something much more traditional. The duet that begins with the andante "Deh non parlare al misero del suo perduto bene" ("Ah, do not speak of the misery of the lost good times") is the first truly lyrical outpouring of the opera. Gilda realizes the depths of her father's sorrow and joins the duet in the minor key. At climactic points they come together at the dulcet interval of a tenth in true bel canto style. As Gilda continues to press for answers, Rigoletto grows more agitated, and the **tempo** accelerates to allegro. The structure outwardly resembles the venerable multipartite aria, but this is something much more subtle than the traditional **cabaletta**. The entire section is a complex sequence of exchanges between Gilda and her father, ranging from recitative-like declamation to sumptuous melody, constantly varying in its relationship with the orchestra. Rigoletto addresses Giovanna, Gilda's nurse, imploring her to guard the innocent girl.

They are interrupted by a sound from outside, and Rigoletto, stopping in the middle of a word, goes out to the street to investigate. The duke slips into the courtyard and hides behind a tree. When the jester returns, the duke learns two salient pieces of information. This is Rigoletto's house, and the girl he has been following is his daughter. Father and daughter sing their farewells, moving from pianissimo to fortissimo with full orchestra, bringing this most traditional number to a blazing close.

Gilda coyly tells Giovanna about the handsome stranger who has followed her from church. When Giovanna speculates that he is probably a grand gentleman, Gilda naively and ironically expresses her hope that he is not a gentleman or prince, but poor like herself. At this moment the duke emerges from hiding and begins their duet: "È il sol dell'anima" ("It Is the Sunlight of the Soul"). Like all of his songlike passages, it is accompanied by a banal, repetitive figure. When Gilda responds, the orchestra abruptly moves to a rapidly pulsating figure that mirrors her excitement.

Just as the duke tells her his assumed name, Gualtier Maldè, the voices of Ceprano and Borsa are heard in the street pointing out Rigoletto's house. The lovers bid each other farewell in a brilliant stretta.

Left alone, Gilda ponders on the name the duke has given her in a recitative that is sensitively accompanied by flute, oboe, clarinet, and horn. This leads to her only aria in the opera, "Caro nome" ("Dear Name"). One of the best-loved sections of *Rigoletto*, its delicate lines with rests between syllables of the words express her innocence and the breathlessness of a first infatuation. The delicate scoring with woodwinds and short solo motives for solo violin inhabits a different world from the noisy orchestration that critics had pointed out in Verdi's early works. His dramatic judgment to forego a standard multipart aria was perfect in this situation. A traditional cabaletta would have undermined the simplicity and naiveté of Gilda's character. Also, by this time he had largely moved away from coloratura passages for vocal display, and the florid passages in "Caro nome" are notably restrained.

Gilda goes inside and reappears on a terrace to watch the duke disappear down the street. As she repeats his assumed name and the first phrase of the aria, the courtiers, now masked, appear on the street and, still thinking that she is Rigoletto's mistress, comment on her beauty.

In the finale of the act Rigoletto, still haunted by Monterone's curse, returns home. He encounters the courtiers, who trick him into aiding in Gilda's abduction. After the deed is done, he tears off the blindfold that they have placed on him and immediately sees his daughter's scarf, which she has dropped. This is accompanied by a remarkable orchestral passage that rises by steps through ten minor keys. Realizing exactly what has happened, he cries, singing the maledizione motive, "Ah! The curse!"

Act Two finds the duke in his palace, distraught at Gilda's disappearance. This situation prompted Piave and Verdi to include the one traditional solo **scena** of the opera. In an extended passage of recitative he sings movingly of his fears for the first one who has moved his heart to constancy. For Verdi, one of the attractions of Hugo's drama was the complexity of the characters of both Rigoletto and the duke. In this and in the **cantabile** that follows, "Parmi veder le lagrime" ("I Can Almost See Her Tears"), he reveals an unexpectedly tender side of this essentially cynical and cruel nobleman.

The duke's musing is interrupted by the arrival of the courtiers, who are celebrating their abduction of Rigoletto's "mistress." This choral interlude provides musical variety, but the information that Gilda is in the palace provides the dramatic impetus for the joyous cabaletta, "Possente amor mi chiama" ("Powerful Love Calls Me"). The tune and its accompaniment are formulaic and somewhat trite, bringing the character down to earth after the exalted cantabile. The courtiers join in the stretta with the duke singing above them. As the orchestra ends the scene, he rushes out the door to find Gilda.

Rigoletto is heard offstage singing a simple, but haunting little tune on nonsense syllables. This melody and its variants become the basis for accompaniment for much of the scene that follows.

He enters the room, trying to seem nonchalant in the presence of the courtiers who have conspired against him. As he banters with them he walks nervously, still singing his childlike song, trying to find some sign of his daughter. When a page, sent by the duchess, inquires about the duke's whereabouts, the lies of the courtiers make it clear to Rigoletto that he is indeed in his bedroom with Gilda. When the courtiers tell him to go find his mistress elsewhere, he shocks them by proclaiming her real identity. When he sings "Io vo' mia figlia" ("I want my daughter"), he moves abruptly to a foreign key with such strength and conviction that the startled courtiers join him in the new tonality.

Rigoletto tries to enter the duke's room, but the courtiers restrain him. In his aria, "Cortigiani, vil razza" ("Courtiers, Vile Breed"), he pours out his scorn and defiance toward his antagonists. Frustrated with his powerlessness, his bravado fades and he implores them to have mercy on his plight. The musical style shifts with his demeanor from stentorian to lyrical. The tempo slows and, now in tears, he sings a poignant melody, joined by a solo English horn, to conclude one of the greatest of Verdi's baritone arias.

Suddenly, accompanied by a joyous ascending line in the orchestra, Gilda rushes from the adjoining room and falls into her father's arms. She expresses her shame and, in order to ensure their privacy, Rigoletto orders the courtiers to leave, and they sheepishly comply. Beginning with the words "Tutte le feste al tempio" ("Every Sunday at church"),

Gilda confesses how she had begun to notice the handsome young man who was watching her as she prayed. She then relates how he had come to their house on the evening before and expressed his love. The tempo increases as she describes the horror of her abduction.

Rigoletto responds despairingly that his hopes and prayers for her have come to nothing. In a new key and slower tempo he sings "Piangi, piangi, fancuilla" (Weep, weep, child") and Gilda responds with gratitude for his consoling words. The duet ends with father and daughter singing in traditional sweet-sounding tenths as they did in Act One.

This tender moment of reconciliation is interrupted by the passing of Monterone, who is being escorted to prison. Singing the maledizione motive, he points out ironically that the duke has not suffered from his curse. But on the same pitch and in the same rhythm, Rigoletto tells him he is wrong and that he will have his vengeance.

This exchange inspires a brilliant cabaletta in which Rigoletto sings "Si, vendetta, tremenda vendetta" ("Yes, revenge, awful revenge"). Gilda repeats the melody a fourth higher, singing "O mio padre, qual gioia feroce" ("Oh father, what fierce joy") accompanied by cries of "revenge" from her father. Shockingly, she begs him to forgive the duke and, aside, declares her love for him despite all that has happened. Returning to his key, Rigoletto relishes the vengeance that he has planned and Gilda, in **counterpoint**, begs for pardon as the act concludes.

The intense confrontation and soaring lyricism of the second act would seem impossible to surpass, but Verdi managed to achieve that in Act Three. This is largely due to the magnificent quartet that is its centerpiece.

Gilda and her father are walking in a forlorn place near the inn of Sparafucile. She repeats her declaration of love for the duke and insists that he adores her as well. Knowing that the duke has been lured to the inn to meet the assassin's sister Maddalena, Rigoletto leads Gilda to a hiding place from which they can observe the scene inside. The duke, disguised as a cavalry officer, asks for a room and some wine. He then sings the most famous melody in the opera and one of the best known in the Italian repertoire: the bawdy song "La donna è mobile" ("Woman Is Fickle").

The song, with its perpetual "oom-pah-pah" accompaniment, begins with an orchestral introduction that states the principal melody. This is repeated between the two identical stanzas. The text is, of course, out-rageously ironic, for the inconstancy that the duke attributes to women is his own most prominent characteristic.

Through the years "La donna è mobile" has been singled out as an example of the banality of nineteenth-century Italian opera, but these critics have completely misunderstood Verdi's intentions. The duke is singing a popular song (canzone) just as a character in a spoken drama might do. It is purposely set in a simplistic manner, amplifying the irony of the text by having an aristocrat sing a decidedly low-class song, albeit one with a very appealing tune.

As the orchestra continues to play the duke's song, the seductive Maddalena enters the room. Sparafucile goes outside to confirm with Rigoletto the plan to kill the duke. The quartet begins with the duke's explanation that he has already seen Maddalena and been smitten with her beauty as with none other. His melody is sung in counterpoint to an equally important one in the orchestra. The fleeting, delicate violin figures recall those in "Caro nome," pointing up Gilda's tragic illusion about the duke. Maddalena coyly protests his advances while Gilda, still in hiding, reacts with horror.

The andante, "Bella figlia dell'amore" ("Beautiful Daughter of Love"), begins the cantabile of the quartet. The duke begs Maddalena to give herself to him, and she reacts coquettishly with fluttering phrases. Gilda cries out in short breathless statements, and Rigoletto solemnly denounces his bitter enemy.

Verdi is at his most masterful in this ensemble writing. The texture of the voices and orchestra is transparent and each character's texts are repeated so that the four disparate texts can be understood and each is perfectly projected in the music. The brilliance of this achievement has often been compared to that of Mozart in the ensembles from *The Marriage of Figaro* and *Don Giovanni*. When *Rigoletto* was produced in Paris in 1857, Victor Hugo, whose original drama was still banned, attended one of the performances and somewhat reluctantly admitted that the opera was superior. Of the quartet, he declared that he would be very pleased if he could have four of his own characters speak simul-taneously and be understood.

The final scene is played against the backdrop of an approaching storm. One of Verdi's central demands of his librettists was that his plots have forward momentum, and this finale is densely packed with human drama. Rigoletto sends Gilda home to disguise herself as a man and flee to Verona. He then summons Sparafucile and pays him for the duke's murder. Lightning flashes across the sky and the orchestra and offstage humming chorus imitate the sounds of thunder and wind. Thinking of the money he will earn for the murder, Sparafucile offers the duke his own room for the night. Maddalena reveals that she has also succumbed to the charms of the intended victim. The duke goes to his room and sings himself to sleep with "La donna è mobile."

Meanwhile, Gilda has returned to the inn in disguise and overhears a conversation between brother and sister in which Sparafucile agrees to accept a substitute victim. Although she recognizes that the duke has betrayed her and realizes what her actions will do to her father, Gilda follows her heart and resolves to die for him. At this point she, Maddalena, and Sparafucile sing together in similar rhythms. Unlike the quartet, in which four wildly different emotions were at play, this trio is perversely united in purpose. Gilda knocks at the door and Maddalena lets her in. Sparafucile waits behind the door with the dagger as the storm reaches its peak in an extended orchestral passage of violent intensity. Then all gradually dies away except for distant thunder and lightning.

Rigoletto appears, savoring his revenge in the most austere of recitatives. As the clock strikes midnight, Sparafucile lets him in and gives him the sack that ostensibly contains the duke's body. As he is about to drag it to the river, he hears the duke, offstage, singing "La donna è mobile." Horrified, he cuts open the sack and a flash of lightning illuminates Gilda's face. Still clinging to life, she speaks to him. As their recitative proceeds, the prevailing key changes almost every measure.

Gilda begs for forgiveness: "V'ho ingannato" ("I have deceived you") and Rigoletto, aside, realizes that she has borne the punishment of his desire for vengeance. When after a long pause she sings of heaven: "Lassù in cielo, vicino alla madre" ("Up in heaven, near my mother"), she moves to the warm key of D-flat major, a tonality that colored a similar reference in the second-act duet. On the word "addio" ("farewell") she makes a stunning momentary shift up to the key of D. She begins to tell her father that she will pray for him ("per voi pregherò"), but dies before she can utter the final syllable. Rigoletto cries "Ah! The curse!" and the opera closes as it began, with the maledizione motive.

❖ ❖ ❖

The premiere on March 11, 1851, was a popular triumph, although several critics questioned some of the innovative elements that they found eccentric. It was soon produced in most of the major Italian theaters. Ironically, it was performed more than one hundred times in Paris in its first season there, despite the fact that Hugo's drama was still banned.

Although Verdi's international reputation was firmly established by 1851, *Rigoletto* was the first of his operas that has consistently remained in the repertoire since its premiere. Its balance between naturalistic declamation and traditional Italian lyricism and its sensitive, colorful orchestration have made it a great favorite of musicians as well as the general public. Even Rossini, the grand old man of Italian opera, pronounced it to be a work of genius.

During the final preparation and first performances of *Rigoletto* a personal drama was unfolding in Busseto. The alienation between Giuseppina and the townspeople had grown worse. In addition, the couple's relationship with Carlo Verdi had worsened. Giuseppe had grown dissatisfied with his father's management of Sant'Agata and ultimately wanted to take up residence there himself. Also both parents disapproved of Giuseppina and of the couple's unmarried status. In April of 1851 father and son signed an agreement that Carlo and Luigia would move out of the house on the estate and that Verdi would provide a pension for them.

During this period Luigia Verdi became ill, and in late June she died. Verdi was devastated by his mother's death, but as always he moved forward both personally and professionally. He and Giuseppina began gradually moving into what was still a very basic farmhouse at Sant'Agata. He supervised an ongoing program of improvements to the house, garden, and farming operations. Although they would temporarily occupy a number of residences in the coming years, the estate was to be their principal home for the rest of their lives.

From January through March of 1852 Verdi and Giuseppina were in Paris, where he negotiated a contract for a five-act grand opera. For her it must have been a welcome reprieve from the indignities she had been enduring in Busseto. Verdi had misgivings about composing such an extended score and dealing with the bureaucracy of the Opéra. He wrote that "An opera for the Opéra is enough work to fell an ox: five hours of music!"[11] He realized, however, that no opera composer could maintain a truly international career without producing a successful French work. He accepted a contract to produce an opera, whose subject was still undetermined, in late 1854.

But Verdi had already been engaged in plans for his next Italian opera even before the premiere of *Rigoletto*. For some time he had been attracted to *El trovador* (*The Troubadour*), a Spanish romantic play by Garcia Gutiérrez (1813–1884). This melodramatic work had been produced in Madrid in 1836 and had made the unknown Gutiérrez famous almost overnight. To prepare this libretto Verdi turned again to the Neapolitan Cammarano. The poet did not respond for several weeks and then expressed a number of doubts about the suitability of the plot. While Verdi was negotiating with Cammarano, he was also dealing with impresarios about a venue. Because of financial disagreements and casting problems both Bologna and Naples fell through, but Verdi finally was able to place the work at the Teatro Apollo in Rome with singers that he found acceptable.

At first Verdi had difficulty convincing his conservative librettist to agree to some of his more progressive ideas concerning the plot, but he eventually prevailed in all but a few trivial details. Suddenly, when everything finally seemed to be in place, Cammarano died. Verdi learned the news from a notice in a theatrical journal and felt an immeasurable loss. Despite all his faults, he had been a poet of skill and taste. He had almost finished a draft of the libretto, but Verdi called upon the young Neapolitan poet Leone Emanuele Bardare (1820–1875) to make a number of revisions. In an act of generosity, he paid Cammarano's widow for a completed work.

IL TROVATORE: SYNOPSIS

The action takes place in fifteenth-century Spain, where a civil war is taking place between the forces of Count di Luna of Aragon and those of Prince Urgel of Biscay. At the beginning servants of the count are in the vestibule of the palace of Aliaferia in Aragon around midnight. Ferrando, a captain of the guard, talks with his men about the count's love for the noblewoman Leonora and his jealousy of a mysterious troubadour who is his rival for her love. He then relates the story of a gypsy woman who cast a spell on the count's younger brother Garzia and then was burned at the stake by the boys' father. To avenge that killing, her daughter abducted Garzia and reportedly burned him at the same stake. The old count maintained hope that the boy had survived and admonished the present count to remain on the lookout for his brother. Neither the gypsy nor the boy has been seen since that day, but Ferrando declares that he remembers every feature of the woman's face.

Meanwhile Leonora and her servant Ines wait in the garden of the palace, where she hopes to see a knight on whom she had placed a victory wreath in a tournament. He now comes regularly at night in the guise of a troubadour to serenade her. This is in fact Manrico, who is a knight of the prince of Biscay, the enemy of Count di Luna. Despite Ines's fears, Leonora declares her love for him.

Disappointed that Manrico has not appeared, Leonora goes inside just as the count appears, hoping to see her. In the distance he hears the sound of the troubadour's song. Just as he vows vengeance on this rival, Leonora rushes out, thinking that the count, who is wrapped in a cloak, is Manrico. She immediately realizes her mistake and boldly tells Manrico that it is he whom she loves. The outraged count challenges the troubadour to a duel, and they exit with swords drawn.

In the mountains of Biscay gypsies are at work with anvils and hammers. Manrico, who has prevailed in the duel but spared his rival's life, has come to the gypsy camp to recover from wounds he received in subsequent warfare between Biscay and Aragon. Azucena, the gypsy woman who abducted Garzia, tells the story of her mother's execution by the old count. Manrico presses Azucena, whom he believes to be his mother, to tell more about her past. Overcome by emotion, she inadvertently reveals that it was her own son whom she killed rather than Garzia di Luna. When Manrico suspects correctly that he is in fact Garzia di Luna, she protests, reminding him of the motherly care she has given him, and begs him, for her sake, never to spare the count's life again.

A messenger arrives with a letter informing Manrico that he is needed on the battlefront and that Leonora, thinking he had died in battle, is entering a convent. Azucena tries to prevent his leaving, but he hurries away.

Meanwhile, Count di Luna, accompanied by Ferrando and several of his other men, is waiting in the cloisters of Leonora's convent, planning to kidnap her. Leonora enters on her way to prayer and is confronted by the count. Just as he is about to seize her, Manrico appears with his followers, who hold off the count's men. While the struggle proceeds, Leonora and Manrico escape.

Manrico takes Leonora to the fortress of Castellor in Biscay. The count and his men set up camp outside, preparing to storm the fortress. A gypsy woman has been captured near the camp, and Ferrando recognizes her as the one who abducted the count's brother. In desperation Azucena cries out for Manrico to come and defend her. Upon learning that Manrico is her son, the count realizes that he can exact vengeance on both the troubadour and the gypsy.

Inside Castellor, Manrico and Leonora prepare to be married. As the sounds of the count's troops are heard outside, Manrico comforts Leonora, assuring her that his forces will triumph. His fellow soldier and friend Ruiz arrives to tell him that Azucena has been captured and is being led to be burned. Manrico vows to save her and rushes off to battle, swearing vengeance on the count.

Some time later the setting returns to the palace of Aliaferia where the triumphant count has imprisoned both Azucena and Manrico in a tower to await execution. Leonora and Ruiz enter, and she asks to be left alone, hoping that she might be able to save her lover. As she reflects on her love, monks intone a prayer for the prisoner's soul. From the tower Manrico bids Leonora farewell. She resolves to save him even if she has to die to do it.

The count appears and orders his men to execute both mother and son at dawn. As he muses on the whereabouts of Leonora, she appears and begs him to spare Manrico. When he refuses, she offers herself to him, but plans to kill herself as soon as the troubadour has been freed.

Inside the tower Manrico comforts Azucena, who again recalls the terror of her own mother's execution. In semiconsciousness she dreams of their return to the mountains of their homeland. Just as she goes to sleep Leonora enters and joyfully announces to Manrico that she has saved him. Almost immediately he guesses that she has given herself to his rival and denounces her bitterly. She collapses and admits that she has taken poison. The count enters and realizes he has been deceived. He vows retribution while Manrico begs for Leonora's forgiveness and

she bids him farewell. As soon as she dies the count sends the troubadour to the scaffold and drags Azucena to the window to see her son's
body. She reveals to him that he has killed his own brother and cries out
to her mother that she has been avenged. Horrified, the count collapses
in front of the window saying: "And I still live!"

The plot of *Il trovatore* has long been considered the ultimate in
operatic excess. The story is extremely complex, even though Cammarano and Verdi omitted some incidental characters and narrative details
from the original. Although most librettos of the time were illogical,
many critics have found the idea that Azucena would throw the wrong
baby into the fire to be impossibly implausible. But it was the bizarre
quality of this story that had fascinated Verdi. Indeed, he considered
Azucena to be the central character. He was attracted to her, as he had
been to Rigoletto, by the paradox of a physically hideous character,
filled with hatred and resentment, who nevertheless possesses great
love for a child. Unlike the jester, Azucena gets her vengeance in the
end, but like him she pays a terrible price. She is one of the most
memorable characters in the repertoire and hers is one of the greatest
of mezzo-soprano roles.

IL TROVATORE: THE MUSIC

Continuing the practice of dispensing with a large-scale overture, Verdi
goes even further here by eliminating a separate prelude altogether.
Instead, a short introduction leads directly into Act One ("The Duel")
with Ferrando and a chorus of male servants. This long narrative passage is necessary to relate the history of the animosity between the
family of Count di Luna and the two gypsy women. It also paints a
frightening picture of Azucena and heightens the drama of her appearance in the second act. Verdi further emphasizes this by giving Ferrando a recurring song that foreshadows in its key, meter, and accompaniment the music that the gypsy herself will sing. Musical variety is
achieved by the dialogue between Ferrando and the chorus.

The second scene introduces Leonora, who tells Ines about the mysterious knight who has come to serenade her. This takes the form of the
great three-part cavatina "Tacea la notte" ("The Night Was Silent").
One of Verdi's greatest melodic creations, the cantabile exploits the

contrasting colors of minor and major and the occasional foreign key. In the *tempo di mezzo* Ines expresses grave misgivings about this stranger above a turbulent and tonally unstable accompaniment. This introduces the brilliant cabaletta in which Leonora reaffirms her love. With its trills and two rapid scale passages that cover more than two octaves, this is a complete throwback to the **bel canto** of early Verdi.

After the dramatic effect he had achieved in the revolutionary scenes at the beginning and end of *Rigoletto*, Verdi had originally planned to similarly eliminate the formal set pieces from *Il trovatore*. In March of 1851 he wrote to Cammarano that if in this opera there were "neither *cavatinas*, duets, trios, choruses, finales, etc., and the whole work consisted of a single number, I should find that all the more right and proper." [12] The conservative librettist found it impossible, however, to completely eliminate the old structures. Ironically, Verdi was partly responsible as well. In the late stages of the opera's composition he decided to enhance Leonora's role and to reinstate this grand cavatina.

After Leonora's exit Count di Luna looks up at the light in her room. Just as he starts to rush up the stairs into the palace he is stopped by the sound of a harp in the distance that he recognizes as that of his rival, the troubadour. Appropriately, Manrico sings a simple song rather than an aria, but the effect of his approach from offstage is suitably dramatic.

Hearing the song of her beloved, Leonora hurries outside and the disconcerting incident of mistaken identity takes place. She quickly asserts her affection for the troubadour, and he reveals his identity to the count. Not only is he a rival for the love of a woman, but he is also the count's political enemy. All of this recitative is sung against a highly agitated accompaniment. It leads to a **stretta** for the three that prepares the way for a duel between the rivals. As in earlier trios of Verdi and others, the two lovers sing in unison with the count threatening in a striking counterpoint.

Act Two ("The Gypsy") begins in the gypsy camp with the workers singing the famous Anvil Chorus. This is another of Verdi's highly effective mostly unison choruses, but it is far removed from the grandiloquence of "Va pensiero." This music, with its irregular accents, use of triangle, and striking of anvils with hammers, is rustic and somewhat coarse. It is not specifically gypsy music, but it has a generic Eastern flavor.

The chorus ends abruptly after two stanzas, and Azucena, who has been sitting by the fire silently, relates a mysterious story of a burning at the stake in "Stride la vampa" ("The Flame Crackles"). This *canzone* (song) complements Ferrando's narration of the events in the first act. It is in the same meter and key, but is by necessity much more dramatic and emotional. The gypsy workers comment on the sadness of Azucena's song and then pack up their tools and exit, singing a reprise of the Anvil Chorus.

Manrico and Azucena are left alone, and he asks to hear the entire story. This prompts an extended narrative, part aria, part accompanied **recitative**, with Manrico interrupting with further questions. When she recalls once again her mother's suffering in the flames, the violins play a reminiscence of "Stride la vampa" against a **tremolo** accompaniment. With Azucena's recounting of casting of her own baby into the fire, the music reaches the extremes of tonal instability in a horrifying tone picture of unspeakable horror.

This information naturally leads Manrico to question his own identity, but Azucena assures him of her motherhood, recounting the care that she has lavished on him. She chides him for the mercy that he showed to the count when he had the chance to kill him in their duel. His response comprises the first section of their duet, "Mal reggendo all'aspro assalto" ("Badly Bearing the Harsh Assault"). This passage, in brilliant C major, epitomizes the strength of Verdi's melodic style at this point in his career. It rises incrementally, finally reaching its apex at the reference to a voice from heaven that commanded Manrico not to hurt his enemy. Azucena responds with fury, insisting that he never again show mercy to the count.

A horn call announces the arrival of a messenger with the news that Manrico must return to Castellor to join his forces and that Leonora is about to take the veil. He prepares to leave, but Azucena protests. Their conflict is played out in a rapid cabaletta that she begins in G minor. Manrico joins in G major and forces her into his key. This is a contest of wills that he will obviously win.

The scene shifts to the monastery that Leonora is about to enter. The count and his companions arrive and he sings movingly of his love for her in "Il balen del suo sorriso" ("In the Light of Her Smile"). The accompaniment, although traditional, is delicate and colorful, with a clarinet playing broken chords, **pizzicato** basses and sustained violas, horn, and bassoon. The sound of a bell signals that Leonora is about to take her vows at the altar. The count orders his men to conceal themselves, and a cabaletta follows in the form of a whispered chorus of the hidden men alternating with another beautiful melody for the count in "Per me ora fatale" ("For Me the Fatal Hour"). After a gigantic climax with baritone and male chorus together, the ensemble ends in near silence as the men take up their hiding places.

From inside the convent a chorus of nuns begins to sing of the joys of taking the veil while the count and his men interject their protests. Leonora emerges with her attendants and sings of her hope to be reunited with Manrico in heaven. In a passage marked by extremely unstable harmony, the action is suddenly compressed. The count appears to interrupt the women's reflections. Then, as the orchestra shifts up a half tone above the prevailing key, Manrico, whom all thought to be dead, suddenly appears.

The act ends with an ensemble tour de force with Leonora, the count, and Manrico, eventually joined by Ines, Ferrando, the chorus of nuns, and that of the count's men. The two rivals sing in unison as the count warns Manrico that the day of reckoning will come and the troubadour insists that God will assist him against an impious enemy. They stop suddenly in midphrase and a long, dramatic pause ensues. The full ensemble continues until Ruiz appears with reinforcements. They restrain the count, allowing Manrico and Leonora to escape together. Before their exit, in a phrase that extends more than an octave and a half, she proclaims: "You are descended from heaven or I am in heaven with you." The entire ensemble and orchestra respond with the final cadence.

Act Three ("The Gypsy's Son") begins at Count di Luna's camp near Castellor, where Leonora and Manrico have taken refuge. Ferrando tells the men that they will soon storm the fortress and they reply with the rousing chorus "Squilli, echeggi la tromba guerriera" ("Let the Battle Trumpet Blare and Echo"). Though not so famous as the Anvil Chorus, it is another of Verdi's stirring unison "choral arias."

Ferrando announces the capture of the gypsy woman. When the count questions her, she tells her story in the same key of E minor and triple meter as the earlier "Stride la vampa." When she expresses her love for her son, she moves to the brilliance of E major with a long, sweeping phrase. First Ferrando and then the count begin to suspect who this woman actually is. When Azucena asks di Luna who he is, he tells her that indeed he is the brother of the baby she abducted. Though terrified, she feigns bravado in the cabaletta "Deh, rallentate, o barbari, le acerbe mie ritorte" ("Ah, Loosen My Harsh Chains, Oh Barbarians"). The triumphant count, Ferrando, and the chorus join in and Azucena repeats the cabaletta. As the orchestra comes to a rousing conclusion, the gypsy is led off by the soldiers.

Within the castle Leonora worries that the preparations for battle are a dark omen for her upcoming marriage. The low strings play a pulsating figure that will recur in the last act as a symbol of death. This prepares the way for Manrico's great solo scene, which is certainly one of the most magnificent and demanding passages for tenor in the literature.

In the cantabile, "Ah sì, ben mio" ("Ah Yes, My Beloved"), he assures Leonora that her love strengthens him for battle, but that if he dies, he will wait for her in heaven. The first two sections are in F minor and A-flat minor, both of which are associated with Leonora. When he refers to his death and to heaven, he moves to the "celestial" key of D-flat major.

After the final cadence and a long pause, an organ is heard in the chapel, suggesting that the wedding will soon take place. But the happy anticipation is cut short by Ruiz, who brings the news of Azucena's capture and impending burning at the stake. This horrifies Manrico and inspires the defiance that he expresses in the famous cabaletta "Di quella pira" ("Of That Pyre"). Bidding Leonora farewell, he, Ruiz, and the other soldiers rush away as trumpets announce the coming battle.

The first scene of Act Four ("The Torture") contains one of Verdi's most celebrated and effective ensembles. The action has returned to the Aliaferia Palace. Manrico and his men have failed in their attempt to rescue Azucena, and mother and son are imprisoned in one of the palace's towers to await their executions. Leonora enters, accompanied by Ruiz, but glancing at a ring on her finger that contains poison, she dismisses him, assuring him that her defense is at hand. In the **romanza** "D'amor sull'ali rosee" ("Love on Rosy Wings"), she expresses her hopes that her feeling for him will bring him comfort in his prison. Beginning in F minor, like Manrico's aria in the preceding act, it moves quickly to A-flat major, the key in which her own "Tacea la notte" had ended. This is one of Verdi's most elegant melodies.

A death bell rings and a choir of monks begins to sing the *Miserere*, a prayer for the souls of those who are about to die. In terms of realism, the presence of the monks is questionable at best, but for musical drama it is a masterstroke. The solemnity of the thick six-voice chords contrasts markedly with the florid aria that precedes it. After one stanza of the *Miserere* Leonora moves to the minor key of the chorus to express the terror that has now gripped her. She is accompanied by the throbbing "death motive" that was heard in the previous scene. When she sings of the beating of her heart, her vocal line breaks into two-note "throbbing" motives separated by rests.

From the tower Manrico, accompanied by harp, sings his farewells in the major key. An exclamation from Leonora wrenches the music back to the minor for the repetition of the monks' chorus. She joins them, followed by Manrico, to create a stunning climax. Because the chorus, Leonora, and Manrico have all sung their texts separately, each is already clear before the three entities come together.

At this point Leonora resolves to give up her own life for Manrico. She expresses her new resolve in the brilliant and demanding cabaletta "Tu vedrai che amor in terra" ("You Will See That Love on Earth"). This is a dazzling showpiece, but is dramatically somewhat anticlimactic after the eloquence of the *Miserere* ensemble.

The count enters and Leonora begs him unsuccessfully to spare Manrico. She falls at his feet and begins the duet "Mira, di acerbe lagrime" ("See the Bitter Tears"). The more she pleads, the more determined he becomes to eliminate his rival. The orchestra alternates between a pulsating chordal accompaniment and dramatic doubling of the vocal lines by both strings and woodwinds. The two end by singing together in a soaring crescendo. Though their musical lines meet in the traditional bel canto tenths, their words are still totally at odds.

Now Leonora has only one alternative. She offers to give herself to the count in exchange for Manrico's life. When he agrees, she takes the poison that has been hidden in her ring and remarks aside that he will have her cold remains. Filled with joy at her triumph, she tearfully begins an ironic duet cabaletta in which she and the count each rejoice in their perceived victories.

The final scene belongs to the gypsy mother and her son. Azucena awakens in the place where they are both imprisoned. Accompanied by the "death motive," she tells Manrico that she already feels the hand of death upon her and that her captors will find a corpse when they come to execute her. The scene grows progressively more dramatic as she envisions the burning pyre. In a **parlante** passage, accompanied by flute and clarinet playing "Stride la vampa," she once again envisions her mother at the stake and becomes so overwhelmed that she collapses. Manrico comforts her and she begins their formal duet with "Sì, la stanchezza m'opprime" ("Yes, weariness oppresses me") in a minor key and with some of the same rhythmic figures that have already been associated with her. Manrico responds with "Riposa o madre" ("Rest, oh mother"), pulling Azucena into the major just as he did with Leonora in the *Miserere* scene.

She now dreams of their homeland in the justly famous, waltz-like "Ai nostri monti ritorneremo" ("We Shall Return to Our Mountains"). The tender duet ends with mother and son harmonizing in the requisite sixths and the tempo slowing as Azucena falls asleep.

The door of the prison opens, and Leonora enters to announce that she has come to save her lover. The joyous reunion ends abruptly, however, when he surmises what she has done in exchange for his freedom. In one of the most dramatic outbursts of the opera, he accuses her of selling herself. She tells him that he will soon learn of her faithfulness and begs him to flee. Their agitated exchange is interrupted in stunning fashion by Azucena, who is dreaming and singing "Ai nostri monti," effectively transforming the duet into a trio.

The finale begins with a dialogue between the two lovers accompanied by a continuous melody in the strings and woodwinds. The action proceeds rapidly in the way that Verdi preferred. Leonora begins to show the effects of the poison, and Manrico realizes what she has done. As he asks her for forgiveness and she takes his hand, the count enters, immediately comprehends that he has been tricked, and orders the guards to execute Manrico. He shows Azucena the scene of her son's death, and she tells him the terrible news that he has just executed his brother. Their exchange takes place above an incessant, hammering rhythm in the orchestra. The opera ends with the E-flat minor chord pounded out repeatedly by the full orchestra.

✿ ✿ ✿

The general evolution of opera in the nineteenth century was marked by a turning away from the formal, multimovement arias of the *opera seria* and *bel canto* traditions toward a more natural and continuous dramatic flow. In the works of Verdi, *Rigoletto* was an important milestone in that progression, but *Il trovatore* represented a return to tradition. Most would agree, however, that it is the richness and diversity of its arias that have ensured its perpetual popularity.

The great tenor Enrico Caruso (1873–1921) famously observed that *Il trovatore* requires the four greatest singers in the world. Indeed, there is at least one elaborate, virtuosic cabaletta for each of the principal characters. In no other work did Verdi achieve such a striking variety of beautiful melodies. His credo was to give the public what it wanted, and this work, perhaps the culmination of bel canto opera, struck a chord with audiences throughout much of the world. He once wrote that "in the heart of Africa or the Indies you will always hear *Trovatore*." [13]

Verdi was under contract to provide a new work for La Fenice less than three months after the premiere of *Trovatore*. Having musically portrayed Rigoletto and Azucena, two characters who were shunned by the establishment, he had become similarly interested in the prostitute Marguerite Gauthier, heroine of the 1848 novel *La dame aux camélias* by Alexandre Dumas the younger (1824–1895) and its 1852 adaptation for the stage.

Presenting a prostitute in a positive light was sure to stir controversy and the scrutiny of the censors, but Verdi realized that in cosmopolitan Venice he stood the best chance of realizing his dramatic vision. Indeed, the only alterations that the management of La Fenice demanded were a change of the proposed title, *Amore e morte* (*Love and Death*), and that Dumas's contemporary drama be moved back in time to the beginning of the eighteenth century. Verdi was especially enthusiastic about the original modern plot, but he reluctantly agreed to the "costume drama." In fact, he was in a weak bargaining position because he was behind schedule and would arrive in Venice too late to supervise the production as thoroughly as usual. During the rehearsals for *Trovatore* in Rome he was feverishly working on the *Traviata* score.

LA TRAVIATA: SYNOPSIS

The opera begins as guests arrive at the Paris home of the courtesan Violetta Valéry. Among them are her longtime acquaintance, Gastone, and his friend Alfredo Germont, who has secretly admired Violetta for some time. Dinner is served and Gastone tells his hostess that Alfredo has inquired about her every day during her recent illness. Slyly, she uses this information to make her "protector," Baron Douphol, jealous.

As the guests move to an adjoining room to dance, Violetta feels faint and excuses herself to recover. Alfredo follows her and confesses that he is in love with her. Although she protests that she is uninterested in love, she agrees to meet him the next day. After her guests have left, Violetta wonders if Alfredo is truly the one whom she could love, but decides that her freedom is more important. As the first act ends, she hears Alfredo serenading her from the street.

Some time has passed and the two are living happily in the country near Paris. Aninna, Violetta's maid, tells Alfredo that her mistress has pawned her jewels in order to keep the country house, and he immediately leaves for Paris to set the financial matters straight. Violetta receives an invitation to a party from her Paris friend Flora Bervoix, but realizes that she has no desire to go back to her old life in the city.

Giorgio Germont, Alfredo's father, arrives and insists that Violetta end the relationship with his son. The scandal caused by their affair has sullied the reputation of his family and threatened the planned engagement of Alfredo's sister. At first Violetta refuses, but Germont prevails. She sends a message to Flora accepting her invitation and writes a farewell message to Alfredo.

When Alfredo returns, Violetta, visibly distraught, tells him how much she loves him and rushes out of the room. As he reads her letter, his father enters, and the sobbing Alfredo falls into his arms.[14] Germont tries to comfort his son, reminding him of their happy family life in Provence. He is unmoved by his father's words and, finding Flora's invitation, assumes that Violetta is planning to attend and decides to confront her there. That evening Alfredo arrives at Flora's soirée, making cynical comments about love. Violetta arrives with Baron Douphol, who challenges Alfredo to a game of cards and loses a large sum. When the guests go in to dinner, Violetta confronts Alfredo and, fearful of a violent exchange between him and the baron, asks him to leave. He demands that she confess her love for the baron and, keeping her promise to his father, she does so. He denounces her and throws his winnings at her feet. Germont has arrived in time to see his son's behavior and reprimands him. The other guests also denounce him, and Baron Douphol challenges him to a duel.

Six months later Violetta is seriously ill and has taken to her bed in her Paris house. A doctor tells Annina that her mistress has tuberculosis and is close to death. A letter has arrived from Germont telling Violetta that Alfredo now knows the truth and is on his way to Paris to ask her forgiveness. She realizes that their reconciliation will occur too late, but when Alfredo arrives, they joyfully plan to leave Paris and start a new life together. Germont and the doctor enter as Violetta feels a surge of strength. She tries to go to Alfredo, but falls dead at his feet.

LA TRAVIATA: THE MUSIC

Like the preludes of its two immediate predecessors, the prelude to *La traviata* is short, but unlike them it makes a complete musical statement that could stand alone. Like the prelude to *Rigoletto*, it begins by foreshadowing the tragic nature of the story. Four first and four second violins play a series of haunting and poignant harmonies whose sense of key is ambiguous. This passage represents Violetta's illness and death, and it recurs in the prelude to the final act. This "death music" is followed by a passionate theme that represents the love between her and Alfredo. Violetta sings this melody in Act Two as she begs: "Amami, Alfredo, amami quant'io t'amo" ("Love me, Alfredo, love me as I love you"). This theme is closely related to another that Alfredo sings in Act One to the words "Di quell'amor ch'è palpito dell'universo intero" ("Of that love that is the pulse of the entire universe"), which is then repeated by both of the lovers. The prelude ends delicately and in a major key, setting the tone for the festive scene that follows.

The party scene is constructed similarly to the opening of *Rigoletto*, with continuous dialogue sung above dance music played by orchestra or banda. The transition between completely declamatory parlante passages and more melodic **arioso** is extremely fluid and natural. Groups of guests are represented by the chorus. When champagne has been served and everyone is seated for dinner, Gaston asks the baron to entertain with a song, but he refuses. He then turns to Alfredo who, with encouragement from Violetta, sings the rousing drinking song (*brindisi*) "Libiamo, libiamo nei lieti calici" ("Let's Drink from the Joyful Chalices"). All the guests echo his last phrase, and then Violetta sings a stanza. The chorus repeats the first section in unison in a lower key, but the two principals take over at the original pitch level, singing alternate phrases. At this point there is little doubt that Violetta reciprocates her new suitor's interest. As with the duke's "Questa o quella" in *Rigoletto*, Verdi has created a simple song with a stock accompaniment figure, but whose melodic and rhythmic vitality give it showstopping appeal.

The banda is heard from an adjoining room playing a waltz. Feeling faint, Violetta sits down to recover as her guests go to the ballroom. Alfredo stays with her and they converse, sometimes singing bits of the waltz tune along with the instruments. He readily admits that he has loved her since the first time he saw her. At this moment the banda is suddenly silenced, and Alfredo, accompanied by strings, begins the duet "Un dì felice" ("One Happy Day"), the second segment of which is "Di quell'amor," whose melody will serve as one of two variants of the "love theme" for the entire opera. In a coquettish vein, marked by sparking coloratura, Violetta chides him and warns him to forget her. The music contradicts her words, however, as she joins him at the end singing in the emblematic thirds, sixths, and tenths above him.

The dance music resumes as Violetta and Alfredo say their goodbyes and plan to meet again the following day. The guests thank their hostess and bid her farewell in an energetic *stretta* that features the orchestral accompaniment from the beginning of the act.

Left alone, Violetta ponders the evening's events in one of Verdi's most famous solo scenes. In a short recitative, "È strano" ("It Is Strange"), she expresses her wonder at experiencing a feeling that she had thought she would never know. Her two-stanza cantabile, "Ah fors'è lui" ("Perhaps It Is He"), is reminiscent of Leonora's "D'amor sull'ali rosee" in *Il trovatore*, with its shift from minor to major. In it she turns her thoughts to Alfredo and his virtues that she has never known in another man. With the shift to the major key she sings the love theme ("Di quell'amor") that Alfredo introduced in the prior scene. This is accompanied by delicate scoring for clarinet and strings.

Violetta's reflections suddenly end as she realizes that for her such passion is madness. Her dilemma almost leads her to hysteria, and the recitative ends with two brilliant **cadenzas**, the first touching the soprano high C and the second the D-flat above it. "Sempre libera" ("Always Free"), the cabaletta that follows, is one of Verdi's most dazzling. For the moment, Violetta decides in favor of her life of pleasure rather than one of commitment. At the end of her first stanza Alfredo is heard from outside, serenading her with another statement of the now familiar "Amor, amor è palpito dell'universo." The triple meter and harp accompaniment are reminiscent of Manrico's offstage singing in the *Miserere* scene of *Il trovatore*. Although Violetta is emotionally moved by her lover's presence outside her window, she once again denounces her feelings as madness and repeats the *cabaletta*. At the end Alfredo repeats his refrain, but this time Violetta joins him by repeating the final words of her aria in a florid coda that floats above his melody. Aside from the inspired melodic content and dazzling virtuoso display for the soprano voice in this great solo scene, Verdi has also exploited the old-fashioned multimovement scena to great dramatic effect as Violetta moves from infatuation in the cantabile to ambivalence in the recitative to resolve in the cabaletta.

Act Two begins at a rented country house outside Paris where Violetta and Alfredo are living together. The gap left in the narrative is typical of Verdi's desire for forward motion and his interest in the kind of human conflict that is the central issue of this act. As the curtain rises Alfredo enters, musing on his newfound happiness. He sings a cantabile, "I miei bollenti spiriti" ("My Ardent Spirits"), in which he declares that he is living as if in heaven. This is interrupted by the entrance of Annina, who reveals that Violetta is selling her possessions to support their life in the country. This revelation prompts a cabaletta, "O mio rimorso" ("Oh My Remorse"), in which Alfredo pours out his feelings of guilt in an impressive series of high notes. As Julian Budden has pointed out, this virtuoso aria hardly seems justified by the turn of events, but a brilliant tenor showpiece was always welcomed by Italian audiences.[15]

Shortly after Alfredo's departure to make financial arrangements in Paris, his father arrives to confront Violetta in the scene that is the crux of the entire opera. Germont tells her that he must ask her to make a sacrifice for the good of his two children, and she asks who the second child is. He responds with the cantabile "Pura siccome un angelo"

("Pure As an Angel"), in which he extols his daughter's goodness and expresses his fears that Alfredo's affair threatens her marriage plans. This is the first of a chain of movements in an extended scene for these two strong characters. In a parlante passage that accelerates inexorably, Violetta asks if this means that she must give up Alfredo only until his sister is married. Germont stuns her by declaring that this is not enough, and she suddenly grasps the full implication of his request. Having reached a breakneck tempo, she refuses to accept this, singing a melodic line of short, breathless phrases. She tells Germont that Alfredo is all that she has and that she is suffering from a serious illness.

Above a repeated "short-short-long" rhythmic figure like the "death motive" in *Trovatore* that portends a tragic outcome, Germont rather cruelly warns her that Alfredo might one day stray from her and that she will have no recourse without the blessing of the church. With this she begins to weaken and, in the almost unheard-of key of D-flat minor, she expresses her lost hope for happiness. Now, in a moving cantabile, "Dite alla giovine" ("Tell the Young Girl"), she begs him to tell his daughter that another woman has sacrificed her life for her happiness. Joining her, Germont praises her sacrifice, and this section ends with the two singing in tenths. They then discuss how she should go about ending the relationship. She arrives at a plan, but refuses to disclose it, telling Germont that he must wait nearby to console his son. In the final cabaletta of the scene, Violetta expresses her wish that when she dies Alfredo will learn of her sacrifice. The key moves from minor to major and the two end together, once again singing in tenths, wishing each other happiness.

Alfredo returns to find Violetta writing him a letter. Their conversation is accompanied by a repeated rhythmic motive in the strings that resembles the one that was associated with Germont in the previous scene. She tells him he must wait to see the letter and tearfully asks him if he truly loves her. His reply, "O quanto!" ("Oh so much!"), evokes a musical response that climaxes in one of the most memorable phrases in opera. As the key resolves again into brilliant major and the wind section joins the strings, Violetta sings "Amami, Alfredo," the "love theme," as it was originally heard in the prelude.

Violetta rushes out, where a carriage is waiting to take her to Paris. An officer brings her letter to Alfredo, who reads it and suddenly cries out as the full orchestra shifts to a foreign key. At this moment his father appears and embraces him. Here Verdi and Piave interpolated a grand bel canto aria for Germont. Trying to comfort his son, Germont reminds him of home and family life in the great cantabile "Di Provenza il mar, il suol" ("The Sea and the Soil of Provence"). The climaxes of its two identical stanzas pose both technical and dramatic challenges for the baritone.

In the recitative that follows, Alfredo reveals that Violetta's letter implies that she has gone back to the baron, and he vows vengeance. Now Germont redoubles his efforts to console his son, assure him of his forgiveness, and convince him to come home to Provence. His cabaletta "No, non udrai rimpoveri" ("No, You Will Hear No Reproach") is somewhat anticlimactic after the power of "Di Provenza," and it sheds no new light on Germont's feelings. Just as the aria is about to end, Alfredo spies Flora's invitation on a table, infers that Violetta has gone to the party, and rushes away.

The finale of the act, set at Flora's party, returns us to the brilliant but empty world of the courtesan, just as it was portrayed at the beginning of Act One. The guests arrive and gossip about Violetta and Alfredo. The entertainment is a masquerade that begins with a gypsy dance, complete with tambourines. The gypsy women are joined by men dressed as matadors and picadors who tell the story of a famous bullfighter named Piquillo who killed five bulls in order to win the hand of a beautiful young girl. Such an interruption of the narrative for this entertainment of dancing and choral singing was a bow to French taste. It seems apropos in this quintessential Parisian setting and provides a moment of welcome stasis within an act of high emotional intensity.

Alfredo arrives, trying to appear nonchalant, and joins in a game of cards. Low strings and clarinets accompany the action with an agitated, rhythmically repetitious passage that reflects the tension in the room. Almost immediately Violetta enters on the arm of the baron. For this final scene of the act Verdi has created a musical structure of complexity and sophistication. Alfredo's dialogue at the card table and the idle chatter of Violetta, Flora, and the baron proceed in the most speechlike *parlante* style. When Alfredo remarks cynically about Violetta, his vocal line becomes more melodic, and when Violetta, aside, pleads for God's mercy in this impossible situation, she sings a long, arching phrase. The bizarre scene unfolds as Alfredo continues to win at cards and is challenged by his angry rival, the baron. Alfredo's good luck continues, but the announcement that dinner is served interrupts the game.

Violetta returns to the salon, having sent a message to Alfredo that she wants to speak with him. She warns him to leave, fearing that the baron will kill him. He replies that he will only go if she accompanies him. She tells him the truth, that she has vowed to leave him. When he questions her, she summons all her courage to lie that she has made the promise to the baron and that it is he that she loves.

Alfredo calls all the guests to come to him. In an abbreviated cabaletta he tells them that Violetta has sold her possessions to support their life together and he has blindly accepted her gifts. Now it is time to repay her. In perhaps the most shocking moment of the opera, he throws his evening's winnings at her feet.

The guests are horrified at his rudeness and cruelty and demand that he leave the premises. During this clamorous chorus Germont enters, assesses the situation, and, in a passage of great power and dignity, condemns his son's cruelty, asking "Where is my son?" In short, breathless phrases Alfredo expresses his anguish and regret. This launches a large-scale ensemble finale. Flora and her guests console Violetta; Alfredo continues to express his remorse; Germont ponders his own responsibility for this turn of events; and the baron challenges Alfredo to a duel. This all unfolds at a majestic tempo, accompanied by full orchestra.

The entire company is suddenly silenced and, with only delicate strings, Violetta sings "Alfredo, Alfredo, you cannot understand all the love that is in this heart." The ensemble reenters, with Alfredo expressing his misery and regrets in *parlante* style and the others offering Violetta their sympathy. At times Alfredo joins with Violetta, singing an octave below her. After a long crescendo, the ensemble ends. As the orchestra concludes the act, Germont leads his son away, followed by the baron.

Act Three, set in Violetta's bedroom, begins with another prelude that opens with the "death music" from the beginning of the opera. This is followed by a new melody that gradually dissolves into a series of descending steps. From seventeenth-century opera to the church music of J. S. Bach, such figures, often likened to sighs, were commonly used to convey despair, weeping, or death.

Violetta's conversation, in recitative, with both Annina and the doctor is filled with optimism, but the "death music" and the descending steps from the prelude recur, making it clear that hope is unfounded. When she is left alone, Violetta takes a letter from her bosom. She reads it in normal speech to the accompaniment of Alfredo's original "love theme," played by seven string instruments. The letter, from Germont, fills in the events that have transpired since Flora's party. Alfredo has wounded the baron in their duel, but he is recovering. Germont has told his son the truth about Violetta's sacrifice, and they are coming together to beg her forgiveness. Her heartrending response, still spoken, is "It is late." She then sings a two-stanza *cantabile*, "Addio del passato" ("Farewell to the Past"), which features a plaintive solo oboe. In it she bids farewell to her hopes of happiness and then prays for God's blessing and forgiveness. At the beginning of her prayer the key shifts from minor to major, but it returns to the darker color for the final phrase. In addressing God she refers to herself as "la traviata" (the lost or fallen one). Just as the orchestra ends the aria, a group of carnival revelers is heard outside singing a lusty chorus. This is a shocking moment of irony, for Violetta has already commented that while the people celebrate "only God knows how many unhappy ones are suffering."

As the crowd moves away, Annina returns with the wonderful news that Alfredo has arrived. He rushes in and takes her in his arms, and they sing an exultant phrase in octaves: "Beloved Alfredo [Violetta], oh joy!" Breathlessly he begs for her pardon, and they both pledge that no "man, demon, or angel" can ever part them again. He helps her to a chair and begins the famous duet "Parigi, o cara, lasceremo" ("Oh My Dear, We Shall Leave Paris"). The rhythm of the waltz with its "oompah-pah" accompaniment poignantly recalls the music of the party where the couple first met. Violetta repeats both text and music of the first section, and then Alfredo introduces a new melody with Violetta adding vocal embroidery above. This is also repeated, climaxing in a short cadenza for the two.

For a moment she deceives herself, suggesting that they go to a church to thank God for reuniting them, but the last word of her sentence is accompanied by the introduction of a turbulent orchestral passage in the minor key. She falls exhausted back into the chair and, accepting the fact that she is growing weaker, she tells Alfredo "If your return cannot save me, then nothing on earth can." She summons the energy to begin the cabaletta "Ah! Gran Dio! Morir sì giovine" (Ah! Great God, to Die So Young"). The almost constant quarter-note rhythm and the pizzicato chords beneath it give it a sense of urgency. But with Violetta obviously near death, Verdi was too sensitive to the dramatic situation to include any coloratura passages. Alfredo joins in, trying to calm her, and they end with an extended passage sung in octaves. Germont enters, ready to take Violetta as his daughter, but he immediately perceives the gravity of the situation and is overwhelmed with remorse. Violetta opens a drawer and takes a medallion from it. At this moment the orchestra moves to D-flat minor, the key that was associated with her submission to Germont's request in Act Two. Accompanied by the "death" rhythm that was introduced in the same scene, she gives Alfredo the medallion to keep as a remembrance of her.

At this point Annina and the doctor join the three principal characters in a brief ensemble in which, for the first time, they all acknowledge that Violetta is dying. Then Verdi achieves a *coup de théâtre*. Violetta feels relieved of her pain and a renewed energy. She sings the phrase "È strano," the same words that opened her first-act scene in which she first recognized her feelings for Alfredo. This is accompanied by the love theme, delicately played by four first and four second violins and two violas. The orchestra changes keys, becoming more agitated as her excitement increases. After a great climax for voice and full orchestra, Violetta falls dead as the others look on, deeply moved, and the orchestra ends in darkest D-flat minor.

* * *

The premiere was, in Verdi's words, "a fiasco." The tenor and baritone who sang the roles of Alfredo and Germont were not in good voice. The prima donna, Fanny Salvini-Donatelli, reportedly sang well, but was too plump to be believable as a character who was dying of tuberculosis. According to some accounts, when the doctor told Annina in the final act that Violetta was "wasting away," some members of the audience began to laugh, thus spoiling the effect of the tragic ending. Verdi was philosophical, writing to Muzio: "*La traviata* was a fiasco, my fault or the singers'? Time alone will tell." [16]

Indeed time proved him right. The following year a new production was mounted at the Teatro San Benedetto, also in Venice. Verdi could not be present, but he made some revisions in the score. Piave was on hand to supervise the preparation, and the cast was stellar. The opera's reception at San Benedetto was as enthusiastic as that at La Fenice had been reserved. From that second premiere on May 6, 1854, *La traviata* joined its two immediate predecessors in the canon of great operas and remains one of the most frequently performed works of the repertory.

5

VERDI THE STATESMAN

Un ballo in maschera, Don Carlos

By the time of the successful second premiere of *La traviata* in May 1854, Verdi was in Paris, working to fulfill the contract he had signed with the Opéra more than two years earlier. Although his *Jérusalem* had not been an unqualified success at its Paris premiere in 1848, several of his Italian operas had enjoyed tremendous popularity in France. Consequently, Verdi had been able to negotiate successfully for generous rehearsal time and total control of the casting for the new grand opera.

More importantly, he had demanded that the text be prepared by Eugène Scribe (1791–1861), the leading French librettist, who had provided texts for *La Juive* (1835), set to music by Fromental Halévy (1799–1862), as well as Giacomo Meyerbeer's immensely popular *Robert le diable* (1831), *Les Huguenots* (1836), and *Le prophète* (1849). With Rossini long retired, Meyerbeer was the only opera composer in the world whose fame and success rivaled that of Verdi. Like his contemporary Richard Wagner, the Italian maestro was eager to challenge the king of grand opera on his home ground, and a libretto by Scribe would be an important asset in that effort.

Verdi's attempts to find librettos that satisfied him had often been tortuous processes, and his dealings with Scribe were no exception. For a year after the contract was signed no progress was made, and Verdi decided to go to Paris to confer in person. Eventually Scribe suggested a revision of his old libretto *Le duc d'Albe* (*The Duke of Alba*), which concerned the tyrannical Spanish governor of the Netherlands in the sixteenth century. It had originally been written for Halévy, who rejected it, and then offered to Donizetti, who began to set it to music but never completed it.

Verdi liked the basic outline of the plot, but not wanting to deal with "used goods," he asked for a change of time and place. Scribe agreed and suggested that a more colorful southern setting such as Naples or Sicily would be more propitious for the work they both envisioned. They settled on a fictional account of an event that took place in Palermo in the thirteenth century. Traditionally known as the Sicilian Vespers, the incident was a spontaneous revolt by Sicilians against the occupying French forces of Charles of Anjou (1126–1285) on Easter Monday, March 30, 1282.

Amid the celebration of the holiday, a French soldier began to flirt with a Sicilian woman, and her jealous husband stabbed him to death. When the other Frenchmen tried to defend their countryman, they were surrounded by armed Sicilians who massacred all of them. This transpired as the church bells rang to signal the start of vespers. According to plan, local men poured through the city attacking the French occupiers. By the next day more than two thousand Frenchmen were dead, and the rebels had taken control of the city. This sparked a general revolt that eventually freed the entire island from French rule.[1]

The libretto, now titled *Les Vêpres siciliennes* and with Guy de Montfort, the French governor of Sicily, replacing the original Duke of Alba, was finally delivered to Verdi in late December of 1853. The story begins with the instigation of the famous uprising in Palermo. The duchess Hélène (Elena), whose brother has been executed by the French, sings a song that enflames the Sicilians and provokes a fight with French soldiers. Guy de Montfort, the French governor, arrives and restores calm. He interrogates Henri (Arrigo), a young Sicilian who has just been released from prison. Later Henri, who is in love with Hélène, and the Sicilian patriot Jean (Giovanni) Procida meet outside the city. Procida, who has been in exile in Spain, knows that Peter, the king of Aragon, will intervene against the French if the Sicilians revolt, and he is trying to bring the insurrection about.

Montfort learns that Henri is his illegitimate son. Hearing this, the young man is divided between patriotic and familial loyalties. At a masked ball he learns from Procida of a conspiracy to kill Montfort and decides to take his father's side. Both Procida and Hélène are deemed to be conspirators and are seized and sentenced to execution. Henri visits them and tells them that now that he has done his duty to his newfound father, he is indeed on the side of the insurrection.

Montfort agrees to free Hélène and Procida if Henri will recognize him publicly as his father. He complies and Montfort agrees to allow his marriage to Hélène. Meanwhile, Procida has planned another attack on the French, the beginning of which will be signaled by the ringing of church bells. In the garden of Monfort's palace the wedding is about to take place. The bridal couple are alarmed when they hear of the plans, but Montfort orders bells to be rung to begin the ceremony. At the sound of the pealing bells the rebels enter and begin their massacre of the French. At this point the curtain descends, with the fate of the principals left to the imagination of the audience. The printed libretto, however, contains a few more lines in which Hélène begs Procida to spare Henri and Montfort. Unmoved by her pleas, he orders the Sicilians to attack all three.

Verdi began to compose with his usual resolve, but found the work difficult. Ironically, in his operas beginning with *Macbeth*, the increasingly natural flow between recitative and aria and the more subtle treatment of the orchestra already showed the influence of the French style, but in *Rigoletto* and *La traviata* he had perfected a type of intimate human drama that was the antithesis of the grand historical pageantry of the Parisian grand opera. Indeed this genre that exploited the size and equipment of the Opéra stage was an impressive but unwieldy art form that could boast few masterpieces in its short history.

In early October the rehearsals began, but the leading soprano, the brilliant and temperamental Sophie Cruvelli (1826–1907), suddenly disappeared. Already uneasy about the whole project, Verdi immediately wanted to cancel the premiere, but the prima donna reappeared. In January 1855 he asked to cancel the contract entirely, mostly due to dissatisfaction with Scribe's libretto.

Verdi had hoped for a dramatic and emotionally moving ending, but he considered the entire fifth act to be weak. He also believed that in adapting the original plot to fit the events of the Sicilian Vespers, Scribe had trivialized the uprising and made the Sicilians seem brutish. Although denizens of the Po Valley at that time would scarcely have thought of Sicilians as their countrymen, Verdi was defensive about their portrayal. Scribe's treatment of the historical figure of Giovanni da Procida (1210–1298) particularly aroused his ire. Procida, a brilliant physician and diplomat, had successfully sought wider European support for Spanish intervention in Sicily. His role as instigator of the Sicilian Vespers itself was a source of disagreement among historians, but Verdi believed that Scribe had portrayed him as a heartless "common conspirator."[2]

The management of the Opéra refused to cancel the project, Scribe made some changes to the libretto, and the disgruntled composer continued with the rehearsals. The premiere on June 13, 1855, was only moderately successful, but many critics and fellow composers praised the music generously. Berlioz wrote of its grandeur and "sovereign majesty."[3] From the beginning Verdi had considered the possibility of an Italian version of *Les Vêpres* but was well aware of the problems a story of an Italian revolt would pose with the censors. Perhaps upon the recommendation of Scribe himself, Verdi decided to change the setting to seventeenth-century Portugal, under Spanish domination. Hélène, transformed to Giovanna, became the title character in what was eventually called *Giovanna de Guzman*. It was first performed at the Teatro Regio in Parma on December 26, 1855, scarcely six months after the Paris premiere of the original. Although the translation by Eugenio Caimi was generally considered to be very weak, *Giovanna de Guzman* was well received and immediately repeated in other Italian cities, including in Milan at La Scala. By 1861 the Italian libretto was revised and returned to thirteenth-century Sicily. This version, titled *I vespri siciliani*, with the removal of the ballet, according to Italian taste, soon became the standard version outside of France.

Unlike his most recent operas, which were introduced by brief preludes, *Les Vêpres siciliennes* is preceded by an extended overture in the classical **sonata form** that was standard in the overtures of Mozart or Rossini. As usual, the principal themes are all derived from vocal passages within the opera. The overture has enjoyed considerable success as a concert work. Verdi's English biographer Francis Toye considered it among his most successful overtures. To meet the requirements of grand opera, Verdi included an extended ballet, "The Four Seasons," as the second scene of Act Three, in which he demonstrated his growing sophistication as an orchestrator.

Verdi's expertise as a choral composer was a formidable asset in this genre that relied so heavily on crowd scenes. The finale of Act Three, in which the conspiracy to kill Montfort is worked out and then thwarted, is a masterpiece of musical tension. There are also several fine arias, the most celebrated of which is Procida's great cantabile for bass, "O tu, Palermo, villa adorata" ("Oh Thou, Palermo, Beloved Land").[4]

Basic weaknesses in Scribe's original libretto and Verdi's essential lack of sympathy for the five-act behemoth that was grand opera have prevented both the French and Italian versions from maintaining a central place in the repertory, but the music has continued to have admirers. The librettist and composer Arrigo Boito (1842–1918), who was not always a Verdi enthusiast but whose librettos were eventually to inspire some of the aged maestro's greatest music, was a staunch supporter of *I vespri siciliani*.

Verdi remained in Paris for several months after the premiere of *Les Vêpres* to recover from the stress of the work's preparation and to deal with some copyright issues. The existing laws were inconsistently written and enforced, and successful composers constantly dealt with pirated productions of their works. Because Verdi was a citizen of the duchy of Parma, he had little diplomatic assistance in cities outside Italy.

In March 1856 Verdi traveled to Venice to prepare and conduct the return of *La traviata* at La Fenice. Because it had played to such acclaim since its unfortunate premiere there, its homecoming was viewed as a new beginning and caused tremendous excitement among the Venetian public. Soon afterward he signed a contract for a new opera for the following year's season. He had already been thinking of another drama by Gutiérrez, whose work had been the source for *Il trovatore*. This new opera was to be an adaptation by Piave of the Spanish playwright's *Simón Bocanegra*, whose title character was a historical figure of the fourteenth century who had given up piracy and become the doge of the republic of Genoa.

In the prologue, which takes place twenty-five years before the main action, Pietro and Paolo, leaders of a people's revolutionary group, are plotting against the patrician rulers of Genoa and support Simon Boccanegra to head the government as doge. Boccanegra has had a love affair with Maria, daughter of Fiesco, a patrician. Her father has kept her confined in his palace because she has given birth to an illegitimate daughter whose father is Boccanegra.

Maria dies and Boccanegra becomes doge. His daughter disappears and is brought up as the child of a patrician family. When, many years later, father and daughter are reunited, she is loved by two men: Paolo, who has been the doge's longtime supporter, and Gabriele, whom she loves, but who is Boccanegra's political enemy. Consequently, the doge is divided between his public position and his paternal love. In the end Boccanegra is poisoned by his former ally and lives only long enough to bless the union of Amelia and Gabriele.

With its implausible occurrences and confusing gaps in chronology, *Boccanegra* presented many of the same dramatic problems as *Il trovatore*. Despite this, Verdi was drawn to the issues of loyalty and betrayal, conflict between the public and private roles of the powerful, and especially to the relationship between father and daughter.

As always the working relationship between Verdi and Piave was fraught with conflict. The situation was exacerbated by Verdi's long stay in Paris during the latter part of 1856 to prepare the French production of *Il trovatore*.[5] Unable to work with Piave by correspondence, Verdi enlisted the aid of Giuseppe Montanelli (1813–1862), a Tuscan journalist and politician who was living in Paris at the time. It is uncertain how much of the final text is by Piave and how much by Montanelli, but the rift between the two longtime collaborators took some time to heal.

Simon Boccanegra had its premiere on March 12, 1857, and was another of Verdi's rare failures. He wrote to Countess Maffei: "I've had a fiasco in Venice almost as great as that of *La traviata*."[6] Negative reaction in other cities followed. In addition to the inherent weaknesses of the libretto, Verdi's constantly evolving style, which had been influenced by French opera, was vastly different from the luxuriant melodic outpouring of *Il trovatore*. Indeed, there is not a single aria for the title character.

For almost twenty-five years *Simon Boccanegra* remained on the fringes of the repertory, seemingly relegated with *Un giorno di regno* to operatic oblivion. But in 1879, at the urging of Giulio Ricordi, Verdi was considering a setting of Shakespeare's *Othello* with Arrigo Boito as librettist. Although Verdi's dealings with Boito had been conflicted, he was impressed with the younger man's literary skill and suggested, as a test of their working relationship, a complete revision of *Simon Boccanegra*. The opera, with significant alterations of both text and music, premiered at La Scala on March 24, 1881, to great acclaim. The most prominent addition was the scene in the council chamber at the end of the first act in which the doge reads a letter from the poet Petrarch urging Genoa to avoid a fratricidal war with Venice. His appeal to the rival Genoese factions, "Plebe! Patrizi! Popolo!" ("Plebeians! Patricians! People!"), is one of Verdi's most magnificent scenes for baritone.

Since 1881 the revised version has been the standard one. Only in the twentieth century, however, has *Boccanegra* assumed a secure place in the operatic canon. The title role has become a central one for great baritones such as Lawrence Tibbett, Tito Gobbi, Sherrill Milnes, and Leo Nucci. In 2009 the legendary tenor Placido Domingo sang the role in Berlin, followed by performances in London and New York.

While he was composing the original version of *Boccanegra*, Verdi was not only dealing with legal issues in Paris, but was also working on the adaptation of *Stiffelio* that he had been envisioning for several years. The original had never been satisfactory to him because of the changes that the censors had demanded. He and Piave changed the setting from nineteenth-century Austria to medieval England, transforming the evangelical minister Stiffelio to the crusader Aroldo, unfortunately eliminating the human drama of the stern man of God and his reaction to his wife's sin.

The premiere, on August 16, 1857, marked the inauguration of a new theater in Rimini, and the occasion was a triumph. Unfortunately the positive response was not shared as *Aroldo* played in various other Italian cities. Although the new music revealed the maturation of Verdi's style during the seven intervening years, the heart of the drama had been sacrificed. In recent times *Aroldo* has been performed even less than *Stiffelio*.

During this period the European political climate was changing rapidly. In 1855, at Cavour's urging, Piedmont (officially the kingdom of Piedmont-Sardinia) joined with England, France, and Turkey in the Crimean War against Russia. Italy had little to gain from this effort to stop Russian aggression in the Black Sea region, but Cavour calculated that Piedmont's participation would invalidate Austria's claim that no Italian entity was capable of governing and defending itself. For the first time the principal European powers began to take the prospect of an independent and unified Italy seriously.

Perhaps even more significant was the reaction among the republican element within Italy that had long resisted the idea of a constitutional monarchy. Cavour convinced the great Venetian patriot Daniele Manin (1804–1857) that the surest route to unification was through a government headed by King Victor Emmanuel of Piedmont. With Manin's aid he also convinced the brilliant and colorful military hero Giovanni Garibaldi (1807–1882) to pledge his support. The tide seemed to be turning toward a cause that, after the setbacks of 1848–1849, had seemed futile.

Verdi corresponded with friends like Countess Maffei about political issues, but was much too occupied with his work to play an active role. Remarkably, along with premieres of a new opera and two revised ones between January and August of 1857, Verdi began to plan a new work for Naples. After years of dreaming of an Italian opera based on *King Lear*, he believed that the time might finally be right. He actually had a libretto in hand by the Venetian playwright Antonio Somma (1809–1864). The two had begun to collaborate on the Shakespeare adaptation in 1853 and had spent more than two years revising and polishing.

Verdi envisioned *Lear* as a grandiose production that would require a large stage that only existed at two Italian theaters: San Carlo and La Scala. Although he had misgivings about Naples, he still adamantly refused to compose a new opera for La Scala.

San Carlo had a strong roster of male singers, and Verdi had spoken with the soprano Maria Piccolomini, already celebrated for her interpretation of Violetta in *La traviata*, about singing the role of Cordelia, but the Neapolitan management failed to sign her for the season. Verdi stubbornly refused to move ahead with the project without Piccolomini and began to consider other subjects for the new work. He eventually settled on *Gustave III, ou Le bal masque*, a libretto by Scribe that had already been set in 1833 by the prolific French composer Daniel Auber (1782–1871). Verdi admired Scribe's original work and asked Somma to adapt the five-act French grand opera into a three-act Italian one. Although the composer had to explain numerous technical details to the still inexperienced librettist, the work went quickly, and the libretto and much of the music were finished in less than three months.

Scribe's original drama was based on a historic event: the assassination of Swedish king Gustav III (1746–1792) by the aristocratic military officer Jacob Johan Anckarström (1762–1792) at a masked ball at the Royal Opera House in Stockholm in 1792. Although he had been a staunch autocrat, Gustav had made numerous liberal reforms, had carried out a successful foreign policy, and had been a strong proponent of arts and letters. Historically, the regicide was politically motivated, but Scribe changed the narrative by inventing a liaison between the king and Anckarström's wife.

Verdi was aware that a regicide onstage would create a problem with the Neapolitan censors. Based on recent experience, however, he assumed that he would only have to alter the setting, as he had in *Rigoletto*. In that instance the change from king of France to Duke of Mantua had not compromised the drama, and Verdi had prevailed on other points that he considered crucial. But the political situation was more precarious in 1858 than it had been in 1851. Two years earlier Ferdinand II (1810–1859), the Bourbon king of Naples and Sicily, had survived an assassination attempt, so there was no chance that an opera about political assassination could be performed in Naples without substantial revision.

Somma suggested changing the locale to the Baltic region of Pomerania and making the central character a duke. The censors had asked for a medieval setting, but Verdi insisted on the seventeenth century. The new title was to be *Una vendetta in domino (Revenge in the Domain)*. Everything seemed to be in order when Verdi, accompanied by Giuseppina and her dog Loulou, arrived in Naples on January 14, 1858. But in a bizarre coincidence, on the previous day Felice Orsini, an Italian revolutionary living in Paris, had thrown a bomb at Emperor Napoleon III as he was on his way to the opera. The paranoia that this event engendered among European rulers made any compromise on Somma's libretto out of the question. Verdi was informed that the entire work would have to be rewritten.

The San Carlo management proposed setting the opera in fourteenth-century Florence with the title *Adelia degli Adimari* (the name of the central female character in this version) with the preexisting music adapted to the new text. Predictably Verdi was furious and refused to be associated with the altered libretto. San Carlo sued him for breach of contract, but he countersued, claiming that the revised text was so far removed from the original that he was being coerced to compose a different opera than the one that had been agreed upon. Verdi argued that *Adelia degli Adimari* violated "the most obvious principles of dramatic art" and degraded "an artist's conscience." The matter was settled out of court, with Verdi agreeing to prepare a new production of *Simon Boccanegra* at San Carlo in the fall.

Assuming that the Roman censors would be less intractable than the Neapolitans, Verdi made an agreement with the Teatro Apollo for the premiere to take place there in early 1859. He expected that the opera would be acceptable in Rome with the libretto that he and Somma had prepared for Naples, thus scoring a moral victory over the haughty and reactionary Neapolitans. He had misjudged the more volatile political atmosphere, however, and discovered that the assassination of a European duke was now as untouchable a topic in Rome as it was in Naples. The censors demanded that the setting be in a non-European country. After some negotiation all the parties agreed to the unlikely setting of colonial Boston, with Gustav becoming the Count of Warwick and British governor of the city.

Verdi was satisfied with the change because it left what he considered the most crucial elements of the drama untouched. For most Italians of the time, life in eighteenth-century Boston was unfamiliar and exotic. Consequently, the inherent absurdity of a lavish court in a Puritan city was irrelevant. With the original narrative now relocated for the second time and titled *Un ballo in maschera* (*A Masked Ball*), the opera was introduced at the Teatro Apollo on February 17, 1859.

Even after political censorship ceased to be an issue, Verdi supported the use of the problematic Boston setting. During the twentieth century, however, many companies began to restore the original and historically accurate Swedish setting. In the Metropolitan Opera production of 2012–2013 the location and names were restored, but the narrative was moved to the early twentieth century. Because the Swedish characters are more likely to appear in contemporary performances and recordings, those names will be used in the synopsis and musical analysis. Names in parentheses are those of the 1859 version.

UN BALLO IN MASCHERA: SYNOPSIS

In the royal palace of Sweden both the supporters of King Gustavo (Riccardo) and those who are conspiring against him, led by Counts Horn (Sam) and Ribbing (Tom), are all waiting for an audience with him. When he arrives, Oscar, his witty young page, hands him a guest list for a masked ball that will take place the following evening. He immediately notices the names of his aide and friend Count Anckarström (Renato) and his wife Amelia and reflects on his secret love for her. When the others leave, Anckarström enters and the king boldly confesses that he is harboring a troubling secret. Oblivious to the king's feelings for Amelia, Anckarström warns him of a plot against him. Relieved that his friend has not guessed the true cause of his worry, he refuses to take the conspiracy seriously.

A magistrate enters and asks the king to sign a decree that will banish the fortune-teller Ulrica, who has been accused of witchcraft. Gustavo asks Oscar what he knows of her, and the page's information arouses his interest. He gleefully announces that he will pay her a visit disguised as a fisherman and accompanied by the men of the court.

The men arrive at Ulrica's dwelling as she invokes the devil to assist her. She reads the palm of Cristiano (Silvano), a young sailor, and tells him that he will receive both an increase in rank and financial reward. When the king hears this, he secretly puts money and a letter of promotion into Cristiano's pocket. When the sailor finds these, he and the others are duly impressed by Ulrica's prophetic powers. A servant, whom Gustavo recognizes to be Amelia's, enters saying that his mistress needs Ulrica's help. The sorceress sends the others away, but the king hides in order to overhear the conversation. Ulrica admits Amelia, who is tormented by her illicit love for the king and wants to be freed from it. Ulrica tells her that she must gather a magic herb that grows at the foot of the gallows where criminals are executed. Fearful, but determined, she vows to gather the herb that night. Hearing this, Gustavo decides to go and meet her there.

Amelia leaves and the courtiers return. Gustavo asks Ulrica to read his palm, and she predicts that he will be killed by the first man whose hand he shakes. As she repeats her prophecy, she stares at Horn and Ribbing, and they fear that she knows of their plot. Confident of the loyalty of his subjects, the king offers his hand to those present, but they all refuse it. Anckarström enters and Gustavo rushes to shake his hand, declaring that the prophecy has been proved wrong because Anckarström is his closest friend.

That night in the desolate place where the gallows stands, Amelia, with her face veiled, arrives to obtain the herb and is soon followed by Gustavo. She begs him to leave, but when he expresses his love for her, she weakens and reciprocates. Anckarström arrives and, not recognizing his wife, warns the king that the conspirators are nearby. Before he flees, Gustavo asks Anckarström to escort Amelia back to the city without lifting her veil. On their way they encounter Horn, Ribbing, and the other conspirators, who make impertinent remarks about the veiled lady. In an attempt to intervene in the confrontation, Amelia drops her veil. The conspirators are amused at Anckarström's situation and he, feeling betrayed by his wife and his friend, decides to join the conspirators in their plot against the king.

The final act begins in Anckarström's house, where he threatens to have Amelia killed for her infidelity. She pleads with him to allow her to see their son before she dies. He lets her leave and, reflecting on the situation, realizes that it is actually Gustavo who has betrayed him. Horn and Ribbing arrive, and they agree to draw lots for the privilege of killing the king. When Amelia returns, her husband forces her to draw the name of the assassin, and he is pleased when his own name appears. Oscar arrives with an invitation to the ball and the conspirators welcome the event as an opportunity to carry out the assassination, but Amelia decides to warn Gustavo.

The king, alone in his study, resolves to give up Amelia and send her abroad with her husband. Oscar brings him an anonymous letter warning him of the assassination plot, but he refuses to heed it.

The final scene is in the palace ballroom, where all the participants are masked. Anckarström forces Oscar to reveal which disguise belongs to the king. Amelia and Gustavo meet, and she begs him to escape. Again he refuses and declares his love for her. As they bid each other farewell, Anckarström stabs the king. As he dies, Gustavo forgives his murderer and assures him of Amelia's innocence.

UN BALLO IN MASCHERA: THE MUSIC

The short prelude features three themes that all appear in the first scene and, in a sense, it encapsulates the spirit of the entire opening segment of the opera. It begins with six very quiet introductory measures dominated by an ambiguous "short-short-short-long" rhythmic figure that sets the tone for the whole opera, which like Mozart's *Don Giovanni* is poised between tragic and comic. This aspect of *Un ballo* has often been described as chiaroscuro, a term in visual art that describes a mixture of light and shade. Throughout the opera Verdi perfectly captures this element, which was present in Scribe's original concept.

Such a juxtaposition of contrasting moods was foreign to the Italian tradition, in which serious and buffa opera had been distinctly separate genres, but comic elements were often present in French grand opera. After his stay in Paris from 1847 to 1849 this French influence had begun to be present in Verdi's works. In 1851 the characters of Rigoletto and the Duke of Mantua had brought a touch of wry comedy to an incomparably dark tragedy.[7]

The first of the principal themes is that of the opening chorus, "Posa in pace" ("Rest in Peace"), in which officers and noblemen praise King Gustavo and wish him peaceful rest. In stark contrast is the second, which is associated with Horn, Ribbing, and the other conspirators. It is aggressive and defined more by its rhythm than by its melody. In almost all of its appearances Verdi utilizes **contrapuntal** writing, perhaps using this most cerebral of musical textures to represent the complex plotting of the conspirators. The third is the theme of the aria "La rivedrà nell'estasi" ("I Shall See You in Ecstasy"), which Gustavo sings when he sees Amelia's name on the guest list. It recurs several times as a musical symbol of their love. All three of these contain references to the introductory four-note motive.

When the curtain opens, the supporters of the king sing "Posa in pace." When their eight-measure passage ends, the conspirators begin their cynical chorus "È sta l'odio, che prepara il fio, ripensando ai caduti per te" ("In Hatred Your Downfall Was Prepared") without an intervening beat. The first group repeats its chorus, so that the two rival factions are singing simultaneously. This must be understood as a standard operatic convention in which both groups, singing very softly, are voicing their thoughts and addressing the audience rather than each other. Cleverly, Verdi binds the two with repetitions of the "short-short-short-long" motive in the accompaniment. As the two groups end their ensemble, the orchestra plays the same six-measure passage that ended the prelude, signaling that the real narrative of Act One is about to begin.

Oscar appears and announces the entrance of the king. In opera buffa the portrayal of a young man by a soprano, famously exemplified by Cherubino in Mozart's *The Marriage of Figaro*, was a long-standing tradition. The two converse above a lighthearted orchestral background. As at the beginning of *Rigoletto*, this scene is dominated by the orchestra, with brief aria-like passages seamlessly interwoven into **parlante** dialogue. Such is the case with Gustavo's sixteen-measure "La rivedrà nell' estasi," whose melody was heard in the prelude. Its powerful lyricism is interrupted abruptly by the choruses of rivals, with the king's adherents now including Oscar. Gustavo repeats a portion of the aria above the chorus of supporters, who continue to praise him, and the conspirators, who whisper that the time is not yet right to carry out their plot.

Oscar ushers the visitors out just as Anckarström arrives. The conversation between the two friends is a prime example of this work's juxtaposition of the serious and the comic. Gustavo states boldly that he has a painful secret, as though he is tempting his friend to guess the truth about his relationship with Amelia. Anckarström is only concerned with Gustavo's safety, and he expresses this simple devotion in the stirring "Alla vita che t'arride di speranze e gaudio piena, d'altre mille e mille vite il destino s'incatena" ("To the Life that Smiles on You, Full of Hope and Joy, the Destiny of Thousands of Others Is Linked"). With its repeated-chord accompaniment and **cadenza**, this is the most traditional aria of the first act, and its contrast with the more sophisticated music that surrounds it reveals Anckarström's apparent guilelessness.

The two friends' meeting is cut short by the arrival of the magistrate with the document whose purpose is to exile Ulrica. Questioned by the king, Oscar defends her as an intriguing figure who is especially adept at predicting the course of love affairs. The musical style of Oscar's role is the closest that Verdi, in his middle years, comes to old-fashioned **coloratura** singing. His defense of Ulrica in "Volta la terrea fronte alle stelle" ("She Turns Her Earth-Colored Face to the Stars") is a sparkling dance-like song in two stanzas, often referred to as a *ballata*. In the refrain he humorously declares that she and Lucifer are always in accord. Between the two stanzas Gustavo wryly comments that the witch and the devil make a charming pair.

The king's announcement that he will pay Ulrica a visit initiates a rollicking finale. It begins as a trio for Gustavo, Oscar, and Anckarström in which the king and the page express delight with this proposed adventure and the careful Anckarström warns of the dangers that are involved. All those present join in a rapid **stretta** to conclude the scene. This extended passage is in the best tradition of both the French and Italian comic repertoire.

The second scene is set in Ulrica's dwelling, where a dramatic introduction punctuated by dissonant chords leads to her incantation "Re dell'abisso, affrettati" ("Hasten, King of the Abyss"). This powerful aria begins on middle C, and each phrase reaches a higher apex. Like the prelude and like all of the "sorcery music" in this act, the sense of key is ambiguous. At the climax Ulrica reaches a high G and, in one measure, descends the full octave and a fifth to the original C.

The ghostly atmosphere lightens momentarily when Gustavo enters, disguised as a fisherman, accompanied by a jaunty woodwind passage. His arrival leads to the second part of Ulrica's aria, in which she announces ecstatically that the spirit of Lucifer is now present. This passage, in a faster **tempo**, replaces the traditional **cabaletta**, although its musical style is much more declamatory than bravura. It begins in a major key, shifts rapidly between major and minor, and ends with a passage that parallels that of the first section. This time, however, the vocal range is extended, and she commands all present to be silent on a low G that is more than two octaves below her highest pitch. Although she only appears in one scene, Ulrica is one of Verdi's most memorable roles for contralto.

The brief episode with Christiano shifts the mood abruptly back to the humorous. After Gustavo has made Ulrica's prediction come true, Christiano and the chorus of women and children sing her praises in the remote, but brilliant, key of C major.

The arrival of Amelia gives Verdi the opportunity to display his mastery of the ensemble. The trio for Ulrica, Amelia, and Gustavo, who is hidden and thus addressing himself, moves seamlessly between declamatory and lyrical styles. At the same time the music becomes increasingly intense.

When Ulrica describes the fearsome place where the magic herbs grow, the trembling Amelia prays for divine comfort in the heartfelt "Consentimi, o Signore" ("Grant Me, Oh Lord"). Here Verdi creates a stunning emotional effect with the simplest of means. Amelia's line is an arch-like rise and fall accompanied by slow-moving harmonies. After one phrase the others join in below Amelia's line, with Ulrica offering encouragement and the king expressing his devotion.

This sublime moment is interrupted by the arrival of the men of Gustavo's court. Amelia exits through a secret door, and the men enter to spirited music much like that which accompanied the king's arrival. When they ask Ulrica to predict the future, Gustavo steps forward with the same request. As if to reinforce his masquerade, he sings a rousing fisherman's song, "Di' tu se fedele il flutto m'aspetta" ("Tell Me if the Wave Faithfully Awaits Me"). As a popular song that lies outside the action it resembles the Duke of Mantua's "La donna è mobile" in *Rigoletto*, but it bears a closer musical resemblance to his equally famous "Quest'o quella." At the end of each of the two stanzas Oscar, Horn, Ribbing, and the chorus repeat his last phrase in unison.

Accompanied by whispered string **tremolos**, Ulrica reprimands the men for their insolence. She then reads the king's palm and reluctantly tells him that he will soon die at the hand of a friend. This exchange occurs against an orchestral background of rich **chromaticism**. At the word "friend" the orchestra plays an almost deafening four-measure passage on a single dissonant harmony. All the bystanders, including Gustavo's enemies, cry "What horror!"

All finally becomes quiet and Gustavo begins an ensemble with the amusing "È scherzo od è follia" ("It Is a Joke or It Is Madness"). Rests between the syllables of words suggest breathless laughter. Juxtaposed against his bravado and wit is Ulrica's disapproval, Oscar's concern, and the conspirators' astonishment at the powers of the sorceress and concern that she is aware of their plot. As usual the music of Horn and Ribbing is primarily rhythmic, and Gustavo's is dominated by **parlando** style while Oscar, sometimes harmonizing with the lower voice of Ulrica, provides the lyricism. The structure, orchestration, harmonic interest, and delineation of the characters combine to make this a dazzling ensemble.

With typical Verdian economy, the final sequence of events in the act, though pivotal to the entire drama, moves rapidly to a climax. Ulrica predicts that the king's assassin will be the first person to shake his hand. Always in character, Gustavo finds this amusing, but none of those present will take his hand. When Anckarström appears suddenly, he grasps his friend's hand, to the great relief of Gustavo's supporters.

The handshake provokes a sudden crescendo and a terrific harmonic shift to a distant key.

Gustavo reveals his identity and pardons Ulrica of her crimes. Christiano reappears and leads a chorus of praise, "O figlia d'Inghilterra" ("Oh Son of England"), that Julian Budden has likened to a national anthem.[8] The king and Oscar, singing in octaves, respond gratefully to this display of loyalty. They are joined by Anckarström, who still expresses fear of lurking danger, and the conspirators, who feel disgust for such a servile display. Christiano and the chorus join in with a repetition of the anthem, bringing the act to a brilliant close.

This scene is the epitome of operatic chiaroscuro, with its alternation between the shadowy world of Ulrica and her companions and the frivolous nature of Gustavo, Oscar, and the courtiers. This juxtaposition is intensified by the conflict that is raging below the surface between the king's supporters and the conspirators.

Act Two begins just before midnight at the lonely field outside the city where the gallows stands. The harmonic tension in the introductory orchestral passage captures the bleakness of the scene. Amelia appears as the melody of her first-act prayer is played by a solo flute. As she kneels to pray, the theme is repeated by more richly scored strings. In a particularly dramatic recitative, she describes her fearful reaction to her surroundings. As she starts to approach the gallows, she sings the aria "Ma dall'arido stelo divulsa" ("When Torn from That Dry Stem"). The introduction is played by a solo English horn without accompaniment. The timbre of the *cor anglais*, often described as "plaintive," provides an apt atmosphere for her troubled state.

In the first three phrases Amelia imagines the power of the herb to rid her of her passion, but then wonders what her life will be like without it. The entire passage is repeated in varied form, with the English horn playing the first phrase while Amelia chides herself in **parlante** style for weakening. She resumes the repetition of the melody for the second and third phrases. As she reaches the cadence, the clock strikes midnight and she sees a phantom-like head rising from the ground. In a dramatic recitative Amelia gives vent to her terror. Falling to her knees, she prays once again, effectively adding a **coda** and a **cadenza** to her aria.

Suddenly the king appears and speaks to Amelia, begging her to be calm. Amelia begs him to let her go, launching Verdi's most passionate love duet to this point. It is approximately at the center of the opera and is its dramatic high point. Although Verdi was generally more succinct than his contemporaries, this scene is one of grand proportions with several contrasting sections. He uses different keys to convey the rapidly shifting emotions. Amelia protests in A minor and Gustavo responds in F major. Weakening, she joins him in F, but immediately begins a desperate prayer in the "heavenly" key of D-flat.

Still struggling with her guilt, Amelia makes one last attempt to resist, but as the orchestra quietly resolves to a luminous A-major harmony and the tempo slows, she haltingly confesses her love. The stunning change of key, the tremolo strings, and the melodic predominance of the orchestra have often reminded listeners of Wagner's *Tristan and Isolde*, although the chromaticism here is less complex. Wagner's great masterpiece was not performed until 1865, but it was composed almost simultaneously with *Un ballo*. Although he was sometimes accused of imitating Wagner during this period, Verdi did not hear a Wagnerian work until the Italian premiere of *Lohengrin* in 1871. But the fact that these exact contemporaries were moving in some of the same directions in their concept of music drama is notable.

A joyous passage in C major, introduced by Gustavo and repeated by Amelia, leads to the duet's brilliant finale. This passage, much of it sung in octaves, is the only true cabaletta in the opera.

After a brilliant ending with Amelia singing a high C, the orchestra ominously drops one tone as the lovers hear the sounds of men approaching. The tonal descent continues as they realize that one of them is Anckarström. He has come to save Gustavo from the conspirators, who know his whereabouts and are on their way to kill him. Despite Anckarström's urging and Amelia's pleas, the king refuses to flee and leave her in danger. She prevails, however, by threatening to lift her veil and reveal her identity to her husband.

After Gustavo has finally agreed to escape and Anckarström has promised to escort the veiled lady to the city gates, the king wavers. They all delay their departures by singing a trio in which the king speculates that perhaps he deserves to die and the other two continue to urge him to escape. Amelia begins in D minor, singing a repeated "short-short-long" rhythmic figure that one who is familiar with the last act of *Il trovatore* recognizes as a "death motive." Unlike in the preceding duet, the trio remains in the same meter and key throughout. The form displays simple classical logic. Amelia and Anckarström sing the same material, sometimes in alternation and sometimes together. The king maintains a separate musical identity until the final section, when he finally succumbs to their pleas and adopts their melodic material.

This ensemble is a brilliant example of the comic irony that characterizes *Un ballo*. A man and his wife, whom he does not recognize even after much conversation, collaborate to save her lover. The implausible use of disguise is a cliché of opera buffa, but because the threat of murder is imminent, the humor takes on a different context.

Gustavo finally flees, and almost immediately Amelia and Anckarström hear the voices of Horn, Ribbing, and their followers singing the rhythmic figure that was associated with them in Act One. When they realize with disappointment that the man they have found is not their intended victim, they taunt him with jokes about his beautiful veiled companion. The taunts turn more serious as they threaten to remove Amelia's veil and Anckarström prepares to defend her. Fearing for her husband's life, she tries to intervene and the veil drops. He cries out her name as the orchestra moves to a huge climax on a major harmony.

This leads to the ensemble finale, in which the conspirators provide a continuous backdrop of laughter while the wronged husband rages at his betrayal in short, breathless phrases and Amelia bemoans her guilt and misery in lines that soar above the others. In a passage of recitative that maintains the rhythm of the conspirators' laughter, Anckarström makes plans to meet with them the following morning. Then, still in rhythm, he grudgingly tells Amelia that he will keep his word by escorting her back to the city gate. All exit, but the conspirators' laughter can still be heard in the distance as they comment on the uproar that this news will cause in the city.

Act Three opens with a furious confrontation between husband and wife in which Anckarström calls her an adulteress and says she must pay with her blood. She responds with the aria "Morrò, ma prima in grazia" ("I Shall Die, but First in Mercy"), in which she asks for time to see their son. A solo cello plays the same role as that of the English horn in her second-act aria. Like the earlier one, it is in a minor key and lacks any of the traditional Italian formal designs. Since the composition of *Rigoletto* and *Il trovatore* Verdi had been freed from the straitjacket of ending every aria of the prima donna with the once obligatory cabaletta.

Anckarström grants Amelia's request, and she leaves the room as oboe and clarinet play the melody from her aria that is associated with her son's love. Her exit sets the stage for a powerful soliloquy by the wronged husband that is the dramatic turning point of the opera. He looks at the king's portrait on the wall and realizes that it is he who bears the real guilt for the betrayal. His aria, "Eri tu che macchiavi quell'anima" ("It Was You Who Stained That Soul"), begins in D minor with a stormy recitation of his betrayal at the hands of his best friend. The climax of the first section moves to F major in preparation for the total contrast of the second. In an outpouring of lyrical melody he remembers the happy times with Amelia. For a moment near the end his rage returns and the music shifts to F minor, but as he ends on the words "O speranze d'amor" (Oh hopes of love"), the major mode returns.

Announced by their "theme" music, Horn and Ribbing arrive. They are shocked that Anckarström is aware of their plot and even more surprised that he wants to join them. Another large-scale ensemble begins, with the three new allies pledging their loyalty to each other in a martial style typical of early Verdi. Although Anckarström keeps his motivation secret, the other two men disclose their very personal reasons for their hatred of the king, with each hoping to be the one to do the deed. Taking a vase from the mantel Anckarström proposes that they draw a name to determine who will be the assassin. While Horn writes the three names on cards and places them in the vase, the orchestra plays a tense passage with multiple repetitions of the "short-short-short-long" figure that began the prelude and that now can perhaps be interpreted as a "fate" or "death" motive.

Amelia enters to announce that Oscar has come with an invitation from the king. Her husband then has the perverse idea that she should draw the name from the vase. As she does this very slowly, another mystical chromatic passage accompanies the action.

When Anckarström's name is chosen, he is exultant. He and his fellow conspirators reprise their martial song while Amelia, who fully realizes what is happening, sings a counterpoint to the unified front of the men.

Oscar enters, accompanied by characteristically light and elegant music. Amelia refuses his invitation to the masked ball that evening, but her husband contradicts her and enthusiastically accepts for both of them. Horn and Ribbing quietly plan to make the ball the scene of the assassination. With a rapid, highly ornamented passage Oscar enthusiastically describes the splendid plans for the evening. Amelia joins him with a minor version of his melody, lamenting the fact that she has abetted the crime. Anckarström and the others gleefully consider the evening's "funeral dance." The irony increases as Amelia wonders if Ulrica can help her prevent the murder while Oscar, oblivious to her misery, tells her she will be queen of the ball.

The second scene finds the king in his study adjacent to the ballroom. The theme of his first-act aria, played by the strings, suggests that his love for Amelia is still of more concern than the imminent threat of assassination. He has decided that his only option is to send her and Anckarström out of the country.[9]

He signs a document that will put his plan into effect and begins the aria "Ma se m'è forza perderti" (But If I Must Lose You"). The first section moves at the end from C minor to D-flat major. Then, as he reflects that this will be the final hour of their love, there is a breathtaking shift to C major, with both vocal and instrumental parts marked *dolcissimo* (very sweetly). The same text is repeated several times, building to a powerful climax.

The sound of the **banda** can be heard from the ballroom, immediately reminding Gustavo that he will probably see his lover there. Oscar enters and hands him a note from an unknown lady warning him that someone will try to take his life at the ball. After reading it he decides that he will not play the coward's role, but will appear as planned. He declares that one last time love will shine for him, referring again to the theme that symbolizes his love for Amelia.

A curtain is opened to reveal the glittering ballroom with many of the costumed guests already dancing. As in the party scenes in *Rigoletto* and *La traviata*, this one is dominated by conversation in recitative against the background of dance music. A chorus of revelers sings of the pleasures of the evening.

Anckarström enters and is recognized by his fellow conspirators, who greet him with *morte* (death) as a password. Perhaps suspecting that Amelia has warned the king, he tells them that their victim will not be there. He then encounters Oscar, who informs him that his master is indeed present. When Anckarström asks him to reveal what costume Gustavo is wearing, the page takes the opportunity to sing a jocular song, "Saper vorreste" ("You Would Like to Know"), in which he boasts of his ability to keep the secret. Each of the two identical stanzas ends with a "tra-la-la-la" refrain. The dance music resumes, and the two are momentarily separated. When they meet again, Anckarström convinces Oscar to describe the king's costume by telling him that he has urgent information for him.

After an extended repetition of the chorus Amelia and Gustavo appear, both masked and accompanied by an elegant minuet-like dance played by a small chamber ensemble. At first he does not recognize her. She urges him to flee, and when he asks her why she cares so much, her sobs reveal her identity. As he recognizes her, the music moves to D-flat and the minuet resumes in that key. Their conversation now continues as a counterpoint to the dance. Together they move into a much more lyrical section with a different accompaniment in which she continues to plead with him to escape and he becomes increasingly overwhelmed by his love for her.

The first part of the duet returns, and Gustavo tells Amelia of his plan to send her away with her husband even though it will break his heart. She calls his name three times and then, at the interval of a third, they bid each other farewell. At the next moment Anckarström steps between them and stabs Gustavo. The crowd asks who the assassin is and Oscar points him out. As they tear off his mask, they all cry out his name.

The bystanders sing a chorus of outrage. As it ends, the minuet resumes as though it had never been interrupted. Gustavo commands the guards to release his attacker and asks him to come close to him. At this momentous moment the dance music gradually begins to die away. In a passage that alternates between recitative and a more lyrical style, the king tells his friend and rival that his wife is innocent. He has loved her, but she has never lost her honor. Amelia and Oscar join in, sharing their despair, and Anckarström bemoans his guilt for such a crime. This final ensemble is interrupted by the dying king, who grants a pardon to all. To the accompaniment of harp, the chorus blesses the dying Gustavo. He summons the strength to bid farewell to his "children," and principal characters and chorus powerfully lament this "night of horror."

❖ ❖ ❖

The premiere of *Un ballo* was received enthusiastically in Rome, but reactions were mixed in later performances. Some Italian audiences objected to the lack of formal arias with cabalettas and thought that the orchestra overshadowed the singers. The opera posed a problem in casting because the three roles of Amelia, Oscar, and Ulrica each demanded a female singer of the first order.

In more recent years the subtlety and sophistication of *Un ballo* have become more generally recognized, and the work maintains a secure position in the international repertory. In a review of the 2012 Metropolitan Opera production, *Philadelphia Inquirer* critic David Patrick Stearns wrote: "The political assassination saga that is *Un ballo in maschera* takes its place among Verdi's great operas without any of the composer's typical breakout tunes, but is full of musical characterizations tapping into an elemental psychology. It transcends its surroundings."[10]

In 1861 Verdi's former student, Emanuele Muzio, conducted *Un ballo* in New York and took the company on tour to Boston. He composed several extra dances for the ball scene so that the most distinguished Bostonian musical patrons could take the stage and join in the ball scene.[11] A performance of the work in New York on January 7, 1955, provided a milestone in American social history when the great contralto Marian Anderson (1897–1993) sang the role of Ulrica along with soprano Zinka Milanov as Amelia and tenor Jan Peerce and baritone Robert Merrill as the male leads. This was the first major performance by an African-American at America's most prestigious opera house.

The premiere of *Un ballo in maschera* occurred just as the Risorgimento was entering its final stage. Cavour had already convinced Napoleon III to ally France with Piedmont against Austria. In April of 1859 war broke out. The peace of Villafranca, signed by France and Austria in July, ceded the province of Lombardy to France with the understanding that it would be transferred to the kingdom of Piedmont. Italian nationalists were outraged that Veneto was to remain in Austrian hands, but despite this the European balance of power now firmly favored the side of Italian unity.

The following year France agreed to the annexation by Piedmont of Parma, Modena, Tuscany, and the Romagna. In the south Giuseppe

Garibaldi and his volunteer "Red Shirts" overthrew the government of Sicily and moved on to Naples. On March 17, 1861, the Kingdom of Italy, which included the entire peninsula except for Veneto, Rome, and other portions of the Papal States, was proclaimed. A regional assembly was established at Parma, and Verdi was elected as a delegate and then as a deputy to represent the Parma region before King Vittorio Emanuele in Turin. A short time later, at the urging of Cavour, he became a member of the newly constituted parliament.

Although he had held strong patriotic feelings since the early years of the Risorgimento, Verdi was a reluctant politician and agreed to run for office only because of his admiration for Cavour, who, like him, was a gentleman farmer. The politically astute Cavour recognized the symbolic value of Verdi's presence in the fledgling government. Early in 1859 someone had recognized that his name could be used as an acronym for Vittorio Emanuele Re d'Italia. At performances of his works and in the streets, crowds cried "Viva Verdi!" For some, the "Risorgimento operas" such as *Nabucco*, *I Lombardi*, and *Attila* had always communicated powerful nationalistic messages, but more importantly, Verdi was now unquestionably the great figure of a revered national art form.

This period also brought change to Verdi's private life. On August 29, 1859, he and Giuseppina Strepponi were married in a small town in the mountains of Savoy after having lived as husband and wife for ten years. Characteristically, the wedding was private and far away from their Busseto neighbors, from whom they were becoming increasingly estranged.

Because of standardization and improved enforcement of copyright laws, Verdi's financial situation had improved markedly by the end of the decade. He was now able to receive royalties for performances of his works in most countries of the world. Although he had been comfortably wealthy for many years, his continuing acquisition of land and improvements on the Sant'Agata estate had necessitated the production of new operas at a breakneck pace, but now he no longer felt driven to compose. He even wrote to Piave "I hope I have bidden farewell to the muses and that I shall never again feel the temptation to take up my pen."[12] After almost two decades in which he had averaged at least one opera every year, between the premiere of *Un ballo in maschera* and its successor there was an interval of nearly three years.

In June of 1861, while he was in Turin for a session of parliament, Verdi received an offer from the Imperial Theatre in Saint Petersburg to provide a new opera for the winter season. The proposed fee of approximately sixty thousand francs was irresistible, and he quickly ended his temporary retirement. Ironically, as one who was seen as the great national composer, he had virtually priced his work out of the Italian market. After *Un ballo* in 1859, no original Verdi opera had its premiere in Italy until *Otello* in 1887.

For Saint Petersburg he first proposed an adaptation of Hugo's 1838 drama *Ruy Blas*, but backed away because of concerns about censorship in czarist Russia. He then turned to *Don Alvaro, ó La Fuerza del sino (The Power of Fate)*, an 1835 drama by Angel de Saavedra, Duke of Riva, that had become a central work of the Spanish romantic theater. Verdi asked Piave to write the libretto for what was to be the last opera by these longtime collaborators. He added some passages from Schiller's *Wallenstein's Lager (Wallenstein's Camp)*, translated into Italian by Verdi's old friend Andrea Maffei. The title became *La forza del destino*, a literal translation of the Spanish subtitle. Piave visited the Verdis at Sant'Agata in July of 1861 to discuss the libretto. The work went quickly, and the opera was essentially complete by November. The premiere was scheduled for January of 1862.

In early December 1861 Verdi and Giuseppina set out on the long winter journey to Saint Petersburg. They traveled in relative splendor with two servants and copious food and wine for their stay in Russia.

Shortly after the rehearsals began the prima donna became ill and the premiere was postponed. It soon became obvious, however, that she would not be able to sing for the entire season, and the performance was rescheduled for November. The Verdis left Saint Petersburg in February, and on one segment of their trip, in present-day Latvia and Lithuania, they endured the Baltic cold in an unheated railway car in which even their wine froze.

Between the two Russian journeys the couple traveled to England for the Great London Exhibition. Verdi had been asked to compose a patriotic work to represent Italy as part of the festivities. He was, as usual, not enthusiastic about this kind of "occasional music," but he believed it was important that his newly created nation be represented along with France, Germany, and the host country. The result was the *Inno delle nazioni (Hymn of the Nations)*, a cantata with one solo voice.

The text, by Boito, celebrated the recent events in Italy and paid homage to the British and French for their support. Toward the end Verdi inserted "God Save the Queen" as well as the future national anthems of France and Italy, "La Marseillaise" and "Mameli's Hymn."

That September the Verdis returned to Saint Petersburg for the rescheduled premiere of *La forza*. This time, with a different soprano, rehearsals went well. The premiere on November 10 was well received by the audience, but critical comment was mixed, particularly from the proponents of the Russian nationalist school who resented the dominance of foreign styles and subject matter.

Verdi himself was dissatisfied with certain aspects of the plot and almost immediately began to consider a revision. The impetus to produce a new version came from publisher Tito Ricordi in 1868. He proposed that a revised *La forza del destino* be presented in 1869 at La Scala, reuniting Verdi with the theater where his career had begun thirty years earlier.

Piave had suffered a stroke the previous year and was unable to prepare the revision, but the journalist, novelist, and one-time baritone Antonio Ghislanzoni (1824–1893) had turned to writing librettos, and Verdi agreed to work with him. Ghislanzoni was appropriately solicitous of the maestro, and their collaboration was a fruitful one. The premiere of the revised work was a success, and the composer, who had boycotted La Scala for twenty-four years, was pleased with the performance. The prima donna was Teresa Stolz (1834–1902), a Bohemian-born soprano who had recently moved to Italy and achieved great success in an 1864 production of *Ernani* at Bologna. Her collaboration with Verdi on the 1869 premiere marked the beginning of an important professional and personal relationship that would continue for the rest of his life.

With few exceptions the 1869 *La forza* is the version that has been performed ever since. The composer and the librettist altered several elements of the plot that had not pleased Verdi in the Saint Petersburg version. Most notably, they eliminated the suicide of the lead male character that had left all the principals dead at the end of the original drama.

The central characters are Leonora, daughter of the Marquis of Calatrava, and her lover, Don Alvaro, the mysterious son of a Spanish aristocrat and an Inca mother. Her father finds them together and challenges Alvaro to duel. Alvaro, unwilling to fight the older man, throws his gun on the floor, but it accidentally discharges, killing the marquis.

The lovers flee, pursued by Leonora's brother Carlo who, disguised as a student, plans to avenge his father. Leonora, in male attire, goes to a monastery and relates her plight to the father superior. He accedes to her request to become a religious hermit and live in a cave.

Now in the military and believing that Leonora is dead, Alvaro saves the life of Carlo, whom he does not recognize, and the two pledge undying friendship. Alvaro is gravely wounded in a battle and asks his friend to burn his private papers when he dies. Carlo begins to suspect Alvaro's identity, and his suspicions are confirmed when he finds Leonora's portrait among his possessions. Alvaro's life is saved by surgery, and Carlo confronts him as the killer of his father. The ensuing duel is stopped by fellow soldiers, and Alvaro resolves to enter a monastery.

Several years later Carlo comes to the monastery where Alvaro is living and demands to see him. Alvaro tries to make peace, but Carlo again demands to fight a duel. Alvaro mortally wounds him and rushes to the nearby cave of the hermit to ask for absolution for the dying man. He and Leonora recognize each other, and together they rush to Carlo's side. With his last bit of strength Carlo stabs his sister. As she dies, she promises Alvaro that she will wait for him in heaven.

The most important musical revision in 1869 was the elimination of the short prelude, by now the norm in Verdi's operas, and its replacement by an extended overture. This is one of Verdi's most successful orchestral works and has long been part of the concert repertory of symphony orchestras. It opens strikingly with a "fate motive" that is associated with Leonora at several key points in the drama. Its striking "short-short-short-long" rhythm is familiar from *Il trovatore* and *Un ballo in maschera*, always representing fate, death, or both. At the beginning of the opera's final scene this passage returns to introduce Leonora's prayer "Pace, pace, mio Dio" (Peace, Peace, My God"). This aria, with harp accompaniment, is perhaps the most famous section of the opera and is one of the great standards of the soprano repertory.

The prominence of choral music, especially for male chorus, was probably a nod to Russian tastes. The expansive four-act structure and the numerous crowd scenes displayed a continuing French influence.

The decade of the 1860s was to be a turbulent period for Verdi, both personally and artistically. A group of young Italian poets and composers who called themselves "the disheveled ones" (*scapigliati*) had begun to call for renewal in the arts. Arrigo Boito, who had supplied the text for *Inno delle nazioni* in 1862, was one of the most vocal members. In 1863 he recited a poem in which he called for young artists to "raise modest, pure art on the altar now befouled like the wall of a brothel."[13] Verdi interpreted this as a personal affront and avoided Boito for a number of years.

As Verdi's productivity slowed during the 1860s, he and Giuseppina began to think about escaping the fog and bitter cold of the Po Valley winters. In 1857 he had become friendly with Angelo Mariani (1821–1873), who had conducted the premiere of *Aroldo*. By this time Mariani had become recognized as Italy's finest conductor. During his short career he was to direct other Verdi productions as well as important Italian premieres of works by Meyerbeer and Wagner. In 1866 Mariani leased two floors of the Palazzo Sauli-Pallavicino in Genoa on behalf of the Verdis so that they could spend the winters there. He subleased an attic apartment from them so that he could be close to his musical idol. Although the friendship with Mariani cooled before his untimely death, the Verdis continued to winter in Genoa until Giuseppina died in 1897.

In 1865 parliamentary elections were held, and Verdi refused to run for another term. The influence of Cavour had been the impetus for the composer's decision to participate in the first government, but he had died in 1861 and with his passing Verdi's direct interest in politics had waned. For the rest of his life he remained a well-informed and intensely interested bystander.

Also in 1865 Verdi's perpetually troubled relationship with his neighbors in Busseto turned decidedly worse. For about twenty years there had been discussions about the construction of a small civic opera house that would bear Verdi's name, but he believed that the town could ill afford to build the theater or to maintain it.

Antonio Barezzi was involved in the project, and undoubtedly he sincerely wanted to honor his famous son-in-law. But as Verdi realized, others were more interested in simply exploiting his name. It was suggested that he might compose a new work for the opening of the house and would use his influence and resources to bring renowned musicians to Busseto for the inaugural season. Naturally some of the proponents also expected him to make a large monetary contribution toward the construction of the theater. They even reminded him that in 1833 the local charitable foundation, the Monte di Pietà, had provided Verdi with a scholarship to study in Milan. The suggestion that he owed the town a specific debt infuriated Verdi and prompted a letter in which he pointed out that the total amount of his stipend had been only twelve hundred francs and that in the thirty years since he had received it he had carried the name of Busseto with honor "into all parts of the world."[14]

Eventually Verdi agreed to have the theater bear his name and donated ten thousand 10,00 lire, for which he received a box. The house opened in 1868 with a performance of *Rigoletto*, but the guest of honor was conspicuously absent. He and Giuseppina increasingly isolated themselves from the townspeople behind the walls of Sant'Agata.

Although Verdi seemed to be content managing his growing agricultural interests and reaping the rewards of his past labors, he was not averse to a new creative challenge. Since the Paris premiere of *Les vêpres Siciliennes* in 1855 "the big shop," as Verdi called the Opéra, had never been far from his thoughts. He was drawn by both the potential financial rewards that Paris offered and by the desire to compose a grand opera that would compete with the handful of immensely successful works of Meyerbeer and Halévy.

In 1865 the revised version of *Macbeth* premiered in Paris, achieving only a moderate success, but Verdi began discussions about a French *La forza del destino* and for a new work to premiere at the Opéra during the Paris Exposition of 1867. The *La forza* revision was eventually to be realized in Italian for the La Scala production in 1869, but the new work for Paris would eventually come to be the greatest of French grand operas.

In his negotiations about a subject for the new opera, *King Lear* was discussed once again. Not surprisingly, Verdi backed away, saying that the drama lacked the potential for the spectacle that grand opera demanded. Eventually all the parties agreed on Schiller's historical drama of the Spanish Inquisition, *Don Carlos*. Schiller's play was the type of grand semihistorical drama that was perfectly suited for the grand opera tradition.

Because the great obstacle that stood in the way of the unification of the Italian peninsula after 1860 was the issue of Rome and the Papal States, this story about the relationship between church and state during the Spanish Inquisition held powerful appeal for Verdi. Also, Schiller's drama, with its intense human conflict between King Philip II, his idealistic son Don Carlos, the fearsome Grand Inquisitor, and the trusted but politically radical adviser Rodrigo, Marquis of Posa, provided the composer with the human elements that he had always found necessary for operatic success.

Schiller's play was to be adapted by Joseph Méry (1797–1866), author of *La bataille de Toulouse*, the drama that had been the basis for Verdi's *La battaglia di Legnano*. Méry died before he completed the libretto, and it was finished by Camille du Locle (1832–1903), the son-in-law and assistant of Opéra director Emile Perrin. Verdi worked on the music at Sant'Agata and Genoa between March and late August of 1866 when he, accompanied by Giuseppina, left for Paris to prepare the production.

When the rehearsals began, Verdi encountered all the bureaucratic inefficiencies that had frustrated him at the Opéra in the past. At the dress rehearsal it became obvious that the sprawling five-act work would be too long to allow patrons to catch the last train to the Paris suburbs, necessitating several cuts.

The premiere, on March 11, 1867, received mixed reviews. Verdi wrote prophetically to his friend Count Arrivabene: "Last night *Don Carlos*. It was not a success. I don't know what the future may hold, but I shouldn't be surprised if things were to change."[15]

Before the second performance on March 13, the opera was cut further. The two early emergency excisions portended a complex performance history for this troublesome but magnificent work. Almost immediately Achille de Lauzières prepared an Italian translation that was performed with numerous cuts in London only a few months after the Paris premiere. That autumn Angelo Mariani conducted the uncut Italian version to great acclaim at Bologna. The following year a production at La Scala, with Teresa Stolz as Elisabeth, was a triumph, but *Don Carlo* did not achieve great success in other venues for several years.

During 1882 and 1883 Verdi shortened the opera again, eliminating the entire first act but restoring some of the original narrative with new dialogue and music. Du Locle collaborated with Verdi on this revision, and Angelo Zanardini made an Italian translation that closely followed the earlier one of Lauzières. This revised work was intended for Vienna, but eventually had its premiere at La Scala in January of 1884 with the

Italian title *Don Carlo*. To complicate matters further, at least two more variants were performed during Verdi's lifetime. [16]

Schiller's complex drama was historically inaccurate in its depiction of Prince Don Carlos (1545–1568) as a heroic figure. Possibly due to intermarriage that was typical among European royalty of the time, he suffered both physical and mental deformity.

DON CARLO(S): SYNOPSIS

Although conceived and composed as a French opera, *Don Carlos* is better known and more often performed in Italian. The synopsis will refer to the English equivalent of proper names when practical, and the musical analysis will use Italian for aria titles except for the opening Fontainebleau act. The narrative, however, will include the original first act, which is often restored in modern performance.

Don Carlo, son of King Philip II (Filippo) of Spain, has secretly arrived in France to see Elisabeth of Valois (Elisabetta), daughter of French king Henry II, to whom he has been betrothed. They meet in the forest of Fontainebleau and fall in love, but soon find out that as a condition of a new peace treaty between the two countries Elisabeth's father has given her to be married to Philip instead of his son. They are both devastated by this news, but Elisabeth knows that she must do her duty. She is taken away and Carlo laments his sad fate.

Carlo visits the monastery of Saint Just (San Giusto), where his grandfather, Emperor Charles V, had gone into seclusion near the end of his life, passing the throne to Philip. Arriving at his grandfather's tomb, he finds a mysterious friar praying there whose voice reminds him of his grandfather's. He then encounters his friend Rodrigo, Marquis of Posa. Carlo tells him of his secret love for Elisabeth, who is now the queen and his stepmother. Posa advises him to forget his love and concentrate on helping the people of Flanders, who are suffering under Philip's oppressive rule and the religious persecution of the Inquisition. The two men pledge eternal friendship and devotion to the cause of the oppressed.

Outside the monastery Princess Eboli, who is in love with Carlo, entertains the other ladies-in-waiting with a Moorish song. Elisabeth arrives, followed by Posa, who gives her a note from Carlo asking for a meeting with her. When they meet, she agrees to his request to ask the king to make him governor of Flanders. When he speaks of his continuing love for her, she rebukes him and he leaves in despair. The king enters and is furious to find the queen unattended. He angrily sends one of her ladies-in-waiting, who he believes is responsible, home to France.

After all the others have left, Philip sends for Posa and asks him why he has never sought advancement at the court. The young nobleman tells him that he has no personal ambition, but only wants to help the people of Flanders. The king respects his honesty and idealism, but tells him that he cannot change his harsh policy toward his Flemish subjects. He warns him that his liberal ideas are dangerous and that he should beware the wrath of the Grand Inquisitor. He also asks him to watch Elisabeth and Carlo. Reluctant to spy on his friend, but still hoping to win the king's help for Flanders, he accepts the charge.

At midnight Carlo comes to the queen's gardens outside the royal palace in Madrid. He has received a note that he believes to be from Elisabeth asking him to meet her. A veiled woman appears and the two embrace. She removes the veil and Carlo is shocked that the woman is not the queen, but Princess Eboli. Seeing his disappointment, she surmises that it was Elisabeth whom he had hoped to meet. Telling him that she has heard the king and Rodrigo discussing his relationship with the queen, she threatens to reveal what she knows. Posa arrives and tries unsuccessfully to convince her not to betray Carlo. She exits angrily, still determined to seek revenge. Posa convinces Carlo to give him incriminating documents about a Flemish uprising for safekeeping.

The scene that follows is an *auto-de-fe* (act of faith) that in this case depicts the burning of heretics at the stake. Such scenes of mass persecutions for religious motives were common in grand opera, and Verdi asked his librettists to add this one to Schiller's narrative. A crowd has gathered in the square of the cathedral. A procession of monks leads the condemned, and the king comes from inside the cathedral. A Flemish delegation, led by Carlo, arrives on the scene to plead for clemency for the heretics. Philip rejects their pleas and also refuses Carlo's request to make him governor of Flanders. This angers Carlo and he draws his sword. Enraged, Philip also seizes a sword, but Posa steps between father and son and takes his friend's sword. As Carlo is led away to prison, the flames rise from the stake, and a heavenly voice welcomes the souls to heaven.

Afterward, Philip, alone in his study, laments his loveless marriage and the burdens of state. He sends for the Grand Inquisitor to ask for advice in dealing with his son. The old priest gives him the church's approval to put Carlo to death. When he recommends the same fate for Posa, the king protests that he is the only man he can trust. The Inquisitor then accuses Philip of having been influenced by liberal ideas that pose a danger to the church.

When the Inquisitor leaves, Elisabeth enters, upset that her jewel box has been stolen. To her surprise the king picks up the box from his desk and demands that she open it. When she refuses, he breaks the lock and discovers a miniature portrait of Carlo. He accuses her of adultery and she faints. He calls Eboli and Posa for help. The men leave and Eboli confesses that it was she who stole the jewel box and also that she has been the king's mistress. The queen commands her to go into exile or enter a convent. The repentant Eboli chooses the latter, but determines that she will try to save Carlo.

Posa comes to the prison to visit Carlo. He informs him that he has allowed the papers about the Flemish rebellion to be found and attributed to him. Since he has taken the blame, Carlo will be released and can go to Flanders and organize the uprising. As Posa is about to leave, an officer of the Inquisition shoots him. As he dies, he tells Carlo that Elisabeth will be waiting the following day at the monastery of Saint Just to say farewell. Carlo falls weeping over his friend's body. The king, Princess Eboli in disguise, other members of the court, and the Grand Inquisitor enter the room. Philip tries to embrace his son, but Carlo refuses, declaring that his father's hands are stained with the blood of innocent people. A mob of dissident subjects arrives to protest Carlo's imprisonment. The king is saved from their wrath by the entrance of the Grand Inquisitor, before whom the crowd kneels. In the confusion Carlo, urged by Princess Eboli, escapes.

In the cloisters of the monastery of Saint Just, Elisabeth prays at the tomb of Charles V. When Carlo arrives, she reminds him of his promise to Posa that he will lead the Flemish subjects in their fight for freedom. They say their farewells and express their hope to meet in heaven. Suddenly the king, the Grand Inquisitor, and the officers of the Inquisition enter. Philip demands that Elisabeth and Carlo be arrested. Carlo draws his sword and moves toward his grandfather's tomb. At this moment the mysterious friar, whom he had previously seen praying at the tomb, appears wearing the crown and robes of Charles V and takes Carlo into the cloister. Philip and the others present exclaim that Carlo's deliverer was indeed his grandfather, the old emperor.

DON CARLO(S): THE MUSIC

The opera begins not with a formal prelude, but with fanfares of hunting horns and two offstage choruses of hunters. Carlo, hidden among rocks and trees, sees Elisabeth and her entourage pass by on horseback. The hunt music gradually dies away and Carlo emerges. Introduced by a plaintive clarinet melody, he sings in free declamation of the gloom of the forest in winter, now illuminated by Elisabeth's smile. The music assumes more tension as he reflects on leaving the Spanish royal court and potentially provoking his father's terrible anger. Thinking again of Elisabeth, he sings the aria "Je l'ai vue et dans son sourire" ("I Have Seen Her and in Her Smile"), accompanied by woodwinds. The simple form and delicate **chromaticism** create the perfect musical image of the immature, but sensitive, young prince.

The hunting horns are heard again, dying away in the distance. In another recitative Carlo wonders how he can find his way through the dark forest to the palace. He hears the voice of Tebaldo, Elisabeth's page, who appears with his mistress leaning on his arm. Carlo is instantly charmed at the sight of her. The page is frightened that they are lost in the forest and startled by this unknown man. Carlo quickly identifies himself as a member of the Spanish ambassador's party. Elisabeth reveals that she is to become the wife of Prince Don Carlo and knows that she will be safe in the care of this young Spaniard while Tebaldo goes to bring an escort for them.

Tebaldo leaves. Carlo bows to Elisabeth and gathers twigs for a fire to warm her. As the fire begins to glow, the music warms as well. In a sudden soaring melodic arch, Carlo exclaims that such a beautiful flame portends either victory or love. Her interest growing, Elisabeth asks him to tell her of the prince who will be her husband and expresses her fears of leaving her country.

Carlo assures her that the prince will be a loving husband and gives her a box that contains an image of him. Tension builds in the orchestra as she looks at the portrait. When she realizes that she is face to face with her fiancé, she exclaims "Great God!" and the music shifts exultantly to the brilliant key of E major. The dialogue that has been steadily moving from speech-like to melodic now evolves into an ecstatic love duet.

In the division of the melodic material between the two lovers, Verdi utilizes most of the procedures of the Italian tradition: one voice finishes or imitates the phrase of the other; the two sing in unison; and they harmonize in thirds and sixths. His mature style is evident, however, in the rhythmic flexibility and the rich chromatic harmony.

The lovers hear the sound of a cannon that signals the signing of the peace treaty between France and Spain. As in a fairytale, the palace of Fontainebleau appears in splendid light in the distance. They rejoice in this apparent omen of their joyful future as the music moves for a second time into the bright region of E major.

Their bliss is short-lived, however. Tebaldo returns and hails Elisabeth as the bride of Philip II and Queen of Spain. She protests, but the page delivers the shocking news that King Henry has pledged her hand in marriage to the king instead of the prince.

The rest of the act is marked by tremendous irony. Tebaldo and all the bystanders rejoice at this happy development, while the two central characters mourn the bizarre twist of fate. They join in a march-like duet that depicts them as participants in a movement over which they have no control.

Count di Lerma, leader of the Spanish delegation, emerges from the rejoicing crowd to proclaim officially what the lovers already know, but he assures Elisabeth that she is free to accept or reject the agreement. The women of the chorus beg her to agree, reminding her of her role in bringing peace to the two countries. Feebly she answers "yes," but to herself, in the lowest part of her vocal range, she whispers that this is "supreme anguish."

The chorus sings a moving prayer of thanksgiving against the lamenting interjections of Elisabeth and Carlo. Then the march resumes and the future queen is borne away in procession on a litter. The crowd follows, leaving Carlo alone to bewail "O destin fatal, o destin crudel" ("Oh fatal, cruel destiny").

The first scene of Act Two (Act One in the four-act 1884 revision) takes place at dawn in the cloisters of the monastery of Saint Just with a chapel that contains the tomb of Charles V. A somber prelude, begun by four horns in unison and then enriched by more winds, introduces a chorus of monks singing, in the style of chanted psalmody, a prayer for the dead emperor. This "Charles V music" returns in the final act when the narrative moves back to the monastery. Although Verdi had used recurring melodies in his operas since the beginning of his career, this procedure is more extensive and systematic in *Don Carlo* than in any earlier work.

The mysterious friar, who kneels in prayer at the tomb, comments on the words of the chorus with the accompaniment of string **tremolos**. Like an Old Testament prophet, he bemoans the emperor's error of desiring earthly power.

At the end of this passage the old monk joins the prayer for mercy as a major key brings a conciliatory tone. The entire scene is reminiscent of the *Miserere* in *Il trovatore*, but has a supernatural quality that was absent in the earlier work.

The chorus of monks exits and the second scene begins with the entrance of the pale and wasted Carlo. He sings of the death, in this place, of his grandfather and namesake and his hope that he too can find peace here. As his thoughts turn toward the love that has been taken from him, he bursts into melody. Such fluid alternation of declamation and lyrical melodic flight had been increasingly present in Verdi's works, but nowhere more than here. In the 1884 score Verdi inserted a slightly revised Italian version of Carlo's aria "Je l'ai vue" ("Io la vidi") from the omitted Fontainebleau act.

The old friar rises from his kneeling position and, in the same tones in which he had commented on the emperor, he warns the young man that peace cannot be found even in the cloister, but only in God. Carlo immediately recognizes the voice and proclaims that the monk is the ghost of his grandfather.

Carlo's terror is quickly defused by the arrival of his friend Posa. The two sing a short, joyful duet expressing their love for each other. A more extended duet was one of the casualties of Verdi's cuts before the premiere. Posa abruptly changes the subject to describe the suffering of King Philip's subjects in Flanders and to express the hope that Carlo can intervene to help them. As he reaches his most intense moment, he suddenly notices Carlo's appearance and asks him why he is pale and has tears in his eyes.

In a rapid passage with breathless, **staccato** notes, Carlo confesses his love for Elisabeth, and the horrified Posa exclaims "your mother!" After this initial shock Posa tries to console his friend. Their duet, "Mio fedel, fratel d'affetto" ("My Faithful One, My Brother"), is in D-flat major: a key that was prominent in the first-act love duet. Certain aspects of the melodic outline also recall the love music. In the ensuing recitative Carlo assures his friend that the king knows nothing of his love for Elisabeth, and Posa advises him to forget his despair and take up the cause of the Flemish.

A bell rings and a group of monks enters, causing Posa to surmise that the king and queen are about to arrive. The two friends join in a martial cabaletta, "Dio,che nell'alma infondere amor" ("God, Who Infuses Love in Our Souls"), harmonizing almost entirely at the interval of a third. This earnest and slightly naive "fraternal duet" is one of the moments in *Don Carlo* that most resemble early Verdi.

The duet ends just as Philip and Elisabeth, preceded by monks, enter regally to the sound of brass fanfares. As they pay their respects at the tomb of the old emperor, the monks intone their prayer from the first scene of the act, and the old friar adds his commentary, "God alone is great." Oblivious to all of this, Carlo pours out his despair at seeing Elisabeth in her role as the wife of his father. Posa brings him back to reality and they reprise the conclusion of their duet, "We shall be united in life and death."

In the second scene several of the queen's ladies-in-waiting amuse themselves on the grounds of the monastery while the royal couple are inside. The women sing a chorus that describes their surroundings. The major-minor shifts and the sound of a triangle add a slightly exotic flavor. Tebaldo and Princess Eboli enter. The page sings a short passage and then joins the ladies in a repetition of their chorus.

Eboli suggests that they devise a game to occupy them while they wait. She asks for a mandolin and suggests that they join in singing "The Song of the Veil." It tells of a Moorish king of Granada who courts a veiled lady in the palace garden only to find that she is his wife. In two stanzas, with the entire party joining in a refrain, the song has rhythmic and melodic figures, including florid **cadenzas** in which a French audience might have detected a hint of Spanish flavor.

The queen emerges from the monastery, and Eboli remarks that a sad thought always occupies her soul. Elisabeth confirms this by commenting to herself that those around are singing happily and that she also was happy in the past. Posa enters and gives her a letter that is allegedly from her mother in France and a smaller note that he urges her to read.

Posa then turns to Eboli and they engage in a trivial conversation about life at the French court. They are both accompanied by a graceful orchestral passage with Verdi's directive that it be played "with elegance." Elisabeth enters the ensemble, but she speaks only to Posa, so that he is conversing alternately with the two women. Elisabeth pours out her heart while Eboli chatters about French style, oblivious to all else.

After some consideration Elisabeth reads the note. It is from Carlo, who tells her to trust the words of Posa. Because of this she tells him she will grant him a royal favor. Posa accepts, but explains that the favor will not be his, but another's. He then proceeds to sing a "song" about Carlo in which he laments his friend's anguish and implores the queen, as his mother, to open her heart to him. Accompanied by **pizzicato** strings with woodwind punctuations, Posa's melody, in two stanzas, reflects the earnestness of his character. Between the stanzas each of the two women reflects on her memories of Carlo.

In his second stanza Posa becomes more specific in his request. He suggests that Elisabeth can save Carlo by showing him the love that he does not receive from his father. The more intense text is matched by a more rhythmically active accompaniment. His lyrical plea moves the queen, and she tells Tebaldo that she will receive Carlo. Eboli, still believing that she is the object of the prince's affections, is escorted away by Posa.

Carlo enters slowly and approaches Elisabeth. Introduced by a softly undulating passage in the woodwinds, he begins this great duet by pouring out all of his anguish at the feet of the woman he loves and begs her to convince his father to send him to Flanders. She surprises him by telling him "with very contained emotion" that he can leave the following day. With increasing agitation he marvels at how coolly she can send him away. Her true emotions eventually take control and she bids him farewell, adding that living on the earth near him has been paradise. This sends Carlo into the "heavenly" key of D-flat, singing parlando against a soaring melody for woodwinds with harp accompaniment. In his last phrase the music moves back to the previous key of B-flat and ends inconclusively as he falls senseless to the ground. Thinking that he has died, Elisabeth bends over him and, in a dramatic accompanied recitative, prays for God to bring him peace, referring to him as her fiancé.

Deliriously Carlo responds to her words with declarations of love that no longer feign propriety or protocol. She cries out in terror at what has been unleashed. His ecstasy is mirrored in the chromatic harmonies in the string tremolos that, like the love duet in *Un ballo*, approach the intensity of passages in *Tristan and Isolde*. The duet reaches its apex as he cries "I love you" three times, ascending a step with each repetition, and takes her in his arms.

Unable to bear this any longer, Elisabeth makes a daring gambit. She almost shrieks that he should kill his father and marry his mother. At this point the accompaniment is at its most rapid. Crying "Oh cursed son," Carlo runs away and the queen falls on her knees, asking God to watch over them. Her prayer ends the duet as it began, in E-flat, but in the major mode rather than minor.

Tebaldo emerges from the monastery and announces the appearance of the king, who enters to a regal march. Philip's anger that his consort is unaccompanied and his subsequent banishment of the lady-in-waiting Countess Aremberg casts an immediate chill on the whole company. Elisabeth sings a wistful aria, "Non pianger, mia compagna" ("Do Not Weep, My Companion"), in which she bids farewell to her old friend and implies that perhaps she envies her opportunity to return to France.

The ladies exit, leaving Philip and Posa onstage. The king's curiosity at why Rodrigo has never sought reward for his loyalty and why he has retired from the military gives the younger man just the opening that he needs. He launches into a graphic portrayal of the horrors of life in Flanders under Spanish rule: "O signor, di Fiandra arrivo" ("Oh Sir, I Have Arrived from Flanders"). The rapidly moving orchestral accompaniment with **syncopated** rhythm mirrors Rodrigo's impatience and the horror of the scene he describes: a land flowing with rivers of blood.

Philip responds with appropriate gravity that only through bloodshed can there be peace in the world. His vocal line is doubled in the orchestra, adding strength and solemnity. The two men argue, but there is no hope for agreement. At this point in the four-act revision a new passage was added in which the king boasts that his Spanish subjects are faithful to God and have no complaint for their king. He desires this same peace for the Flemish. With devastating honesty and bravado, Posa declares that this is the "peace of the tomb." With his final word the low strings, winds, and timpani begin a powerful tremolo that commences with the stark **dissonance** of two notes a step apart. The distance between them gradually widens as the dynamic level diminishes and Posa whispers: "Oh King! May history never say of you: he was a Nero."

Posa maintains this level of passion and outrage in the aria that follows, "Quest'è la pace che voi date al mondo?" ("This Is the Peace That You Have Given the World?"). This begins as a dialogue between the baritone and the low strings and woodwinds. The orchestral texture thickens and the harmony becomes chromatic to a degree that would have been unthinkable in Verdi's music a decade earlier. The kaleidoscopic series of key changes finally arrives at a firm, brilliant E major at the words "date la libertà!" ("give liberty!").

Calling Posa a dreamer, Philip cynically tells him that he would feel differently if he knew the hearts of men as he does. In the foreign key of F-sharp major he assures him that he will not hold him responsible for his inflammatory words, but as the orchestra descends in pitch and **crescendos** in sound, coming to rest in C major, he warns him to beware the Grand Inquisitor.

The king now changes his tone abruptly as he realizes that Posa is the only man he can trust. He confides that he suspects that his wife loves Don Carlo. He asks Posa to keep watch over the queen and the prince. As he expresses his satisfaction that he has found a trustworthy ally, the music shifts from minor to major. To himself Posa observes with great joy that the king has found hope. The obvious implication is that he will now be led to show mercy on the people of Flanders. In a final excursion into distant keys, Philip repeats his warning to beware the Grand Inquisitor. Posa kneels before his sovereign and kisses his hand as the full orchestra reasserts the major harmony and the curtain falls.

Act Three in the original Paris score begins with a scene for Elisabeth and Eboli on the night before King Philip's official coronation. The queen tells Eboli that she wants to spend the evening in prayer rather than participate in the entertainment that has been planned and that she must take her place. The two purposes of this scene are to reveal Eboli's plan to invite Carlo to a midnight tryst and to introduce the *Ballet of the Queen* or *La peregrina* (*The Wanderer*). The dance scene, so central to the Parisian tradition, was deleted from the 1884 revision, but is occasionally restored in modern performance.

Act Two (1884) opens with a prelude based on the beginning of Carlo's earlier aria "Io la vidi." The use of **counterpoint**, chromaticism, and muted string tremolos displays Verdi's wholehearted embrace of late Romantic musical style at this point in his career.

After the 1884 prelude all versions coincide for the remainder of the act. Carlo appears at midnight in the palace garden, reading a note that he believes to be from Elisabeth, asking him to meet her there. The veiled Eboli arrives and, believing her to be the queen, Carlo sings passionately of his love for her. She responds ecstatically and the two join in a soaring passage in octaves.

Eboli removes her veil and Carlo reacts visibly to the mistaken identity, accompanied by a sudden change of key. In the duet that follows she shocks him by reporting that she has overheard the conversation concerning him between his father and Posa. She declares her love for him and assures him that she can save him from the cruel intrigues of the court.

Carlo praises her goodness, but confesses that any love between them is only a strange dream. Suddenly she realizes the truth and, without accompaniment, she cries "You love the queen!" In a state of near frenzy he responds "Pietá!" ("Mercy!").

At this moment Posa rushes in and begins a heated exchange with Eboli. She tells him that she now knows Carlo's secret. She recognizes Posa's influence as a confidant of the king, but boasts that she has power of her own. She threatens revenge for being scorned, singing in short, breathless phrases that are supported by staccato chords. Posa's vocal line is more coherent and controlled as he declares that only heaven knows the human heart. Carlo, more to himself than as a part of the conversation, laments his foolishness. The rhythmic activity becomes increasingly frantic. As the emotional level intensifies, the two men begin to sing as a unit against Eboli's increasingly hysterical threats of revenge.

Eboli turns to Elisabeth as the target for her venom. In a sinuous melodic line that is doubled in octaves by the orchestra, she mocks the saintly image of the queen that was only a mask of virtue. Her words are so offensive to Posa that he draws his dagger to kill her, but Carlo restrains him.

The final section of the scene begins with Posa in the lead, declaring that if Eboli seeks revenge, God will punish her. She and Carlo provide declamatory commentary: he lamenting his great sorrow, and she with the incessant warning that he should tremble at the thought of her vengeance. The musical motion continues to intensify until Eboli storms out, warning Carlo that soon the ground will open under his feet.

Left alone with Carlo, Posa asks him to entrust potentially incriminating documents to him. The entire request is sung on a single pitch. Responding on the same note, Carlo is doubtful about trusting an intimate of his father, provoking surprise and disappointment in his friend. The entire exchange encompasses only four pitches. Carlo quickly has a change of heart and, expressing his total confidence, agrees to give him the papers. They embrace and the full orchestra plays the triumphal theme of their "fraternal duet" from the previous act.

The finale of this act is the grandiose *auto da fé* scene: a genre that was dear to Paris audiences in the works for Meyerbeer and Halévy. The curtain opens on the great cathedral plaza. A grand stairway leads to the doors of the church, and the top of a stake can be seen in an adjacent square. Bells are chiming and a large crowd is gathering.

After a fanfare-like introduction a chorus of people sings praises to the king. This joyous passage recurs like a refrain, interspersed between other sections of the scene. Considering the central purpose of this scene, both text and music are distinctly ironic. Suddenly this ends and a somber funeral march begins, punctuated by the short-short-short-long "death figure" that by now is ubiquitous in Verdi. Monks accompany the condemned heretics toward their execution. The monks begin to sing in counterpoint with the march as they proclaim the terror of the day, but extol the righteousness of its purpose. The tone changes as they announce that those who repent in their final moments will receive pardon after death. This is intoned in *parlante* style above an arching melody that moves from one section of the orchestra to another.

As the monks lead the victims to the stake, the chorus of the people is repeated and Posa, Elisabeth, Tebaldo, and other members of the court walk in procession from the palace. A march is played by a **banda** (*musique sur le theater* in French), sometimes in alternation with the orchestra and sometimes with it. After another repetition of the people's chorus, the royal herald demands that the doors of the cathedral be opened to reveal the king to his people. They repeat his request unaccompanied and in the style of church music.

The orchestra and *banda* play a grandiose passage as the king walks beneath a canopy carried by monks. In stentorian tones he proclaims that in taking the crown he pledges to avenge sins against God by sword and fire.

The music moves from majestic to agitated as Carlo appears, leading a Flemish delegation who kneel at the feet of the king. In an aria-like unison passage the six deputies beg him to hear their people's complaints. Philip brazenly pronounces them to be infidels, and his judgment is echoed by a group of monks. Elisabeth, Carlo, Posa, and Tebaldo, supported by the chorus, beg him to extend his hand to these supplicants. This sets in motion a huge ensemble in which the king and the monks express their unwavering condemnation and the others beg him for mercy. The musical texture grows increasingly complex as the deputies repeat their plea and each of the other groups takes up its own melodic line. A massive climax is reached and a sense of finality attained, but after a long silence Carlo faces his father. He has chosen this highly inopportune moment to express his frustration at his preparation for his future role of king and to request that he be granted responsibility over Flanders.

The king reacts angrily, and Elisabeth and Posa look on with horror. Carlo draws his sword, and in a line that ascends to the top of his vocal range he announces that he will be the savior of the Flemish. All the onlookers cry that the prince is delirious, and Philip orders that he be disarmed. As tension increases in the orchestra, the king waits while both guards and courtiers show reluctance to lay a hand on the prince. Finally Posa steps forward and asks for the sword. As two clarinets very softly play the theme from the "fraternal duet," Carlo hands him the sword and whispers: "Oh heavens! You, Rodrigo!" Presumably he is then arrested and taken away.

Immediately Philip grants Posa the title of duke and announces that they will now go to witness the execution. Orchestra and *banda* play the martial music from the opening of the scene, and the royal party processes toward the flames of the stake. This is followed by a final reprise of the people's chorus that completes the musical symmetry of this enormous scene. But a surprise occurs before the end. A "voice from on high," accompanied by the heavenly sounds of harp and **harmonium**, is heard by the audience but not by those on stage. The voice comforts those who are about to die, offering them pardon before the throne of God. The passage combines two musical ideas that were heard in succession earlier. The monks are repeating their funeral march, singing of the terror of the day while the mysterious celestial voice sings the melody that accompanied their earlier offer of mercy for those who repent. The voice continues to console while the Flemish deputies comment on the horror of what is transpiring in the name of religion, and all the others join the king in singing "Glory to God!" The flames rise and the curtain falls to the tumultuous music of orchestra and banda.

Act Four (1884, Act Three) takes place in the king's study where a troubled King Philip reflects on his loneliness and the limitations of power. The contrast of private doubt with the prior scene's public glory is stunning. The orchestral prelude, scored as delicately as chamber music, demonstrates how Verdi, by this period, has become a master of instrumental writing. Philip delivers a heart-rending recitative to the accompaniment of the prelude music. He knows that Elisabeth has never loved him, and as the light of dawn becomes visible through the windows, he realizes that he has not slept all night.

After a long pause he begins the aria "Dormirò sol nel manto mio regal" ("I Shall Only Sleep in My Royal Mantle"). Although the traditional Italian set piece is almost absent from *Don Carlo*, this is one of the most celebrated of all bass arias. The king muses that he will eventually find sleep as his body lies under the stone vaulting of the Escorial. He laments that royalty cannot possess the power to see into the hearts of men. The aria moves seamlessly from minor to major and through several relatively remote keys. A rich orchestral background is maintained throughout without a hint of old-fashioned Italian accompaniment figures.

Just as the musical climax is reached, Philip whispers that a traitor waits for him to sleep so that he can steal his wife and his honor. He then repeats the aria, almost intact. At the same climactic point he pauses and, in a **cadenza**, reiterates obsessively, "She does not love me."

In this scene, with its natural declamatory rhythm, strong melody, and rich harmony, Verdi has humanized this man who could be viewed as a monster. Along with its dramatic integrity, there is overarching strength in its musical architecture.

As he sinks back into his meditation, the Count di Lerma enters the room with the ancient Grand Inquisitor, followed by two Dominican friars. His entrance is accompanied by a slow, pompous march played by low woodwinds and strings and punctuated by trombones and timpani. To this accompaniment the two basses carry on a dialogue in which Philip tells the Inquisitor of Carlo's numerous betrayals of him and asks the old cleric's sanction to have him put to death. The Inquisitor replies coldly that the price of peace in the world is the blood of a rebellious son. He reminds him that God himself sacrificed his son to save the world.

With the king's dilemma easily dispatched, the Inquisitor now turns to what he considers to be a more pressing issue. He tells the king that Posa, his friend and confidant, is a heretic, more dangerous than the immature Carlo. All of this is sung with restraint, but as he reflects on his own power, mightier than the throne, he grows more emotional. His line rises in a long crescendo above tremolo strings and brass outbursts. Over a descending stepwise line, Philip glumly declares that in his whole court he has been able to find only one man who is a true friend. Cynically the Inquisitor asks how he can call himself a king if he needs such a confidante. The king loses his temper, uttering the famous line "Tais-toi, prêtre!" ("Silence, priest!"). One reason often suggested for the mixed early reception of *Don Carlos* was the reaction of the Spanish-born Empress Eugénie (1826–1920), wife of Napoleon III, who was offended by the opera's portrayal of the Inquisition. On the evening that she attended, when the king commanded the Grand Inquisitor to be quiet, she turned her back to the stage in protest.[17]

The conflict between the two authority figures becomes increasingly antagonistic when the old man demands that Posa be handed over to the Inquisition and the king refuses. Ominously, the Inquisitor declares that if he had not been summoned to the palace, the king would have been called before the tribunal the following day. He reminds Philip that he has installed two kings on the Spanish throne, and now this one is destroying a life's work.

The Inquisitor turns to leave, accompanied by the lugubrious march that had announced his arrival. Philip, the most powerful man on earth, is completely cowed by this adversary. He begs for peace between them, but the old man can only answer "perhaps." Defeated, Philip observes cynically that the throne must bow to the altar as this dark scene ends ironically on a major harmony.

Elisabeth enters and throws herself at the king's feet. She has come to protest the treatment she has received from her perceived enemies at the court and to seek his help in recovering her stolen jewel box. As Philip produces the box and presents it to her, a fanfare-like passage precedes each of his short statements, ominously descending a step each time. He forces the lock of the box and produces a portrait of Carlo.

Accused of infidelity, Elisabeth counters that she had possessed the image in France from the time that she was originally betrothed to the prince. The dialogue and the accompaniment grow increasingly intense. When Elisabeth tells Philip that she pities him, he replies: "You pity me, adulterous woman?" Hearing this, the queen faints. This is all punctuated by a dramatic harmonic shift that takes the music to a foreign key.

The king cries for help, and both Posa and Eboli rush in, horrified at the sight of the unconscious queen. She expresses guilt for what has happened, and he boldly declares to Philip that although he controls half of the world, he cannot control himself.

In a passage in which the sense of key is very unstable, Philip bemoans his suspicion as the work of a demon. Eboli joins in and they both whisper words of regret in *parlante* style accompanied by a long, mostly stepwise melody in bassoon and cellos. Now a traditional ensemble finale for three and then four characters begins. Eboli continues to express her remorse for the betrayal of her mistress, and Posa, unheard by those on stage, makes the fateful decision that he will die for the future of Spain. Philip joins in, singing the melody that has just been heard in the cellos and bassoon, which essentially becomes his "theme" in the ensemble. He expresses his newfound confidence that Elisabeth has never been unfaithful.

Elisabeth revives and sings of her sorrow at being an exile in a foreign land. Although this is a heartfelt lamentation, the melody is a dulcet one in a major key with the accompaniment of broken chords played by a flute. This ensemble has the stunning dramatic effect of the great quartet from *Rigoletto*, but its rhythm is more fluid and its harmony richer.

Philip and Posa exit, leaving Eboli alone with the queen to confess two betrayals. She stole the jewel box out of jealousy of Elisabeth and to punish Carlo for spurning her advances. The more serious confession, however, initiates a change of key and a highly agitated rhythmic figure in the orchestra that supports her breathless phrases. Vacillating wildly between a scream and a whisper, she announces that she has committed adultery with the king. The quietness of the queen's restraint belies the power of her words. Reinforced by a sustained pitch from the horn, she pronounces Eboli's choice: exile or the cloister. Without a further word she exits, leaving Eboli alone to reflect on her fate.

The great scene that begins with "O don fatale" ("Oh Fatal Gift") emphasizes Eboli's remarkable vanity as she blames her great beauty for her downfall. But as with King Philip's "Dormiró sol" at the beginning of the act, the warmth and sincerity of Verdi's music have given this unlovable character a glimmer of humanity. After a declamatory section that ends with a spectacular two-octave descent as the princess curses her beauty, the tempo slows for her tender farewell to the queen whom she has wronged. A ravishing melody against a colorful harmonic background finally humanizes this villainess.

Suddenly Eboli's thoughts turn to Carlo, whose death seems imminent. The pace suddenly quickens as she determines to do whatever is necessary to save him. Near the end, a declamatory passage takes flight in a thrilling melodic line as she realizes that Carlo's salvation will bring about her own rebirth.

This concludes one of Verdi's most ambitious scenes, whose musical symmetry should not go unnoticed. In a great musical arch, it moves from solo to duet to quartet and then back to duet and solo.

The second scene takes place somewhere in the precincts of the palace where Carlo is imprisoned. He sits with his head in his hands, lost in thought. Solemn chords in the orchestra match the gloomy setting. A solo oboe's reminiscence of the love duet from the Fontainebleau act illuminates the subject of the prince's thoughts.

Posa enters and Carlo pours out his frustration that his ill-fated love for Elisabeth has taken away his strength, leaving him unable to help the cause of the Flemish. Shockingly, Posa informs him that he has saved his life and obtained his freedom. He sings a short aria that expresses his joy at saving his friend and the prospect of their being reunited in heaven. In the succeeding recitative he explains that he has allowed Carlo's incriminating papers to be found in his possession and he is now the condemned man. Unnoticed by the friends, two men have come down the stairs. At that moment Posa sings a march-like passage relating his hopes for the freedom of Flanders under Carlo's rule. A shot rings out and, mortally wounded, he falls into Carlo's arms.

Posa then sings a second aria in which he rejoices in the hope that Spain can become a place of happiness. The accompaniment features the harp and contains still another statement of the theme from the friends' "fraternal duet." With his last breath, he bids Carlo farewell and begs him to save Flanders.

The king rushes in with various members of his court. He gives Carlo back his sword, but his son rejects him with savage contempt, telling him that he is covered with the blood of an innocent and that he no longer calls himself his son.

At this point all the versions of the opera vary in some details. Because the perpetual problem with *Don Carlos* was its length and complexity, Verdi eventually decided to move expeditiously to the end of this exceedingly intense act. In the 1884 revision he condensed the narrative, but attempted to maintain the plot's integrity.

After Carlo's forceful condemnation of his father, a great commotion is heard outside. Count di Lerma announces that the people are rebelling, storming the palace, and demanding that Carlo be freed. Philip orders that the palace gates be opened, and the crowd rushes in. At this moment Eboli, wearing a mask, enters and urges Carlo to flee. The crowd demands the prince and Philip points to him. In the earliest version the crowd takes Carlo away, accompanied by Eboli.

Suddenly the Grand Inquisitor appears and orders the mob to fall prostrate before the king. The awestruck crowd obeys, and Philip cries "Glory to You, great Lord!" The act concludes with a huge sonic climax with Philip praising God, the crowd praying for pardon, and the courtiers glorifying the king,

Act Five (1884, Act Four), like Act Two, is set in the cloister of the monastery of Saint Just. The prelude, played by low brass, is an instrumental version of the monks' chorus of prayer for Emperor Charles V. Elisabeth enters and kneels at the emperor's tomb. Almost entirely without accompaniment, she addresses him as one who turned away from the vanity of the world and found peace in the grave. Abruptly the key moves from minor to major and Elisabeth prays that the emperor will carry her tears to the feet of God. The melody, with its ascent of more than an octave and a half in its opening phrase, is one of the most poignant in the entire score.

In a short recitative she explains that she has promised Posa that she will watch over Carlo. Returning to lyrical style, she observes that his path will be a blessed one, while her own life will end. She begins to think of France and Fontainebleau, accompanied by reminiscences of the first-act love duet. She then addresses the gardens of Spain, asking that they sing to Carlo of her memories of him. The music grows progressively more agitated as Elisabeth bids farewell to her youth and longs for the peace that can only be found in death.

This thought reminds her once again of the old emperor and initiates a return of her apostrophe to him from the beginning of the scene, supported by a richer orchestral palette than before. Just as her aria ends, Carlo appears and whispers excitedly, "It is she." He tells her passionately of his plan to go to Flanders and erect a monument to Posa such as no monarch has ever been granted.

All versions of the score now proceed with a duet for Elisabeth and Carlo. The 1884 version is somewhat abbreviated and the music revised, presenting a kaleidoscope of strong emotions. Carlo sings tenderly of his memories of Posa, but the happy thoughts are quickly replaced by those of his death and of the burning of heretics. This inspires Elisabeth to a march-like passage, reminiscent of the now familiar Carlo-Posa duet, in which she encourages him to heroism for a dying people. Carlo joins in, bolstered by her passion for his mission, and becomes ecstatic at the thought that their love has been purified by this common cause.

Suddenly the tone darkens as bassoon and cellos play a descending two-note motive that for centuries had signified sighing or weeping. Carlo notices that Elisabeth is crying, and she professes that they are the tears that women always shed for heroes.

In the final section of the duet, in brilliant B major, they sing their farewells and their hopes for a better life to come. As they end their final phrase, "per sempre" ("forever"), sung together in the traditional sixths, the king, the Grand Inquisitor, and officials of the Inquisition enter. Philip takes his wife's arm, saying "Yes, forever!" In the most devastating statement of the opera, taken virtually intact from the last line of Schiller's play, he turns to the Inquisitor and, accompanied by string tremolos, says: "I have done my duty. And you?" The Inquisitor commands the Holy Office to do its work.

○ ○ ○

The 1867 version extends Schiller's narrative with the addition of a brief trial scene in which Carlo's crimes are enumerated. In 1884 this was omitted and the Inquisitor immediately commands the guards to seize Carlo. Over a melodramatic passage in perpetual motion he cries that God will be his avenger. He struggles and moves toward his grand-father's tomb.

The old friar from Act Two appears, wearing the crown and robes of Charles V and singing the same music and text as before. The Inquisi-tor, echoed by his acolytes, intones "It is the voice of Charles V!" The king cries "My father!" and Elisabeth shrieks "Oh heaven!" as the ghost-ly friar pulls Carlo into the cloister. The "Charles V music" rings out in the low brass as the opera ends.

The appearance of the dead emperor as the *deus ex machina* who saves Carlo has perplexed audiences and elicited criticism since the work's premiere. *Don Carlo* was ostensibly set in the 1860s, after Charles's death in 1558. Is this then the ghost of Charles V, or is the audience to believe that the emperor had feigned his death, remaining in seclusion in the monastery?

The figure of Emperor Charles is a powerful presence in Acts Two and Five of *Don Carlo*, as it was in the Spanish Empire during the reign of Philip II. It was through Charles's Habsburg inheritance that Spain acquired her territory in the Netherlands. He was a native of Ghent and spoke Flemish. Consequently, despite his central position in the Coun-ter-Reformation, he was viewed more favorably among his northern subjects than his son was. Thus the conceit that he might have been more sympathetic to them and to his grandson's crusade for their liberty, though without historical basis, is not inconceivable.

Charles had come to Busseto in 1542 to meet with Pope Paul III to discuss plans for the Council of Trent. The emperor granted Busseto the honorary status of imperial town, and the event became a point of pride in the small town's history. A plaque on the wall of the collegiate church of San Bartolomeo commemorates that event. The emperor's visit to his hometown was certainly known to Verdi. During the negotiations during 1865 that eventually led to the creation of *Don Carlos* Verdi had written to Emile Perrin that it was "an excellent idea to make Charles V appear."[18]

Because of discrepancies among its various revisions, texts in two languages, and its extreme length, even in the four-act version, *Don Carlos* failed to become a repertoire staple until well into the twentieth century. When Rudolf Bing (1902–1997) became general manager of the Metropolitan Opera in 1950, he chose the Italian *Don Carlo* to be the first work that he produced. The choice was considered to be unorthodox because the opera had not been performed at the Metropolitan since 1922.[19] With a stellar cast that included tenor Jussi Bjoerling, baritone Robert Merrill, and bass Jerome Hines, the production scored a great success. *Don Carlo* was heard often during Bing's tenure, and it could be argued that he is the person most responsible for its acceptance as an important part of the Verdi canon.

During the second half of the twentieth century increased recognition by the public was accompanied by the attention of the scholarly community. The culmination was the 1977 Ricordi publication of the critical edition of *Don Carlos* in both the five- and four-act versions and with French and Italian texts.[20] Since that time new productions have taken advantage of authoritative texts of all the music Verdi produced for the work with both French and Italian librettos.

6

RETURN TO MILAN

Aida, Manzoni Requiem

The lukewarm reception of *Don Carlos* in Paris caused Verdi more consternation than any of his professional setbacks since that of *Un giorno di regno* in 1840. Also he was depressed at the political situation, in which the pope had refused to cede political control of Rome, thereby standing in the way of real Italian unification.

A great personal loss that occurred during the same period was the death of Antonio Barezzi in the summer of 1867. The most constant friend in Verdi's life, Barezzi had loyally tolerated his former son-in-law's unorthodox lifestyle with Giuseppina, his stubborn refusal to take an active role in the opening of the new Busseto opera house, and his general hostility to the town's citizens.

In order to escape her husband's dour humor and the boredom of the isolated countryside, Giuseppina concentrated on the decoration of the apartment they had leased in Genoa. In May of 1867 she went to Milan to shop for furniture and while she was there called on her husband's longtime friend and confidante Countess Clara Maffei. The two strong women had never met, but they had much in common and instantly became friends. The countess proposed that she introduce Giuseppina to Alessandro Manzoni and, aware of Verdi's veneration for the great poet, Giuseppina accepted enthusiastically.

Like Verdi, Manzoni was basically a private man who avoided most of the social events of the Milanese elite. Consequently, Italy's greatest poet, now in his eighties, and its greatest composer had never been in each other's presence. When Giuseppina returned home, she brought a photo of Manzoni on which he had written: "To Giuseppe Verdi, a glory of Italy, from a decrepit Lombard writer."[1] Verdi was embarrassed but strongly moved and reciprocated by sending the countess a photograph of himself to deliver to Manzoni. He inscribed it to "one who did true honor to this strife-torn country of ours. You are a saint, Don Alessandro!"[2]

In the spring of 1868, at Clara's invitation, Verdi went to Milan for his first extended visit in twenty years. During his stay he finally paid a visit to Manzoni. Although there is little documentation of what transpired between the two intensely private men, Verdi came away from their conversation with his saintly image of Manzoni reconfirmed.

That autumn Rossini died in Paris. Though the two composers had never been close friends, their relationship had always been one of great mutual respect. Verdi considered the older man to be, like Manzoni, one of the great treasures of Italian culture. He immediately proposed that the leading Italian composers collaborate on a requiem mass in Rossini's memory. He suggested that the participants be chosen in a kind of lottery, and each would provide one movement. The requiem would be performed on the first anniversary of Rossini's death in Bologna, the city in which he had been educated and had begun his career. Both the composers and performers would provide their services without remuneration as a tribute to great man. This met with enthusiasm on all sides, and Verdi was selected to compose the final movement, the "Libera me." Angelo Mariani, the country's leading conductor, would direct the performance.

During the subsequent months Verdi spent considerable time in Milan preparing the production of the revised *La forza del destino*. The opening, on February 27, 1869, with Mariani conducting and Teresa Stolz in the role of Leonora, was the first Verdi premiere at La Scala since that of *Giovanna d'Arco* in 1845. His return to the historic theater marked a turning point, with Milan once again becoming his musical home and the scene of the triumphs of his later years. Ironically, the success of the new *La forza* occurred almost exactly a year after Boito's opera *Mefistofele*, conducted by the composer, had suffered a miserable failure at its La Scala premiere. Because of Boito's 1863 recitation about the state of Italian opera that had so offended Verdi as well as certain harmonic innovations in *Mefistofele* that many Milanese found too Wagnerian, there was a near-riot at the opening night, and the production closed after only two performances. Verdi did not see either performance and refused to comment on Boito's opera. This public rejection of the major work of one of the principal proponents of a "new Italian school" followed by Verdi's success with *La forza* marked the beginning of a rapprochement between the putative rivals that would eventually lead to one of the great collaborations in operatic history.

Verdi quickly finished his assigned movement for the *Messa per Rossini*, but difficulties were encountered in assembling an unpaid chorus and orchestra that were capable of performing the work. The whole project was eventually abandoned, much to Verdi's embarrassment. The mass was not performed in its entirety for more than a century. Although the Bologna impresario was probably most responsible for the fiasco, Verdi blamed Mariani for not organizing the performing forces, and this was the beginning of a gradual deterioration of their relationship.

Despite his negative feelings for the Paris Opéra, Verdi had enjoyed his collaboration with Camille du Locle on *Don Carlos*, and the librettist continued to send him ideas for opera plots in an effort to tempt him back to France. Despite his determination never to compose for the Opéra again, he dutifully read everything that du Locle proposed.

Finally in 1870 du Locle sent Verdi an Egyptian story that aroused his interest. The idea had been evolving for more than a year, since the inauguration of an opera house in Cairo had been part of the celebration of the opening of the Suez Canal in November of 1869. Verdi had turned down the request of the khedive of Egypt to compose an ode for the occasion, and the theater had opened with a performance of *Rigoletto*. Still eager to sponsor a premiere by the world's most successful opera composer, the khedive turned to the French archaeologist Auguste Mariette (1821–1881), who was serving him as the superintendent of all Egyptian excavations. Mariette sketched a scenario for the opera and sent it to his friend du Locle. This story of a general in ancient Egypt who falls in love with the daughter of an enemy king was to become the basis for *Aida*, a work that would quickly join *Rigoletto*, *Il trovatore*, and *La traviata* among the most successful of all operas.

Through the years there have been numerous questions about the originality of Mariette's story. It is generally believed that it had its roots in Egyptian legend. But in his study of Verdi's operas Charles Osborne points out similarities between the plot of *Aida* and that of Metastasio's libretto *Nitteti* about a love triangle in ancient Egypt, which was set to music by several composers during the eighteenth century. *Nitteti* may have been known by Mariette, and it would likely have been familiar to du Locle. The basic premise of the plot is such a common one in literature, however, that suspicion of deliberate plagiarism by any of the parties seems exaggerated.

Verdi was immediately drawn to the story. Aside from the juxtaposition of human drama and political conflict that always appealed to him, he also saw the potential to create a grand opera in Italian and away from the confines of the Opéra. He probably was also influenced by the fact that Mariette made it known that he and the khedive were prepared to approach either Gounod or Wagner if Verdi decided not to participate. In addition, the financial reward was astounding; he asked for and received 150,000 francs for the Cairo production.

Du Locle came for several days to Sant'Agata, where he and Verdi completed the narrative for *Aida*. Then, through the agency of publisher Giulio Ricordi, the composer secured the services of Antonio Ghislanzoni, who had revised *La forza del destino*, to help him transfer the scenario into Italian verse. As the librettist sent him the text in installments, Verdi revised it substantially and set it to music with his old alacrity. The premiere was scheduled for January of 1871, and all of the music for the massive work was written between July and November of 1870.

While Verdi was working feverishly on the score, historic events were taking place in Italy. Vittorio Emanuele had decided to send an army to take Rome. On September 20 the pope made a symbolic, but futile, effort to defend his patrimony, and the city fell to the king's troops. The dream that patriots had held for decades of incorporating Rome into a united Italy had finally been achieved. For Verdi, however, this momentous news was clouded by the almost simultaneous siege of Paris by Prussian troops in what came to be known as the Franco-Prussian War. Verdi viewed the possibility of a French defeat by the forces of Kaiser Wilhelm I to be a threat to the liberty of the entire continent.

The situation in France had a direct effect on the preparations for *Aida*. All of the sets for the Cairo production were being constructed in

Paris, but with the city under siege it was impossible to ship them to Egypt, and the premiere had to be postponed until December 24, 1871. The Italian premiere at La Scala, already scheduled for the Carnival season of 1871, also had to rescheduled for February 1872.

As always, Verdi was actively involved in the selection of conductor and cast. Despite the debacle of the Rossini requiem, Verdi still considered Mariani to be the finest conductor in Italy and wanted him to prepare the Cairo premiere. Involved in other projects and still offended by his former hero's hostility concerning the Rossini debacle, Mariani refused the offer. Stolz was Verdi's choice for the role of *Aida*. She was unavailable for the Cairo performance, but agreed to sing in Milan.

A month before the Cairo premiere Wagner's *Lohengrin* became the first work of the German master to be produced in Italy. The performances, in Bologna, were conducted by Mariani, and they inspired immense curiosity among both Wagner's admirers and his detractors. Verdi attended one of them, trying unsuccessfully to be unnoticed in the audience. He brought a score of *Lohengrin* on which he made copious notes, both positive and negative, about the opera and its performance.

In Cairo, despite the absence of the composer, who was averse to a sea voyage in the winter, the khedive did everything in his power to make the long-awaited premiere of *Aida*, on Christmas Eve, a glittering occasion. Admission to the performance was by invitation only, so the audience was mainly composed of the khedive and his harem, diplomats, high-ranking officials, and European journalists.

AIDA: SYNOPSIS

The action occurs in Egypt during the time of the pharaohs. At the royal palace in Memphis, Radamès, captain of the pharaoh's guards, learns that Ethiopia is threatening to attack. He expresses the wish that he could command the Egyptian troops and return triumphant to his beloved Aida, the Ethiopian slave of the pharaoh's daughter Amneris. The princess is in love with Radamès, but suspects that he loves Aida. The pharaoh and his entourage arrive and announce that the Ethiopians are advancing toward Thebes. The pharaoh appoints Radamès to lead the Egyptians into battle.

Unknown to the Egyptians, Aida is the daughter of the Ethiopian king Amonasro, and it is to rescue her from captivity that he is leading his army to war. Left alone, she ponders the conflict she feels between loyalty to her country and to her Egyptian lover. Radamès goes to the temple of Vulcan where priests and priestesses pray for victory and consecrate his sword.

The battle takes place and the Egyptians are victorious. Amneris prepares for the triumphal return of the army. Aida enters and the princess first tells her that Radamès has been killed and then that he is still alive. From Aida's contrasting reactions she can tell that her suspicions have been correct and that her slave is also her rival.

A great victory celebration is held in a square in Thebes. Radamès enters in triumph followed by the Ethiopian captives, one of whom is Amonasro, dressed in an officer's uniform. He secretly signals to Aida not to reveal his identity. As his reward the pharaoh gives Radamès the hand of Amneris in marriage and grants his request that all the prisoners except Amonasro be freed.

In the moonlight Ramfis, the high priest, and several guards escort Amneris to the temple of Isis on the banks of the Nile to prepare for her wedding. Nearby, Aida, waiting to meet Radamès, thinks fondly of her homeland. Amonasro appears and convinces his daughter to find out from Radamès where he plans to lead his army against the Ethiopians the following day. When he arrives, Aida tells him that their only hope to be together is to escape to her country along with her father. Like her, Radamès is torn between his beloved and his country, but agrees to go with her. In discussing their route he reveals the location of his army. This is overheard by Amonasro, who leaves his hiding place and reveals his identity. Ramfis and Amneris come out of the temple and see Radamès talking with the enemy. Denounced as a traitor by Amneris, he surrenders to Ramfis and the guards.

As he awaits trial Radamès refuses Amneris's offer to save him if he will give up Aida. When he is condemned to execution, she loses control of her emotions and curses the priests who have sentenced him.

Radamès is buried alive in a vault below the temple of Vulcan, where he discovers Aida waiting for him. The lovers sing farewell to earth and anticipate being together in heaven while, in the temple above them, Amneris prays for peace for Radamès.

AIDA: THE MUSIC

The prelude begins with an ascending stepwise melody played by muted violins that will be associated with the title character and her love for Radamès throughout the opera. Although it begins in D major, the melody's **chromaticism** provides the basis for considerable ambiguity of key. A second theme, which will represent the priests, is a foil to that of Aida. It is first heard in low strings rather than violins; it descends; and it is in B minor, the relative key to D. Both themes are treated **imitatively** and then, in a powerful passage for full orchestra, the two are played together as though in conflict. This short prelude with its harmonic and **contrapuntal** subtlety hints at the orchestral richness that pervades the entire score.

Act One opens with a conversation between Ramfis and Radamès concerning the anticipated attack on Thebes by the Ethiopians and the selection of a commander to lead the Egyptian troops. Their recitative is accompanied by continuous imitative counterpoint. Such a musical texture traditionally connoted profundity, spirituality, and seriousness, all of which could be considered reflections of Ramfis in his role as high priest.

Ramfis exits and, accompanied by martial brass fanfares, Radamès dreams of the glory of returning in triumph from a military victory. All of this, he asserts, would be for the sweet Aida. Thoughts of her lead to the famous **romanza** "Celeste Aida" ("Heavenly Aida"), which has become one of the signature arias of the tenor repertory.

The first section is based on a constantly rising line, befitting the key word "heavenly." The second turns to the minor for a melancholy reference to Aida's homeland. The duet for oboe and bassoon adds a poignant and exotic color. A return to the opening section precedes a **coda** in which Radamès vows to build her a "throne near the sun." On the word "sol" ("sun") Verdi requires the tenor to sustain a high B-flat, beginning very softly and then dying away. This has proved impossible for most tenors, and Verdi provided an easier, but unsatisfactory, ending for a later performance in Parma. Many modern singers choose to follow the composer's markings, but to transpose the aria down a step.

Amneris enters to the accompaniment of strings, playing a lilting melody that will be associated with her and her jealousy. In this passage the orchestra is the melodic element while the princess sings in declamatory style, only occasionally doubling the instruments' phrase endings. Coyly she tells Radamès that she has noticed a look of joy on his face and wonders what has inspired it. He explains his hopes to assume command of the army, but she is not satisfied. She asks if he doesn't have a sweeter, more tender dream.

Startled, Radamès asks himself what the princess may have discovered about what is in his heart. The agitation in the music reflects his fears, and the opening orchestral melody returns to represent her jealousy. They join their voices while both ostensibly sing to themselves. Their lines, sometimes in rhythmic conflict, sometimes moving together, express the irony of their situation.

A solo clarinet plays the "Aida theme," and Amneris quickly observes Radamès's agitation as his beloved approaches. The "jealousy theme" betrays the princess's true feelings, as she addresses her servant with feigned tenderness, calling her a sister. She now begins a cross-examination of Aida that parallels what she has done with Radamès.

Aida tells her that she fears for her country as it prepares for war. Again, Amneris presses for another reason, and once more she and Radamès carry on a "silent" dialogue, as she inwardly pours out her venom toward Aida and he becomes more convinced that she knows the truth.

The key moves to brilliant E major as Aida enters the ensemble, singing to herself "Ah no, sulla mia patria" ("Ah no, upon my country"). Her long phrases contrast markedly with the short utterances of the other two. As the emotions become more intense, the texture of the trio thickens and Aida's rhythms conflict with the prevailing meter. Just before the end, the ensemble shifts ominously back to the minor.

Fanfares announce the entrance of the king. In hushed tones he announces the arrival of a messenger bearing grave news. In even quieter declamation than the king, the messenger describes the devastation that the invading Ethiopians have wrought on the Egyptian borderlands. When he speaks of their fierce leader, Amonasro, the members of the court cry: "The king." But Aida whispers: "My father."

The messenger assures the people that Egypt is ready to defend herself, and they cry out for war. The king announces that the goddess Isis has chosen the leader and that he is Radamès. The king ends on a C; the people sing the first two syllables of his name on that pitch; and then they ascend to D-flat on the final one. The next seven measures remain in that key, which Verdi had so often used to represent exaltation, majesty, or heaven.

The king orders Radamès to go to the temple to receive his consecrated sword. He begins a stirring battle song, "Su! Del Nilo" ("On the Nile"), in which the people join. Like the duet of Carlo and Posa in *Don Carlos*, this stirring march is a throwback to the early Verdi of the Risorgimento operas. The tune recurs several times in various guises as a unifying factor in this grand and complex ensemble.

Radamès and Aida join the ensemble. He sings the march tune triumphantly to the words "Sacro fremito di gloria" ("Holy thrill of glory") while she wonders "Per chi piango?" ("For whom do I weep?"), singing a contrasting melody that suggests weeping.

Amneris presents Radamès with a military flag; the king repeats the battle song; and everyone onstage contributes to the great clamor. Suddenly all is silent and, without accompaniment, Amneris, turning to Radamès, sings a rising line on the words "Ritorna vincitor" ("Return a victor"). This is echoed by the entire company, providing the departure point for the famous soliloquy of Aida, who is left alone after the crowd has marched away.

Aida repeats "Ritorna vincitor," using the same pitches that Amneris had sung except for the last one, which is a half step lower. This subtle alteration completely changes this defiant phrase and illuminates Aida's terrible dilemma.

The entire scene is comprised of five sections, each becoming slightly more melodic than its predecessor. In the opening recitative, "Ritorna vincitor," she questions how she can utter such sacrilegious words when an Egyptian victory would be a defeat for her father, whom she pictures as a prisoner behind the chariot of Radamès.

In "L'insana parola, o Numi, sperdete" ("Dispel, Oh Gods, the Foolish Word") the rhythmic intensity increases, the vocal range expands, and Aida's vocal line is doubled at an octave below by low strings and winds. Momentarily overwhelmed by her loyalty to family and country, she prays that her country's oppressor be destroyed. Then, on the highest pitch of the passage, she realizes what that would mean for her lover. As she asks "What am I saying?" the tempo slows and a clarinet plays the "Aida theme" as her thoughts return to Radamès. She joins the clarinet with "e l'amor mio?" ("and my love?").

The agitation returns with "I sacri nomi di padre d'amante" ("The holy names of father and lover"), in A-flat minor, marked "sadly and sweetly." This section melts away into the final one, a cantabile prayer in A-flat major. Aida sings "Numi, pietà del mio soffrir!" ("Gods, have pity on my suffering!"). The melody is one of Verdi's most beautiful. The long arching phrases dissolve into two-note fragments on "pietà" and "soffrir," with a sudden shift to the minor near the end followed by a return to major on Aida's final note, sustained above a whispered string **tremolo**.

The second scene takes place in the temple of Vulcan where Ramfis, along with priests and priestesses, are invoking the god Fthà. The high priestess sings a melody that is intrinsically minor, but some of whose pitches are altered to produce an exotic sound. Verdi was not utilizing an authentic Egyptian scale, but to most European ears the effect was probably sufficient to suggest local color. Ramfis sings with the male chorus in standard Western harmony that is reminiscent of the *Miserere* from *Il trovatore*.

The priestesses then perform a "sacred dance" whose main melody contains the same altered pitch as the chant of the high priestess. The exoticism is heightened by the sound of three flutes playing in close harmony. During the dance Radamès enters and a silver veil is placed over his head. Ramfis charges him with his country's fate, gives him a sword, and expresses his hope that it will strike the enemy with terror and death. On the word "morte" Ramfis and all the priests come together on a high F.

With the solemn accompaniment of a trio of trombones Ramfis begins an ensemble of prayer for Egypt. Radamès and then the priests imitate his melody at various pitch levels. Just as a climax is reached, the priestesses reenter with the exotic invocation that opened the scene. This is then heard in counterpoint against the prayer of the male chorus, bringing the act to a majestic close.

Act Two begins in the apartments of Amneris, where she is surrounded by female slaves. Radamès and his forces have defeated the Ethiopians, and Amneris is being dressed for the celebration. The scene is set musically by a passage of chords played by the harp. The slaves sing of the glory of victory with numerous references to the rising melody of "Ritorna vicitor." In an impassioned descending chromatic line Amneris appeals to Radamès to return and bless her.

This is followed by a dance of young Moorish slaves. The music is in the "Turkish" style that is familiar from certain music of Mozart and Beethoven, characterized by the sound of side drum and triangle. This is followed by a slightly altered return of the preceding ensemble. The "Aida theme" sounds in the orchestra, and simultaneously Amneris announces her slave's approach. She is torn between her sympathy for a woman whose country has been defeated and her overwhelming jealousy for a rival. She resolves to learn the truth about her slave's feelings toward Radamès. The confrontation that ensues between the two princesses is one of the most compelling such scenes in the Verdi canon.

Amneris begins the duet by expressing her sympathy. She declares that time and, eventually, love will heal her anguish. Beginning with her own theme, Aida expresses to herself the dual nature of love: joy and torment, sweet elation and cruel anxiety.

Amneris begins to probe more deeply, suggesting that perhaps Aida is in love with one of the Egyptian soldiers. She casually adds that not all of them died in battle as their leader did. This provokes an almost hysterical outburst from Aida. The key shifts to the minor, the tempo increases, and the harmony becomes more chromatic. She reveals that if Radamès is dead she will weep forever. Amneris has now received the response she was both expecting and dreading. As the orchestra rolls turbulently through foreign keys, she admits that she was lying and that Radamès is alive. Aida falls to her knees, repeating the word "vive" ("He lives").

Finally Amneris has all the evidence she needs and tells Aida that they are rivals. Aida's pride takes control for a moment, and she almost reveals that she too is a princess. She quickly realizes that this revelation will only do her harm and, kneeling before Amneris, she admits the truth and begs for mercy in a lovely cantabile, "Pietà ti prendi dal mio dolor" ("Take Pity on My Sorrow"), which begins the more formal section of the duet.

Over tremolo strings, Amneris warns her of the consequences of her love, singing precipitously descending phrases. Aida continues to plead for mercy, and the two emotionally and musically conflicting lines come together.

Fanfares are heard in the distance, signaling the return of the army. A full chorus begins to sing "Su del Nilo," the king's battle song from Act One. Above the sound of the jubilant people, Amneris taunts Aida with the visions of the two of them at the celebration: she on the throne and Aida on her knees. Aida resumes her pleas for pity, but her rival is merciless. At the climax of the scene she cries that her love will only die in the tomb. On the word *amore* (love) she ascends to the soprano high C. Ominously, Amneris, in her exit line that ends on a high A-flat, tells Aida that she will show her what it means to vie with her.

At the end of the phrase "war and death to the foreigner," sung by the chorus, Verdi achieves a strikingly beautiful theatrical and musical effect. Above the mass of chorus and **banda** Aida begins a reprise of her ravishing prayer, "Numi, pieta." After her first note the orchestra is silent except for the most delicate of tremolo strings.

After this poignant and intimate prayer, the finale of Act Two provides a startling contrast. This is the celebrated "triumphal scene" in which the victorious Egyptians return to a hero's welcome whose ceremonial pomp and grandeur would have done credit to Meyerbeer and the Paris Opéra.

This scene is familiar to many who have never seen or heard the entire opera. Thousands saw it for the first time, filmed at La Scala, for the first Cinerama film, *This Is Cinerama*, in 1952. As Charles Osborne has pointed out in his study of the Verdi operas, the fame of this scene has obscured the fact that much of *Aida* is a work of intimacy and delicate orchestral scoring.[3]

The setting is a city gate of Thebes with a temple and a throne covered with a purple canopy. Pyramids and sphinxes can be seen in the distance. A crowd of bystanders is on the stage.[4]

Fanfares from the banda are answered by a march theme (later represented as section A) played by the orchestra. As the music continues, the king enters with priests and officials followed by Amneris with Aida and her other slaves. The king takes his place on the throne and his daughter sits beside him.

The chorus sings the hymn "Gloria all'Egitto" ("Glory to Egypt") (B). The khedive was so moved by this passage that he toyed with the idea of making it the national anthem. Without abandoning the martial background, the women of the chorus sing a more lyrical melody (C) as they ask for laurel and lotus to be brought for the victors.

A chorus of priests calls for the people to give thanks for the victory (D). They sing the "priests' theme" that was heard in the prelude, and again each vocal part enters separately in imitation. The entire crowd then sings a variant of C.

The soldiers begin to file in, accompanied by the famous "Triumphal March" (E), whose melody is introduced by three "Egyptian" trumpets. Verdi designed these unusually long instruments and had them made to order in Milan.

The melody of the "Triumphal March" is one of the most famous in all opera. Its apparent simplicity is deceptive, for its rhythm and phrase structure are surprisingly sophisticated, and the shift from the key of A-flat to B and then back provides a striking bit of color.

Young girls bring trophies taken from the Ethiopians and perform an extended ballet. As in the earlier dance of slaves, Verdi employs the sounds of triangle along with piccolo to create a convincingly exotic atmosphere.

The march theme (A) returns, sung by the chorus of people, with the priests providing striking interjections on a single pitch. The priests then deliver another variant of D followed by the people's chorus singing fragments of A and C.

Radamès enters to the sounds of D as the crowd cries "Glory!" and the king comes down from his throne to embrace him. Without accompaniment he sings: "Savior of the country, I salute you!" to the rising tune of "Ritorna vincitor." Amneris comes forward to present him a crown. The king promises to grant him any wish, and Radamès asks that before he makes a request the Ethiopian prisoners be brought in. The priests' chorus sings another repetition of D as the captives are led in. As Aida recognizes her father among them and rushes to embrace him, the entire throng cries "her father!" When the Egyptian king asks him who he is, he repeats "her father." Then, in a dramatic arioso, he tells his concocted story. As an officer he fought alongside his king. They were defeated and the king was killed. Turning to the Egyptian king as the major key emerges, he pleads for mercy, reminding him that someday he may find himself in the same position. Aida takes up her father's petition, accompanied by a chorus of prisoners.

Ramfis and the other priests protest, singing their ubiquitous theme (D), advising the king to close his heart to them. This begins another grand ensemble in which the Ethiopians continue to beg for clemency, the king expresses sympathy, and the priests protest. Amneris, oblivious to all else, notices passionate glances between Aida and Radamès and expresses her determination to seek vengeance for her rejection.

Radamès enters, single-handedly pulling everyone into a new key. Singing to himself, he lovingly observes that the pain in Aida's face only makes her more beautiful. The musical texture becomes increasingly dense with Aida's pleas soaring higher and higher and finally reaching a high C just before the final cadence.

An extended conversation between Radamès, the king, and Ramfis follows. The vocal lines flow freely between austere declamation and lyrical melody, with the punctuation of the competing choruses of priests and prisoners. Radamès announces that his request of the king is the release of all the Ethiopian captives. Ramfis protests, but eventually advises the king to free all the prisoners except Aida's father.

The king accepts this advice and then, in a surprising gesture, gives Amneris to Radamès as his wife and proclaims that they will someday rule as king and queen. The final line of this passage belongs to Amneris, who gloats to herself at her victory over her rival.

All the people join to sing "Gloria all'Egitto" (B). Above the hymn, Aida and Radamès lament the tragedy of the king's decree, and Amneris rejoices in her victory. After a long contrapuntal passage of considerable complexity, the "Egyptian trumpets" and banda end the act with a reprise of the "Triumphal March."

The great crowd scenes in grand opera were always conceived to provide audiences with a maximum of thrilling spectacle, and any attempt at musical sophistication was secondary. The "triumphal scene" shares many of the stereotypes of its genre, but by 1871 Verdi's skill was so refined that he was able to transcend the most flagrant excesses. Aside from several truly memorable melodies, the musical success of the scene depends upon a solid musical architecture. The structure of the whole can be represented as follows:

Fanfares A B C D C E Ballet A D A C D Dialogue D
Dialogue/arioso D Ensemble dialogue B Ensemble E

In addition, the solo sections contain numerous references to melodic motives from earlier in the opera. Thus Verdi was able to combine an enormous diversity of musical ideas and performing forces into a coherent entity.

Act Three begins with the justly celebrated "Nile scene." The temple of Isis stands on the banks of the river, bathed in moonlight. This colorful musical portrayal of an exotic night opens with muted strings playing fast-moving repetitions of the same pitch in alternating octaves. As other instruments enter on different pitches, the static, solemn, and placid atmosphere is maintained.

A chorus of priests sings praises to Isis as a goddess of chastity. A single priestess answers in another key. As priestess and priests begin to chant together in unison, Amneris and Ramfis, followed by servants and guards, arrive in a boat. They have come to pray to Isis for a blessing on the princess's wedding to Radamès. She expresses her heartfelt hope that he will eventually give her his heart as she has given hers to him. Both in her words and in her arching melody, Amneris displays a tender and vulnerable side that is affecting. They enter the temple while the priests and priestesses repeat their chant.

With the stage void of people, the sound of Aida's theme, played by flutes, announces her arrival. She enters and in short, breathless phrases makes it clear that she has come to meet Radamès and is fearful that he might be coming to bid her farewell. If this happens, she will drown herself in the Nile. When she sings the word "Nile," the low strings begin a whirling chromatic figure.

As she ponders the fate of dying in Egypt, her thoughts turn to her native country. A solo oboe plays a melody of ambiguous key that introduces her second great recitative and aria, "O patria mia" ("Oh My Homeland"). The delicate shifting between major and minor and excursions into remote keys displays how far Verdi had evolved in the preceding twenty years. The entire aria section is repeated with subtle alterations, the second time reaching a high C, to be sung extremely softly, on the phrase "non mai più non ti vedrò" (no, nevermore shall I see you"). As with the soft tenor B-flat at the end of "Celeste Aida," Verdi seems to be trying to eliminate the tendency of the star singers to deliver their high notes at high decibel levels when the emotional effect demands the opposite.

The orchestra begins a delicate postlude, but it is interrupted at the beginning of its second phrase when Aida sees her father appear. This allows no opportunity for applause for this magnificent and difficult aria. For years Verdi had been moving toward a seamless flow throughout a scene. By this time Wagner had almost eliminated the aria as a set piece. Later, Giacomo Puccini (1858–1924) would increasingly omit the rousing endings that had traditionally elicited ovations for the principal singers, interrupting the flow of the drama.

Amonasro reveals that he has observed her and knows everything that is in her heart. He implies that he has a plan that will allow her to defeat Amneris, return home, and live with her lover. He begins their duet, "Rivedrai le foreste imbalsamate" ("You Will Again See the Balsam Forests"). Their alternating phrases repeat or complement each other until they join together in a traditional passage in tenths on the final phrase.

Amonasro then begins to reveal his plan in a section that is full of fury. He tells her that the Ethiopian army has reassembled and is ready to engage the Egyptians in another battle. They only need to know what route the enemy is taking. Naively Aida asks who could possibly obtain that information and, over an ominous minor chord, he answers "Aida." When he explains that she has the power to get the information from Radamès, she is horrified and refuses unequivocally.

This provokes Amonasro to vent all his hostility toward the Egyptians in a passage that resembles a "rage aria" in Baroque opera. His anger erupts in rapidly moving notes, with the accompaniment dominated by brass. Aida tries to protest, but he repulses her, telling her that the destruction of her country will be her fault. With the orchestral fury unabated he evokes the image of her mother rising from the grave to condemn her as a traitor. In a final, devastating statement he tells her "You are not my daughter. You are the slave of the Pharaoh."

The orchestral storm subsides as Aida falls to the ground and crawls to the feet of her father. Low strings and bassoon play a sinuous melody in D-flat minor as she undergoes a change of heart. The minor key brightens to major as Amonasro tells her to think that she alone can save her people. For this single moment Verdi portrays Amonasro as a loving father rather than as a vindictive warrior. As usual he chooses D-flat major to suggest transcendence.

Finally Aida sings a rising line on the devastating words "Oh country! How much you cost me." Victorious, Amonasro tells her to have courage and quickly hides among the palm trees as Radamès approaches.

He greets Aida with a jaunty tune, but she dismisses him, saying that all hope for them is gone. With feigned anger she accuses him of being unfaithful to her and asks him how he could give up Amneris and defy the will of his king and country.

He interrupts her to explain his strategy. Over a repetitious motive played by a pair of trumpets, he tells her that her people are threatening Egypt once more. He will again command his country's forces, and when he wins a second victory, the king will reward him by recognizing his love for her.

Aida realizes the futility of this dream and tells him that they have only one hope to be together. When he questions her, she utters a single word: *fuggir* (to flee). This evokes two dramatic chords in the orchestra and an outburst of shock from Radamès as he repeats "fuggir" with an ascending octave leap. In a recitative, accompanied by a single oboe, she brightens as she thinks of their life in her native country.

In a passage of recitative Radamès resists the thought of leaving Egypt and his gods, but with typical Verdian economy he changes his mind quickly. When he reaches the phrase "il ciel de'nostri amori" ("the heaven of our love"), he ascends to a very soft, tender high B-flat that leaves little doubt about the fateful choice that he will eventually make.

Radamès wavers momentarily and Aida proves that she possesses some of her father's strength and cunning. Declaring that he does not love her, she commands him to go back to Amneris. With an element of cruelty she sarcastically tells him to "drop the axe" on both her and her father.

With this, Aida has achieved the victory. Without accompaniment Radamès cries "Ah no! We shall flee!" He then begins a passionate duet, "Si, fuggiam da queste mura" ("Yes, We Shall Flee from These Walls"), that is the first old-fashioned **cabaletta** in the opera. Verdi knew his audiences and realized that they would expect an extended lyrical duet movement to mark this crucial turning point in the lovers' relationship. On the phrase "Come with me to flee from this land of sorrow," the two join their voices in octaves in an expansive line that encompasses the high and low extremes of both of their vocal ranges.

They begin to exit, but Aida pauses to ask coyly what route they should take to avoid encountering the Egyptian army. Innocently he tells her the exact location of his forces and immediately Amonasro steps forward, identifies himself as the Ethiopian king, and announces triumphantly that his army will be waiting. Scarcely able to believe what he is hearing, Radamès despairs of his unintentional betrayal of his country. Amonasro tries to convince him that he bears no guilt for what has occurred. He reminds him that he now has Aida and will one day become a king of Ethiopia, but Radamès will accept none of it. During this masculine conflict Aida can only utter short outbursts of dismay. Amonasro begs Radamès to come with them too and even attempts to force him physically, shouting "vieni!" ("come!") three times on a single D-flat.

Stunningly, the voice of Amneris cries out from the temple, beginning on a D-flat two octaves above Amonasro and then ascending a step on the word *traditor* (traitor). Amonasro rushes toward her with a dagger, but Radamès restrains him, calling him insane. At a breathless pace with perpetual motion in the orchestra, Ramfis appears and summons the guards. Radamès tells Aida and her father to flee quickly, and Ramfis orders the soldiers to pursue them.

The orchestra is silenced and, in a stentorian phrase, Radamès delivers the final line of Act Three: "Priest, I remain with you." An extended passage of turbulent music for the full orchestra brings the curtain down.

Act Four opens in the royal palace. The prelude to the act begins with a descending passage for woodwinds that recalls the king's granting of Amneris to Radamès as a bride. As the princess appears, her theme from the first act is heard. In an extended recitative passage she reflects on her unbridled hatred for Aida, but expresses conflicted emotions about Radamès. Repeating a melody from their first duet, she confesses to herself that she still loves him insanely. She decides that she must try to save him and orders the guards to bring him to her.

They lead the prisoner in and Amneris begins an emotional duet. She tells him that the priests are about to decide his fate, but if he will deny the charges against him, she will intervene with her father to save him. Radamès responds, singing the same melody in a different key. He will not do what she suggests, but will take responsibility for his deed and maintain his honor.

As the music intensifies, Amneris's pleas become more passionate. She would give up her country and her throne for him. With the same melody and in the same key, he reminds her that he has given up his country for his love for Aida. Assuming that she has been killed, he accuses Amneris of being responsible for her death. Almost hysterically, she reveals that Amonasro has been killed but that Aida has escaped.

Throughout this passage the bass line has been rising rapidly by steps, creating a constant flux in the sense of key. The motion pauses in the radiant key of B major as Radamès quietly prays that the gods will take Aida safely home and that she will never know that he died for her. For the second part of the statement the melody moves to the minor.

In an almost comic instance of poor judgment, Amneris asks him to swear that if she saves him he will never see Aida again. She continues to ask him to renounce his love, and he grows increasingly vehement in his refusal. Now enraged, Amneris virtually explodes into a cabaletta in which she warns him of her revenge. In bright C major he tells her that death poses no fear for him. They sing together with Radamès basking in his "immense joy" and Amneris savoring the thought of revenge. In the course of the movement she twice ascends to a B-flat at the extreme of the mezzo-soprano range. The guards come to take Radamès away, and the scene ends with a march-like postlude that is built over a repeated descending bass line.

As usual in Verdi the narrative moves toward its end without undue prolongation. Amneris is left alone in despair at the prospect that Radamès will be condemned to death. The "priests' motive" is heard in the double basses. They enter in procession and move to an underground room where the trial will take place. They chant a prayer for the guidance of the gods. Amneris responds by offering her own prayer for Radamès's deliverance. This short, lyrical passage begins with the words "Numi, pietà," which were sung by Aida in her first-act aria.

Radamès is brought into the hall and the examination begins. Brass fanfares punctuate the scene. Amneris listens and reacts from above. In unaccompanied recitative Ramfis enumerates three charges—treason, desertion, and rebellion—and for each he asks the accused to defend himself. For each of the three parallel passages his declamation moves up a step. The other priests reinforce and echo his words. Each of these segments is followed by Amneris in a prayer for mercy. As with Ramfis, each of her invocations ascends by a step. Through it all Radamès remains silent.

The inevitable verdict is delivered. Radamès is guilty on all counts and will be entombed alive beneath the altar of Vulcan. This provokes a frenzied outburst of dissonant chords from the orchestra and a furious condemnation of the priests from Amneris. As they emerge from the subterranean room, repeatedly chanting "traitor," she tells them that they are punishing an innocent man and then, summoning all of her resources, reminds them that this is a man she has loved and that they will be cursed by her. Verdi adds to the obvious irony of the situation by referring throughout Amneris's interjections to the rising six-note figure of "Ritorna vincitor" that she introduced in Act One. After the priests have exited, she repeats the motive once more as she invokes the aid of heaven to carry out her curse. She runs out in disarray as the orchestra moves to a starkly powerful close.

The great final scene is set in the temple of Vulcan. The stage is divided into two levels: the ornate temple itself and the dismal vault beneath. Radamès is on the stairs leading to the depths of the crypt, and two priests are above, lowering the stone that will seal him inside. The whispered "long-short" motive in the orchestra matches the visual gloom. In recitative that alternates with this orchestral figure Radamès reflects on his fate. He thinks lovingly of Aida and hopes that she can live happily and never know what has happened to him. Then he hears the sound of weeping and at first thinks he is hallucinating. As he realizes that another human is in the crypt with him, the accompaniment grows more agitated. He finally realizes that it is Aida, and she confirms simply "Son io" ("It is I").

In a simple **arioso** she explains that she had assumed that he would be put to death and has come to the temple to die in his arms. She is accompanied by the repetition of a single pitch from the low strings and woodwinds and with the chilling sound of bass drum. Radamès responds in a beautiful passage, "Morir! Sì pura e bella" ("To die! So pure and beautiful."), which is delicately accompanied by **pizzicato** strings and two clarinets playing in dulcet thirds. He is moved by her desire to die with him, but protests that one of such youth and beauty should not have to end her life.

Aida responds in Verdi's celestial key of D-flat that she can already see the angel of death. In a series of ascending phrases she almost deliriously envisions the ecstasy of their eternal love.

From above, the priests and priestesses chant a prayer to Fthà that is almost identical to that of the priestess in the first act. Aida observes that for the two of them this is a hymn of death. As the chanting grows in intensity, Radamès, with one last hope for life, tries to move the stone. Seeing the futility of this effort, Aida observes that "all is finished for us on earth."

They now begin their final farewell, "O terra addio" ("Oh Earth Farewell"), for which Verdi reserved one of his most eloquent and sublime melodies. Aida sings the entire melody alone, and then Radamès repeats it, accompanied by her tender bits of commentary. On the final note of his melody the priests resume their chant. The women and men sing in octaves, and above them the two principals do the same, proclaiming that "heaven is opening."

During this passage Amneris appears in the temple and kneels on the stone that seals the crypt. Aida and Radamès sing "O terra addio" together, supported by tremolo strings. Amneris intones a prayer for peace and for her beloved Radamès. The priests join the ensemble, settling into a single chord just as Aida dies in the arms of her lover. Two violins repeat the first phrase of "O terra addio" as the curtain falls slowly. Amneris, on a single tone, continues to pray for peace.

✿ ✿ ✿

Verdi was gratified by the reports of *Aida*'s success in Cairo and the positive reviews of the European critics who had attended, but he was more personally interested in the Milan performance six weeks later. For this production he added Aida's recitative and aria "O patria mia," and he was actively involved with all aspects of the rehearsals. This gave him another opportunity to work with Teresa Stolz, who sang the title role. Like Giuseppina, Stolz was a prima donna of taste and intelligence, and Verdi was powerfully drawn to her. After the La Scala premiere he went back to Milan for several more performances and spent time with Stolz. In the years that followed she was a frequent visitor to Sant'Agata and sometimes traveled with Verdi and Strepponi.

To the outside world Stolz and the Verdis maintained the appearance of a friendly threesome, but remarks in Giuseppina's correspondence indicate that she was troubled and occasionally angered by her husband's attentions to another woman. Nineteenth-century Italy was still a very old-fashioned society in which a distinct double standard existed for the behavior of men and women. Also a diplomatic woman like Strepponi had become accustomed to making allowances for a man of such genius. She kept up the appearance of a sisterly friendship for the rest of her life, and Stolz remained close to Verdi until his death in 1901.

On May 22, 1873, Alessandro Manzoni died at the age of eighty-eight. Verdi proclaimed that "with him ends the most pure, the most holy, the greatest of our glories."[5] His funeral in Milan was a state occasion. Verdi was too moved by his hero's death to attend, but a week afterward he paid a solitary visit to the grave. While he was in the city he proposed to the mayor, with the help of Giulio Ricordi, that he compose a requiem mass to be performed on the first anniversary of Manzoni's death.

Verdi was determined to avoid the problems he had encountered with the *Messa per Rossini* by composing the entire mass himself and assuming full responsibility for preparing and conducting the performance. He and Giuseppina spent the summer of 1873 in Paris, where he began to compose the *Requiem*. He revised the "Libera me" that he had created for the Rossini earlier work as the final movement of the new one.

Verdi had few models for a large-scale requiem for chorus, soloists, and orchestra. Mozart's requiem, left incomplete at his death in 1791, was the first of the great "symphonic" settings of the mass for the dead. Luigi Cherubini (1760–1842), who, like Rossini, was an Italian opera composer who moved to Paris, produced two requiems: one in 1816 to commemorate the anniversary of the execution of King Louis XVI and the other in 1836, to be performed at his own funeral six years later. Hector Berlioz (1803–1869) composed a grand, dramatic requiem in 1837 in memory of those who had been killed in the July Revolution of 1830. Notably, Mozart, Cherubini, and Berlioz were all important composers of opera.

The traditional requiem contains four of the so-called ordinary texts that are components of every mass: Kyrie (Lord Have Mercy), Gloria

(Glory to God in the Highest), Sanctus (Holy, Holy, Holy), and Agnus Dei (Lamb of God). To these are added the Introit, *Requiem aeternam* (Eternal rest); the long, multisectional medieval hymn "Dies irae" ("Day of Wrath"); the Offertory, *Domine Jesu Christe* (Lord Jesus Christ); the *Communion*, *Lux aeterna* (Eternal Light); and a responsory, "Libera me" ("Free Me"). Like his fellow agnostic Berlioz, Verdi rearranged the texts to serve his musical purposes.

The performance took place at the church of San Marco in Milan, whose acoustics Verdi deemed most suitable for the four soloists, chorus of 120, and large orchestra. Teresa Stolz was the soprano soloist. The requiem was an enormous success and, due to public demand, was soon repeated three times at La Scala.

MESSA DA REQUIEM: THE MUSIC

The hushed opening of the requiem is a masterpiece of descriptive musical setting of words that is commonly called "text painting." It begins with muted cellos playing a descending motive that contains the three notes of a minor chord. Although no text has been uttered, there is little question that this motive implies the word "requiem." The chorus then intones the word, with each of the vocal parts repeating a single pitch. For the first full sentence of the text, "Grant them rest Oh Lord and let eternal light shine upon them," Verdi musically "paints" each idea using melody and harmony. On the word "dona" (grant) four sopranos sing a descending two-note figure that for centuries had represented sighing, weeping, or pleading. At "lux aeterna" (eternal light) there is a sudden shift to the major key.

"Te decet hymnus, Deus, in Sion" ("A hymn befits you, God, in Zion"), taken from Psalm 64, is set for unaccompanied choir singing contrapuntally. This is a reference by the composer to the old Renaissance church style that was often used by later composers for venerable texts such as psalms. The opening returns verbatim except that the final phrase provides a transition into the Kyrie.

Because this section contains only three different words, "Kyrie eleison" and "Christe eleison," composers since the Renaissance had traditionally set the text in elaborate, **florid** style, and Verdi followed suit. The anticlerical composer had little interest in liturgical ritual, but as in so many of his operas, he related viscerally to the cry of the dying for mercy. Tenor, bass, soprano, and mezzo-soprano soloists enter separately, each on a different pitch, singing the same soaring phrase. The quartet rises to several dramatic climaxes with the voices essentially maintaining their independence as in an operatic ensemble. In a stunning gesture, the four suddenly come together on the word "Christe" to form an F-major chord that is audibly foreign to the prevailing key. On the final "eleison" the home key returns as the movement ends, as it began, in a whisper.

The most famous component of the requiem, which occupies about one-third of the entire score, is the "Dies irae." In this graphic and terrifying thirteenth-century depiction of the judgment day, Verdi obviously found the kind of dramatic intensity that he appreciated in a good libretto. He provided music for all the stanzas of this very long poem, dividing them into groups and setting each one as a chorus, solo, or ensemble. As in *Don Carlos* and *Aida* each section usually flows into the next without a break.

The opening "Dies irae" passage still possesses the power to shock the listener with its massive orchestral chords, its turbulent perpetual motion, and the hammer strokes of the bass drum on the offbeats. This section returns twice to contribute to the structural unity of the movement and even makes a surprising reappearance in the "Libera me."

The fury abates as the chorus sings very softly in octaves. The short phrases are interrupted by silences to portray the text "Quantus tremor est futurus" ("What trembling there will be"). Suddenly four trumpets in the orchestra and four others "from afar" begin a dialogue that eventually includes all the orchestral brass in a gigantic climax that leads to the chorus "Tuba mirum spargens sonum" ("The wondrous trumpet sounds"). The principal idea, first stated by the basses on a single pitch, imitates the trumpet calls. The largely contrapuntal choral sound contrasts with the massive sonorities of the orchestra, still dominated by the trumpets.

The bass soloist sings an accompanied recitative on the text "Mors stupebit et natura" ("Death and nature shall be amazed"). The orchestral background is a funeral march with the bass drum, again playing on the weak beats of the measure, but this time very softly. At the end the bass intones the word "mors" three times, descending a step with each repetition. After a long pause, with only the continuous pulse of the bass drum, he continues his descent on "stupebit."

The mezzo-soprano soloist sings "Liber scriptus proferetur in quo totum continetur" ("A book will be brought forth in which everything is contained") in a dramatic arioso. As she proceeds, the chorus begins to interject whispers of "Dies irae." They become increasingly insistent until a slightly altered version of the beginning of the movement returns.

The storm of the "Dies irae" dies away once more and the mezzo begins the trio "Quid sum miser tunc dicturus?" ("What shall I, wretched one, say then?"). She is joined by tenor and soprano with the same melody. The accompaniment, dominated by a winding line played by solo bassoon, is silenced for a short passage in the middle of the trio and again at then end The soprano ends alone before the choral outburst of "Rex tremendae majestatis" ("King of awesome majesty"). This begins with the choral basses singing a phrase that descends precipitously by more than an octave and a half with a pronounced "long-short" rhythmic figure that traditionally suggested royalty and majesty. The tenor section responds in three-part harmony. A bass solo begins a contrasting section with the heartfelt plea "Salva me, fons pietatis" ("Save me, fount of pity"). As all the soloists and the upper parts of the chorus take up this petition, the basses reiterate the "Rex tremendae" in striking counterpoint. Then Verdi creates a sublime, operatic moment. Beginning with bass solo and then moving up through the chorus, with each part entering separately, all join in the cry of "Salva me," making the universal plea of the text into a series of personal prayers.

"Recordare, Jesu pie" ("Remember, dear Jesus") is a lush duet for soprano and mezzo-soprano. The shift of the object of the prayer from the God of majesty to the compassionate Jesus inspired what is perhaps the most traditional Italianate movement of the requiem. Near the end, on the words "grant me pardon," the two sing a short but florid cadenza straight from the bel canto tradition.

"Ingemisco tamquam reus" ("I Groan Like One Condemned") is one of the composer's great tenor arias, but decidedly in the late Verdi style, with more emphasis on declamation and refined orchestration than on florid singing. The final, climactic stanza of the text: "Give me a place among the sheep and separate me from the goats, setting me on Thy right hand," features a dialogue between tenor and oboe accompanied by tremolo strings. The last phrase rises by steps to a high B-flat on the first syllable of "dextra" ("right").

The short "**scena**" for bass, "Confutatis maledictis" ("When the Cursed Have Been Confounded") begins with a recitative followed by a three-part aria with a melody of great dignity and nobility. At times the sense of key is uncertain, and the soloist's final pitch coincides with a sudden shift to a foreign tonality and the dramatic return of the "Dies irae" chorus.

Like the finale of an opera act, the "Lacrymosa dies illa" ("That Day Will Be One of Weeping") is the culmination of this great movement, uniting soloists, chorus, and orchestra in a complex ensemble. The basis of the opening section is a reworking of some of the excised music from Act Four of the original *Don Carlos*.

The solemn melody is first stated by the mezzo-soprano. The baritone repeats it while the mezzo sings single notes separated by rests that rise by steps, creating a graphic musical depiction of weeping. The soprano, accompanied by the female voices of the chorus, pleads "Huic ergo parce, Deus" ("Therefore spare him, God"). For this single line Verdi moves from B-flat minor to glowing D-flat major. Soloists and chorus repeat the "Lacrymosa" melody, with the soprano floating above the rest of the ensemble.

Verdi explores the key of G-flat on the words "Pie Jesu Domine" ("Merciful Lord Jesus") in a striking unaccompanied passage for the solo quartet. The main melody returns and is developed by the chorus, soloists, and orchestra, eventually dying away with the repeated repetition of "Dona eis requiem." The final masterstroke is the ascent to the very distant key of G major for the "Amen."

After the high drama of the "Dies irae," the Offertory, *Domine Jesu Christe* (Lord Jesus Christ) for soloists and orchestra, is an oasis of serenity. Notable are the use of contrapuntal church style for the reference to the patriarch Abraham and the chant-like "Hostias" ("Sacrifices") for the tenor. The orchestra provides a hushed ending with a fourfold repetition, with varied harmony of the movement's opening melody.

The Sanctus (Holy, Holy, Holy), from the book of Isaiah, is the most ancient text of the Ordinary of the mass and traditionally was composed in the old contrapuntal style. Verdi follows suit by setting it as a great **fugue** with the chorus divided into two separate groups. The modern element is the powerful role of the orchestra in this exuberant hymn. The brilliant major key and lively tempo of the Sanctus provide a buoyant contrast to the somberness that surrounds it.

The serene Agnus Dei (Lamb of God) begins with soprano and mezzo singing in octaves without accompaniment. The chorus repeats the melody, supported by bare octaves in the orchestra, but still without harmony. In the several repetitions, delicate contrapuntal interplay between soloists, chorus, and orchestra is introduced, but the final statement of "Dona eis requiem" returns to the two soloists as at the beginning with hushed fragments of commentary from the chorus.

Lux Aeterna (Eternal Light) is a trio for the three lower solo voices that juxtaposes the petition for eternal light with a repetition of the plea for eternal rest. Appropriately, the first is set in a major key and the second, in minor. The mezzo begins with a recitative accompanied by string tremolos. With the entrances of the others a more melodic style evolves. The predominantly soloistic texture alternates with two passages of unaccompanied counterpoint. At the end the two prayers are combined, with the mezzo repeating her plea for light while tenor and bass, singing "requiem aeternam," fill in the harmony, now fully affirming the brightness of the major.

Verdi made several revisions and additions to the "Libera me" from the earlier requiem. It begins in a most austere fashion with an unaccompanied monotone intonation of "Libera me, Domine, de morte aeterna" ("Free me, Lord, from eternal death") by the soprano. She is answered by the chorus on a repeated chord instead of a single pitch. The soprano continues, moving from accompanied recitative to a very dramatic arioso as she describes the fear and trembling that will precede the last day. Her voice drops to the softest whisper on the word "timeo" ("I fear"). After a long silence the "Dies irae" chorus returns in all its fury. As in its earlier appearances, the tempest subsides into profound calm, but the peace is punctuated by two orchestral statements of the short-short-long "death motive" that Verdi had used so often in the operas.

Perhaps the most sublime moment of the requiem arrives with a repetition of the opening "Requiem aeternum" text for soprano solo and unaccompanied choir. She sings a beautiful melody that begins with the "requiem" motive that was heard in the cellos at the beginning of the mass. Once again, the word "light" prompts a shift from minor to major. On the final iteration of the word "requiem," Verdi requires the soprano to ascend an octave to a high B-flat at the softest possible **dynamic** level. Perhaps he had admired Teresa Stolz's performance of the similar hushed ascents in *Aida* and had composed this difficult passage with her in mind.

After another soprano recitative, the altos of the chorus begin a second massive choral fugue, repeating the "Libera me" text. This one is considerably longer and more complex than that of the *Sanctus*, and Verdi displays enormous contrapuntal mastery. The final statements abandon the counterpoint and turn to massive chords for the choir while the soloist ascends to the soprano high C.

A lesser and perhaps more orthodox composer might have chosen this glorious moment to end the work, but Verdi selected an unexpected and ultimately more dramatic option. The soprano returns to her monotone chant from the beginning of the movement, singing a full octave lower than before accompanied by the chorus on a C-major chord. Finally all come together in octaves on two repetitions of "Libera me." The severity is brightened only by the glowing C-major harmony played by the orchestra.

Although the public reaction to the *Manzoni Requiem* was almost unanimously positive, the work was not immune to criticism. The church eventually condemned it for its unorthodox manipulation of the texts and for the intrusion of secular musical style.

One of the most infamous attacks on the requiem was that of the eminent German conductor, pianist, and Wagner devotee Hans von Bülow (1830–1894), who was in Milan at the time of the premiere, but was not in attendance. He wrote, however, that Verdi had presented "an opera in ecclesiastical garb" and called him a "corrupter of Italian taste." Of the numerous reactions to Bülow's condescension was that of Johannes Brahms (1833–1897), who wrote: "Bülow has made a fool of himself for all time; only a genius could write such a work."

Since Verdi's time the *Manzoni Requiem* has assumed the status of a universal symbol both of mourning and of the desire for peace and hope. In 1943 and 1944 it was performed sixteen times by the Jewish inmates of the concentration camp at Terezín, near Prague. In a gesture that transcended sectarian boundaries, the performance represented a triumph of human spirit in darkest of times.

7

THE FINAL MASTERWORKS

Otello, Falstaff

By his sixtieth birthday in 1873 Verdi was unquestionably the greatest living Italian composer, and his international reputation was continuing to grow. After its premieres in Cairo and Milan, *Aida* had soon been performed in most of the world's musical centers from Paris to Buenos Aires. The *Manzoni Requiem* was equally successful, with seven performances in Paris after the original series in Milan.

In addition to his stature as a composer, Verdi was increasingly recognized by his countrymen as a patriotic icon. With Cavour, Mazzini, Manin, and Manzoni all dead, Verdi was almost alone as one of the fathers of the Risorgimento. In 1874 he was awarded an honorary seat in the Senate for life.

The private life of Verdi and Strepponi had settled into a satisfying routine. The Sant'Agata estate had evolved into a comfortable country house, and the couple continued to enjoy their winter stays in Genoa. Gradually Giuseppina grew to accept the role of Teresa Stolz in her husband's world and treated her as a beloved part of the family for the rest of her life.

The Verdis were also finding great satisfaction in their new role as parents. In 1867 they had adopted Maria Filomena, the eight-year-old granddaughter of Verdi's father Carlo's younger brother. In 1878 she was married at Sant'Agata to Alberto Carrara, a local attorney who had done legal work for Verdi and of whom he was very fond. Their descendents, taking the name Carrara-Verdi, would preserve the estate, continue to live there, and eventually open several rooms as a museum.

At this point Verdi seemed content with the assumption that the *Requiem* would be his last work. Although he had probably never been serious when he spoke of retirement in earlier years, now he was extremely wealthy and, with *Aida*, had finally scored the unmitigated triumph with a grand opera that had eluded him for years. He seemed content to manage his estate and to oversee the occasional performance of one of his works. In 1875 he conducted the *Requiem*, with Stolz as soprano soloist, on a tour that included Paris, London, and Vienna.

Verdi's reluctance to begin another project also stemmed in part from his sensitivity to a small group of critics who had characterized *Aida* as being an imitation of Wagnerian style. One even called it "the Italian *Lohengrin*."[1] Although these views were in the minority and *Aida* continued to be an enormous popular success, Verdi was particularly rankled at the suggestion that he had copied another composer's style. He wrote to Giulio Ricordi: "A fine result after a career of thirty-five years, to end up as an imitator!"[2]

Some of Verdi's friends were troubled with the idea that this vigorous man who was at the peak of his creative powers would give up composing. The most vocal of them was Clara Maffei, his great confidante since the early days in Milan. When she suggested in a letter that it was his moral duty to continue working, he replied firmly that "the account is settled."[3] He had done his duty for the public and they had rewarded him for it.

Verdi's eventual change of heart largely resulted from the efforts of Giulio Ricordi. Now the head of Italy's most prestigious music publisher, Giulio was the third generation at the Casa Ricordi, and Verdi had worked with all three. The relationship had been fruitful, but sometimes contentious. Composer and publisher had often clashed about financial matters, and on the occasions that Ricordi had both printed an opera's score and produced its performance Verdi had sometimes complained that they had sacrificed artistic quality for higher profits.

Giulio's father Tito was Verdi's contemporary and had dealt with him as an equal, but the son treated him with deference and diplomacy. Even though Italian musical tastes were changing and productions of the works of Wagner and other foreigners were proliferating, Ricordi realized that a new work by Verdi would be assured of financial success.

Ricordi was a close friend of Arrigo Boito, whose career had increasingly evolved from composer to librettist. His *La Giocanda* (1876), based on Victor Hugo and set to music by Amilcare Ponchielli (1834–1886), had quickly become a major success. Boito had also evolved from a harsh critic of the old school of Italian opera that the younger Verdi had represented to an admirer of the mature maestro. This was due both to the younger man's maturation and the more progressive style that had emerged in *Don Carlo* and *Aida*. Boito, whose literary taste was extremely refined, revered the works of Shakespeare and knew that Verdi shared that enthusiasm.

In his efforts to persuade Verdi to consider another opera, Ricordi enlisted the aid of the composer and conductor Franco Faccio (1840–1891), who had become general director of La Scala. Cleverly, he also sought the support of Giuseppina. In June of 1879 an opportune time presented itself. Verdi and Strepponi were in Milan, where the composer conducted a benefit concert for victims of flooding of the Po River.

After the performance Faccio conducted members of the La Scala orchestra in an impromptu serenade outside the Grand Hotel, where the Verdis had a suite.[4] On another evening he and Ricordi dined with the couple at the hotel. During this visit they mentioned the idea of a collaboration between Verdi and Boito on Shakespeare's *Othello*.

The maestro agreed to meet with Boito, whom he had not seen in many years, the following day. The meeting went well and three days later Verdi had a scenario for *Otello* in hand.[5] He liked it so well that he asked Boito to put it into verse.

Despite this positive development, Verdi had decided to move very deliberately. At the end of August, Ricordi suggested that he and Boito come to see him at Sant'Agata to discuss the project and deliver the libretto. Verdi wrote to him that he preferred that he come without Boito because he didn't want to feel pressure to agree to the project. He chided Ricordi for moving too quickly but also asked him to send him Boito's libretto.[6]

For its preparation Boito studied Shakespeare's original text. Due to his limited understanding of English, he also worked with several Italian translations. The source he followed most closely, however, was a French version by François-Victor Hugo (1828–1873), son of the more famous Victor. The younger Hugo had translated the complete works of Shakespeare into French.

Months went by and although he seemed to be pleased with the libretto, Verdi continued to procrastinate. Desperate to nurture the collaboration, Ricordi suggested that Verdi and Boito prepare a revision of *Simone Boccanegra*, a work that had languished since its Venice premiere in 1857. Agreeing that *Boccanegra* had never reached its potential, Verdi agreed to work on the revision, with a production at La Scala planned for March of 1881. Although Boito faced a daunting task in reworking what was generally recognized to be a weak libretto by Piave, he and Verdi worked well together. The new version was well received in Milan and effectively replaced the original in the repertoire.

After the success of this collaboration all of the concerned parties expected that Verdi would immediately begin to work on *Otello*, but he was still reluctant. He was approaching seventy and perhaps wondered if the Shakespeare masterpiece was too daunting for a man of his age. Also Rossini had composed a setting of *Otello* in 1816 that Verdi admired. As Rossini himself had learned with *The Barber of Seville*, producing an opera with the same title as a successful earlier work (in his case, that of Paisiello) could prove to be dangerous.

Much of Verdi's correspondence in the early 1880s was pessimistic in tone. In addition to the deaths of numerous friends, including Andrea Maffei, and the prospects of his approaching old age, he was deeply depressed about the political direction of the country. The generation that was now in power was moving the country away from its ties to republican France in favor of the more authoritarian, imperialistic stance of Bismarck's Germany. In 1882 Italy had joined the Triple Alliance with Germany and Austria. Despite his conflicted history with the Opéra, Verdi loved Paris and believed that France was the cradle of European liberty

Another death that touched Verdi was that of his almost exact contemporary Richard Wagner in Venice on February 13, 1883. Having been compared unfavorably to Wagner by certain musical progressives and then criticized for imitating him in *Aida*, Verdi could hardly have avoided carrying some resentment towards the German titan. On the day after his death, however, Verdi wrote to Ricordi to express his shock at hearing the news. He declared that Wagner's was "a name that leaves a most powerful mark in the history of art."[7]

Finally, in the autumn of 1884, after completing the substantial revision of *Don Carlo*, he began to set Boito's libretto to music and, despite all of his misgivings, the work progressed extremely well. On November 1, 1886, he wrote to Ricordi: "It is finished! Salutations to you (and also to Him!!!)."[8]

Verdi prepared the performance himself with the vigor that had been characteristic of him in the decades before. Faccio conducted, and in the orchestra was a nineteen-year-old cellist from Parma named Arturo Toscanini (1867–1957). Within a few decades he would preside over one of La Scala's most glorious periods and eventually become the most famous conductor of the early twentieth century.

OTELLO: SYNOPSIS

The drama takes place on the island of Cyprus in the late fifteenth century. The island is a Venetian possession, but the Turks are about to invade. As the curtain rises a fierce storm is battering the Venetian fleet that has been sent to defend Cyprus. The Moor Otello, who is a Venetian general and governor of the island, arrives and announces that the Turkish fleet has been defeated.

Iago, Otello's ensign, speaks privately with the wealthy Venetian Roderigo, who confesses that he is in love with the governor's bride Desdemona. Iago reveals that he hates Otello because he has passed over him for an expected promotion in favor of Cassio, who is now a captain. He assures Roderigo that Desdemona will soon tire of her husband.

During the ensuing celebration of Otello's victory, Iago proposes a toast. When Cassio refuses to drink, Iago warns him that it would be ungracious not to drink a toast to Otello and his new bride. Cassio relents and proceeds to drink too much. Iago then provokes a fight between him and Roderigo.

Otello enters and breaks up the skirmish, reacting with anger to the behavior of his subordinates. As Desdemona enters, disturbed by the conflict, Otello revokes the promotion that he has granted to Cassio. Iago is secretly pleased with this turn of events because his strategy for revenge is already taking shape.

Otello orders everyone to go away, leaving him alone with Desdemona. They recall happy events from the past and declare their love for each other.

Iago advises Cassio to ask Desdemona to intervene with her husband to restore his promotion. Cassio agrees, and after he leaves, Iago soliloquizes about his cynical view of life.

Cassio speaks to Desdemona, but their conversation is interrupted by the arrival of her husband. When Cassio leaves and Desdemona brings up the subject of his demotion, Otello becomes angry and complains of a headache. She offers him her handkerchief to cool his head, but he furiously throws it on the ground.

Desdemona's loyal servant Emilia, who is Iago's wife, picks up the handkerchief, but her husband seizes it from her. Everyone exits except Otello and Iago, who tells the governor that Cassio has expressed his love for Desdemona in his sleep and also that he has seen him with her handkerchief in his hand. Otello is enraged with jealousy and vows to seek revenge. Iago kneels beside him, pretending to share his outrage, and swears to aid him in his plan.

In the great hall of Otello's castle a page announces the arrival of Venetian representatives. Iago tells Otello that he will bring Cassio to the castle so that he can observe his behavior. Desdemona enters and the couple attempt to behave normally until she again brings up the name of Cassio. He demands that she give him the handkerchief that, unknown to her, Iago has stolen and placed in Cassio's house. She lies that she has not lost a handkerchief, and he insists that she produce it. When she cannot, he accuses her of adultery and orders her out of the room.

Iago enters with Cassio, and Otello hides in order to observe his actions. Iago encourages the unsuspecting Cassio to speak about Bianca, the woman with whom he has a relationship. According to plan, Otello believes that he is speaking of Desdemona. Cassio boasts that someone else must admire him because he has found a woman's handkerchief in his home. Iago takes it from him and waves it in the air for Otello's benefit.

Otello becomes hysterical with rage and decides to murder Desdemona. Lodovico, the Venetian ambassador, arrives and informs Otello that he is being recalled to Venice and that Cassio will replace him as governor. Furious at this turn of events, Otello vents his rage on Desdemona by throwing her to the floor. Amid the confusion, Iago advises him to proceed quickly with her murder and convinces Roderigo to kill Cassio. Otello orders everyone to leave and collapses before his throne, leaving Iago to gloat over the success of his plot.

Desdemona anxiously prepares for bed and says her prayers. When she falls asleep, her husband enters and wakes her with a kiss. He tells her frankly that he is about to kill her because of her love for Cassio. She protests her innocence, but he strangles her brutally. Emilia arrives to announce that Cassio has killed Roderigo. Horrified at what has happened, she goes to seek help for her mistress. Iago, Lodovico, and Cassio arrive, and Emilia challenges her husband to explain his accusations about Desdemona. When Otello mentions the handkerchief, and Emilia immediately realizes what has happened, she reveals that Iago took it from her. It is then learned that the dying Roderigo has exposed Iago's entire plot. Now understanding everything, Otello pulls out a dagger and stabs himself. Dying, he crawls to the bed and kisses Desdemona's hand.

OTELLO: THE MUSIC

Otello begins without a prelude, but with a thirteen measure orchestral depiction of a furious storm. It is reminiscent of the opening of the "Dies irae" of the *Requiem*, with the listener hurled into a maelstrom of terrifying sound. The effect is strikingly modern, with the reiteration of a **dissonant** chord, sustained pitches in the very low register of an organ, the bass drum imitating thunder, and the high woodwinds suggesting lightning. Without traditional melody or harmonic movement, this music anticipates the revolutionary "tone paintings" of Claude Debussy's impressionistic style, which was to appear in the subsequent decades. It continues as Act One begins with a chorus of Cypriot men who spy a Venetian ship approaching the harbor. A trumpet call and the sound of a cannon are heard, and Cassio declares that this indicates the return of the general Otello. Women of the town enter and join the chorus, marveling at the power of the wind, waves, and lightning.

The full chorus turns toward the sea and bursts into a fervent prayer for the deliverance of the ship. Iago appears with Rodrigo and immediately displays his hatred of Otello by whispering that he hopes that his ship will sink. He begins this statement with an upward leap of the dissonant and disjunct interval of a ninth.

As soon as Iago ends his phrase, the orchestra and chorus move from great ambiguity of key to brilliant E major as the danger passes. Soon Otello walks up the steps from the shore, followed by a large entourage of sailors and soldiers. His first word, "Esultate!" ("Rejoice!"), delivered above a triumphant C-sharp-major harmony, provides one of the most striking entrances in all opera for one of the greatest tenor roles. He announces that the Turks have been defeated and their pride "buried in the sea." As the chorus praises his victory, he proceeds into the castle with Cassio and the other soldiers, leaving Iago and Roderigo outside.

The storm is now subsiding and the musical depiction of its dying away is as graphic as that of its fury, approaching even more closely the sound of impressionism. The townspeople bring branches and light a bonfire. Against this backdrop Roderigo tells Iago of his love for Desdemona. In a shockingly racist statement, the ensign assures him that Desdemona will soon grow tired of "the kisses from the swollen lips of that savage." This exchange is set with the barest of accompaniments, standing in stark contrast to the outpouring of music that has preceded it. Then a breathless-sounding and somewhat humorous melody emerges, to which Iago suggests that he has a plan to help him.

Slipping back into bare recitative he reveals his hatred for Otello and jealousy of Cassio, whose promotion to the rank of captain should have gone to him. In a line filled with foreboding he sings, "If I were the Moor, I would not want to see Iago around me."

The bonfire is now burning brightly, and the townspeople sing a massive, complex chorus, "Fuoco di gioia" ("Joyous Fire"), with orchestral accompaniment that suggests the flickering of the fire. As the flames die away and the chorus ends, Iago, Roderigo, and Cassio reappear and group themselves around a table that has been set up for further festivities.

In a subtle **parlante** passage in which the orchestra hints at motives from the preceding chorus, Iago, with cunning efficiency, convinces the reluctant Cassio to drink a toast to Otello and his victory and, as the wine takes its effect, to sing the praises of Desdemona. Roderigo also falls into Iago's trap by believing that Cassio is another rival for Desdemona's affections.

As the wine continues to flow, Iago begins a drinking song that recalls the *brindisi* in the first act of *La traviata*. Cassio, Roderigo, and a chorus of soldiers join in the rousing song, which consists of three stanzas, each followed by a refrain. The prevailing major key is clouded by Iago's lines, which hint at the minor mode and briefly explore **chromatic** harmonies.

Cassio, now almost in a drunken stupor, begins to enter the ensemble at the wrong time. Encouraged musically by Iago, he begins to sputter hiccup-like two-note fragments and the chorus responds with hearty laughter. As the ensemble increases in excitement, Iago prods Roderigo to start a fight with the tipsy Cassio. Montano, the former governor, arrives to summon Cassio to guard duty and is dismayed to find him drunk.

Roderigo takes Iago's bait and insults Cassio. The two begin to fight and Montano tries to separate them. Cassio draws his sword and wounds Montano. In total control of the situation, Iago instructs Roderigo to sound an alarm. Bells are rung and Otello makes a dramatic appearance that produces a stunned silence. In a stentorian line that recalls that of his first entrance, he commands the two to put down their swords. He asks Iago who is responsible for this outrage.

Replying "I don't know," Iago's feigned innocence is parodied by the orchestra with its sudden shift to the most simplistic of harmonies. When Otello discovers that Montano has been wounded, he is filled with rage as **tremolo** strings emphasize the tenseness of the situation. Seeing that Desdemona has also been awakened and has come out of the castle, his jagged melodic line evolves into a more lyrical one as he addresses her. In quick succession he revokes Cassio's promotion, instructs Iago to calm the townspeople, and asks others to care for Montano. During this dialogue the orchestra has settled into a calm, string-dominated passage in F major. This continues as the stage empties and the orchestra paints a musical picture of the shimmering starry night.

A solo cello and then four muted cellos introduce the great love duet that Otello begins with "Già nella notte densa s'estingue ogno clamor" ("Already in the thick night all clamor has ceased"). The brilliant British jazz musician and essayist Spike Hughes aptly described the duet as "a string of exquisite tunes which meander through one unlikely key after another."[9] The impact of this duet is heightened because it is the first truly lyrical section of the opera. In *Otello* Verdi has completely eliminated the venerable tradition of the formal entrance aria.

Desdemona begins to recall the past in a highly chromatic accompanied recitative, but when she asks her husband "Do you remember?" both she and the orchestra move without preparation into radiant C major. The two lovers alternate with contrasting melodic ideas until they finally come together as she exclaims "I loved you for your adventures" and he responds "I loved you for your mercy."

The dramatic climax is reached as Otello declares that if death were to come, it would be welcome at this sublime moment. Reflecting his emotional state, the orchestra moves frenetically from key to key, dominated by tremolos in the strings. The music becomes even more ecstatic as he asks for a kiss and she can only respond by calling his name. He asks for another kiss and then another. The "kiss music" will return with great poignancy in the final act.

As he had done before in so many sublime moments, Verdi now moves to D-flat major as Otello sings in a whisper near the top of his vocal range "Come, Venus is shining." Beneath a high violin **trill**, the cellos recall their passage from the introduction as Desdemona and Otello enter the castle.

Before the curtain rises on Act Two the orchestra plays an extended prelude whose principal theme appears in fragments in low strings and winds and evolves into a complete melody as it moves to the higher instruments. When the curtain rises, revealing Iago and Cassio in a hall of the castle, traces of this music are interspersed with their conversation. Its general lightness and pleasantness reflect the glibness and ease with which Iago lies. He tells Cassio that Desdemona has great persuasive power over her husband and suggests that he ask her to help him regain his promotion. Cassio is easily convinced, and Iago sends him outside to wait for her in the garden.

Left alone, Iago begins his celebrated blasphemous soliloquy, "Credo in un Dio crudel" ("I Believe in a Cruel God"), in which he espouses his nihilistic philosophy. Iago's "Credo," often performed in concert by baritones, is a striking example of the late Verdi style in which there is virtually no distinction between recitative and aria.

The opening parlante is delivered above two contrasting orchestral themes: one in commanding octaves and another that is composed of a winding descent (a) followed by a rapidly ascending scale and then another fall on **pizzicato** strings (b). These passages return in different guises throughout the scene.

When he compares the strength of his faith in evil to that of a widow in church, his vocal line becomes mockingly melodic, in unison with the orchestra. Finally he declares that after all of life's mockery there is only death. On the word *morte* the orchestra plays two tritones, the interval between two pitches that divides an octave in half that medieval musicians considered diabolical. The second of the recurring instrumental passages reenters furiously as he asserts that death is nothingness and heaven, an ancient fable. From the height of Iago's final note, the orchestra dies away as it repeats the two descending segments of b, finally sinking into a void like the nothingness of death.

Iago sees Desdemona and Emilia walking into the garden and urges Cassio to approach her with his request. At this point the action in the garden is observed in the distance by the audience with Iago providing a running narration. His short notes and the dancing accompaniment emphasize his glee at seeing his plan continue to fall into place. He describes the increasingly intimate conversation between Cassio and Desdemona.

Just as Iago has expected, Otello arrives and observes the scene. With his back to Otello and pretending not to see him, Iago mutters that he is displeased by what he has just seen. In masterful fashion he begins to intimate that Cassio is not to be trusted. Masterfully Verdi intersperses melodic fragments amid the recitative. Exerting his control of the situation, Iago continually manipulates the music from one key to another. The climax arrives when he voices the central theme of the opera: "Beware, my lord, of jealousy" over a startlingly chromatic series of chords played in a whisper by the orchestra. This precipitates an outburst from Otello in which he demands proof of Iago's intimations. This culminates in his stunning ascent of more than an octave and a half to the tenor high B.

From the garden a dulcet chorus of men, women, and children is heard praising the goodness of Desdemona. It is accompanied by mandolins, guitars, harps, and the delicate Renaissance woodwind instrument called a cornamuse. Against this, Iago sings an ironic **counterpoint** as he warns Otello to watch his wife and Cassio. Desdemona sings naively of the joy this outpouring brings, and Otello ponders how such beauty could harbor deceit. Iago observes to himself that he will shatter this harmony.

The chorus exits and Desdemona goes inside to speak with her husband. She immediately broaches the issue of Cassio's demotion. This exchange begins in the same innocent tone as the chorus that preceded it, but as Desdemona presses Otello to forgive Cassio and the seeds of suspicion that Iago has sown take hold, the music becomes increasingly agitated.

When Desdemona asks Otello why his voice is so dark, he claims to have a pain in his temple. Both rhythmic and harmonic tension increase in the orchestra as the drama's decisive act unfolds. She offers to tie her handkerchief around his head, but he angrily throws it on the ground. As Emilia retrieves it, Desdemona sings a descending declamatory line that begins the statement "If I have unconsciously offended you." In midsentence there is a musical shift to pure melody as she continues "give me the sweet and happy word of pardon."

This initiates a quartet for the three central characters and Emilia. As in the traditional Italian ensemble, the characters express their contrasting sentiments about what is taking place, but this one is enhanced by the supple juxtaposition of various vocal styles that is central to Verdi's late works.

In soaring melodic lines Desdemona innocently expresses her loyalty to her husband and her dismay at his unhappiness and coldness. In phrases that are more rhythmic than melodic, Otello speculates sarcastically to himself on what has caused him to lose Desdemona's love.

In a completely separate conversation Emilia, fully aware of her husband's character, accuses him of plotting to bring about this situation, but his only concern is to obtain the handkerchief from her. Although the text is divided between the two sparring couples, Desdemona dominates musically with her long lines floating above the fast-moving dialogue of the other three. Just after she reaches her highest pitch, Iago tears the handkerchief away from Emilia and gloats over his triumph.

Desdemona repeats her plea for a word of pardon that began the quartet, but with a different melody. The first violins accompany, playing her original vocal line in counterpoint. Otello sends the women away as the orchestra continues to play fragments of Desdemona's melody. He collapses into a chair, lamenting her alleged treachery as Iago considers his plan to hide the handkerchief in Cassio's house and gloats that his poison is working.

Iago now approaches Otello with feigned politeness, but is angrily rebuffed. The Moor expresses the wish that he had never learned of Desdemona's infidelity. He begins a nostalgic soliloquy about the happiness of his past military life. Verdi sets this text as a military march that ironically expresses no sense of triumph. The **dynamics** are mostly quiet, and as Otello becomes more agitated the key moves down by steps three times as he bids "addio" to his past glory. The familiar "short-short-long" death motive is heard several times in the brass.

Iago bids him "peace," instigating one of the great confrontations of the opera. The music grows more rhythmically active and more chromatic as Otello demands proof of the implications about his wife. He eventually grabs Iago by the throat and throws him down, accompanied by violent descending octaves.

Challenged to prove his veracity, Iago concocts his blatant lie about Cassio's dream in the **arioso** "Era la notte" ("It Was Night"). This passage, with delicate strings doubling the vocal line, is the polar opposite of the brutally honest "Credo." Here he is all charm as he whispers his concocted story of Cassio's addressing Desdemona in his sleep, declaring "Heaven's ecstasy overwhelms me." This is accompanied by an amazingly unorthodox passage of very delicate parallel major chords that descend stepwise, completely obscuring any sense of key.

Sensing the triumph of his ruse, Iago delivers his masterstroke. Asking Otello if he knows a handkerchief embroidered with flowers, he learns that indeed he had given it to Desdemona. Haltingly, as though reluctant, he whispers that he has seen it in Cassio's hands. This instigates an outburst from the orchestra and an anguished cry from Otello. Nearly losing control of himself, he repeatedly calls for the blood of the guilty.

Otello kneels and begins an oath, "Sì, pel ciel marmoreo giuro" ("Yes, by the marble heaven I swear it"), that will be the finale of the act. Beginning in parlante style, this section evolves into one of the most traditional passages of the opera. At the repetition of the text Iago joins in and, always in control, he takes over the melody. At the end they join together, with Iago encouraging Otello's calls for revenge. Their final phrase, a call for the aid of God as avenger, sung in thirds, provides a brief touch of the earlier Verdi style. The orchestra finishes the act with full force, but after three measures in the home key it begins to descend stepwise as in the previous passage associated with Iago's story of Cassio's dream. Instead of the earlier gentle depiction of ecstasy, the progression now suggests Otello's impending collapse.

Act Three begins with a prelude based on a theme that earlier was associated with what Iago termed "the dark hydra of jealousy." As the curtain rises on the great hall of the castle, a herald announces the arrival of a ship bearing the Venetian ambassador. Iago has asked Cassio to come to the castle and suggests that Otello observe his actions. He starts to leave, but sees Desdemona approaching and cannot resist making one more mention of the handkerchief.

Desdemona's entrance is accompanied by a graceful passage for strings that expresses none of the irony of the music that precedes it. With characteristic innocence she lovingly greets her husband and at first he mirrors her behavior, asking politely that she give him her hand. Soon his true thoughts emerge as he begins to make double entendres about the warm softness of her hand, and the music gravitates away from her bright major key into the darker regions of the minor.

Once again Desdemona chooses an inopportune time to bring up the subject of Cassio. As at the earlier mention of his name, Otello complains of a headache and asks for her handkerchief. When she cannot produce the one in question, he accuses her of losing it and threatens "Woe if you lose it," ominously repeating the word "guai" ("woe"). Frightened by his anger, she lies that it is not lost and then, with almost unbelievable naiveté, asks that he consent to receive Cassio. She makes this request in a short lyrical and lilting passage that Verdi marks "with elegance" and "with politeness." She persists in her purpose, but he is reduced to repeating, more and more emphatically, "the handkerchief." The level of tension increases until he finally accuses her of being impure.

The orchestra builds to a furious climax, eventually coming to rest on a dissonant harmony. Accompanied by a sustained pitch on the oboe and the death motive in the trombones, she whispers that she feels the fury in his words, but does not understand them. Beginning to weep, Desdemona sings a poignant **cantabile**: "Io prego il cielo per te con questo pianto" ("I Pray to Heaven for You with this Weeping"). Verdi's sure command of chromatic harmony strengthens the effect of her straightforward melodic line.

Otello is unmoved by her pleas and the dramatic tension builds inexorably to a climax. All becomes calm, the major key returns, and with the same ingratiating music as before he asks for her hand. In a statement of almost maniacal sarcasm he asks her forgiveness if he has confused her with "that vile courtesan who is the wife of Otello." On the word "courtesan" the music shifts drastically from serenity to violence, and he sings his highest pitch of the opera, the tenor high C. With this he pushes her out of the room.

Left alone, Otello delivers his soliloquy, "Dio! Mi potevi scagliar tutti I mali" ("God! You Could Have Flung All the Evils at Me"). As though all his strength has been consumed in the confrontation with Desdemona, he begins in a breathless whisper on a single pitch with uncharacteristically bare and austere accompaniment. At the line "Ma, o pianto, o duol! M'han rapito il miraggio" ("But, oh weeping, oh sorrow! They have stolen my mirage.") the key moves to major, and the vocal line becomes more lyrical with the support of tremolo strings. Otello temporarily lapses into fond memories of his past with Desdemona. In this passage Verdi arouses sympathy for this troubled character as he did in the great soliloquy for Philip II in *Don Carlos*.

Becoming agitated again, he demands a confession. At that moment Iago appears and announces that Cassio is approaching and leads Otello to the terrace to observe his actions. The scene that follows, for two men in conversation and one commenting from his hiding place, is carefully stage-managed by Iago. Addressing Cassio as "Captain," he leads him to mention Desdemona, who is trying to get that title restored. At this point the tempo quickens and the rhythmic figures suggest the perverse game that Iago is playing. This scene provides a semblance of comic relief amid this dark drama.

Iago then encourages Cassio to recount his amorous exploits with his lover Bianca, making sure that he pronounces her name out of the earshot of Otello. This causes Cassio to laugh, inciting Otello's rage.

At this point the central section of the trio begins. Verdi's music here is in the style of the eighteenth century with lucid, transparent orchestral texture and dance-like rhythm that emphasizes the humor of the situation. Now Cassio, changing the subject from the hilarity of his dalliance with Bianca, has another matter to relate. He believes that he now has a secret admirer, for someone has left an embroidered handkerchief in his place of lodging. Anticipating this revelation, Iago has already moved him farther away from Otello, who becomes even more vexed at not being able to hear.

Iago asks to see the handkerchief and then takes it from Cassio and holds it behind his back so that Otello can see it. He continues to tease Cassio and to revel in the consternation that the situation is provoking in Otello.

The trio ends with a spirited **stretta**, "Questa è una ragna" ("This Is a Spider's Web"), featuring rapid-fire delivery of text that recalls the "patter" arias of opera buffa. Against the banter of the other two men, Otello can only repeat "tradimento!" ("betrayal!").

This is suddenly interrupted by the sound of distant trumpets announcing the arrival of the ship bearing the Venetian ambassador. To provide a realistic effect, Verdi stipulated that pairs of trumpets be positioned in different positions onstage and off.

Cassio exits and Otello, now determined that Desdemona must die, approaches Iago to ask him how the murder should be accomplished. As distant voices hail the "lion of St. Mark," the two continue their gruesome conversation. Otello asks Iago to bring him some poison, but he cynically suggests that she should be strangled in her bed, where the sin was committed. He also offers to "provide" for Cassio, and, gratefully, Otello grants him the coveted promotion to captain.

To avoid suspicion, Iago goes to bring Desdemona to the ambassador's reception. A grand public scene ensues with the entry of Lodovico, the ambassador, and his entourage. Iago, Desdemona, Emilia, and Roderigo arrive, accompanied by soldiers, trumpeters, and townspeople to the strains of a grandiose chorus of welcome. Lodovico formally presents Otello with an official document. While he reads it, a conversation takes place between the others. Declamatory passages alternate seamlessly with bits of melody.

Lodovico asks why Cassio is not present, and Iago explains that Otello is angry with him. Still hopeful, Desdemona suggests that he may soon be restored to favor and adds that she has great affection for him. This provokes an angry whisper from Otello, who commands her to keep quiet. With tension building in tremolo strings, he starts to strike her, but is restrained by Lodovico as the bystanders react with horror.

Having finished reading the document from Venice, Otello demands that Cassio be brought to him. When he enters, the orchestra begins an agitated chromatic passage that climaxes with five dramatic chords to announce the reading of the document. Above prolonged tremolo chords Otello reads the orders of the Venetian Senate. He is to return to Venice and his successor in Cyprus is to be Cassio. This surprising news provokes an outraged curse from Iago.

Desdemona approaches her furious husband, and he throws her down, crying "To the ground and weep!" As everyone stands frozen in terror, the orchestra plays a passage whose chromaticism is as radical harmonically as anything Verdi ever composed. Comparison of late Verdian harmony to that of Wagner has become a convenient cliché, but here it seems inevitable.

After this moment of tremendous musical ambiguity Desdemona begins the opera's most complex ensemble with a moving lament. She expresses three contrasting ideas, each with its own music in a different key. In the accompanied recitative, "A terra! Sì, nel livido fango" ("On the Ground! Yes, in the Discolored Mire"), she bemoans her tragic situation and senses the portent of death. "È un dì sul mio sorriso" ("One Day upon My Smile") is a nostalgic reflection on the love she and Otello shared in the past. It begins in a bright major key, but quickly lapses into chromaticism as she mourns for what she has lost. In "Quel sol sereno e vivido" ("The Serene and Vivid Sun"), she bewails that even the sun that lights the sky and the sea cannot soothe her pain. Melodically related to the previous passage, this one is in a higher key and reaches a passionate climax on a high C-flat.

Emilia, Lodovico, Cassio, and Roderigo sing in unaccompanied chords, the first two expressing sympathy for Desdemona and each of the other two reflecting on what this turn of events means to him. Desdemona enters the ensemble with a repetition of her "È un dì sul mio sorriso" passage.

Iago approaches Otello and advises him to act quickly to murder Desdemona and that he will do the same with Cassio. The orchestra repeats a motive that is full of tension, both in its strong, persistent rhythm and in its chromatic harmony. Desdemona breathlessly sings short fragments of the text from her earlier solo while the chorus continues to express their horror at Otello's cruelty.

Iago begins to manipulate Roderigo to arrange Cassio's murder. He tells him that Desdemona, whom he still loves, will be leaving Cyprus the following day, but if something were to happen to Cassio, Otello would have to remain on the island as governor. Iago's scheming takes place below the surface of the continuous commentary of the full ensemble. Above it all Desdemona continues to repeat text from her lament with variants of its melodies.

The tempo accelerates and the texture becomes more complex as six characters and the chorus all sing in counterpoint. Only Otello remains silent. When the enormous ensemble reaches its climax with everyone singing together, he rises abruptly, turns to the crowd, and commands them in a "terrible" voice to flee. With this single word the key is wrenched into a region that is totally foreign to what has prevailed throughout the scene. Desdemona rushes to him crying "My husband!" but he curses her. A fanfare from trumpets and trombones is heard offstage along with a very ironic choral cheer.

The entire company, frightened by Otello's apparent madness, makes a hasty exit, with only Iago remaining. Deliriously Otello rages at the thought of Desdemona and Cassio together. He then focuses on the handkerchief and sings that word three times in a stepwise descent. He is accompanied by the descending parallel chord progression that was originally heard in Iago's story of Cassio's dream of Desdemona. At this point it seems to reflect Otello's descent into near insanity.

The act concludes with tremendous irony. Otello faints and Iago gloats "My poison is working." In the distance, accompanied by trumpet fanfares, a crowd cries "Glory to the lion of Venice!" Iago stares at the motionless form of Otello and observes, "Here is the lion." Blaring chords bring the curtain down.

Act Four takes place in Desdemona's bedroom. As in the final act of *La traviata*, with its similar setting, Verdi begins with an extended prelude that perfectly sets the tone for the tragedy that is about to unfold. In the thirty-five years that had elapsed since the earlier work, however, Verdi's command of harmony and orchestration had changed profoundly. Here the musical material is stripped to the barest essentials, and out of it grow the components of the scene that follows.

The prelude is for woodwinds and horns only. The English horn begins with a forlorn melody without accompaniment. While it sustains the last note of its phrase, three flutes play a six-note weeping motive. Two clarinets, low in their range, play the hollow-sounding, desolate interval of a fifth to prepare for a repetition of the English horn theme.

Desdemona asks Emilia to lay her white wedding dress on her bed and, accompanied by a change of key, she instructs her that when she dies she would like to be wrapped in one of its veils. Her unfortunate situation reminds her of the "Willow Song" that she learned as a child and now proceeds to sing it for Emilia.

Boito translated the "Willow Song" virtually intact from Shakespeare. Desdemona explains that she learned it from her mother's servant Barbara, who had been abandoned by the man she loved. The song depicts a woman whose situation is similar. She is seated by a river, weeping as she sings to a willow tree whose funereal branches will comprise her garland.

Like the duke's "La donna è mobile" in *Rigoletto* and Eboli's "Song of the Moor" in *Don Carlos*, the "Willow Song" is a set piece inserted within the narrative. Shakespeare indicated that it was to be sung in the spoken drama. Unlike the earlier songs, however, it is not in popular style, but in the sophisticated musical language, reminiscent of *Aida*, that lies between aria and recitative.

The song is unified by an introductory passage for woodwinds that recurs three times and then by the striking, unaccompanied refrain "Salce! Salce! Salce!" ("Willow"). The first phrase, "Piangea cantando" ("She weeps, singing"), is a variant of the English horn melody that began the prelude to the act. The most lyrical moments are the three statements of the word "Cantiamo" ("Let us sing"). When Desdemona sings "cantiamo" the first two times, the octave leap to its second syllable is accompanied by a D-major chord that contrasts brilliantly with the prevailing F-sharp minor. The third time, the same melody notes are harmonized with the even brighter chord of B major.

Throughout the song Desdemona's asides to Emilia add naturalism to the scene. So too does the ending, in which the introductory passage leads directly into her heartbreaking farewell. After a long sustained note in the clarinet, whose effect is to further cloud the already ambiguous key, the orchestra settles into F-sharp major.

After an entire scene marked by the greatest delicacy of sound, an enormous climax occurs at the words "Ah! Emilia, Emilia, addio!" The sound dies away and the orchestra plays a postlude that is entirely based on the weeping motive of the prelude.

The "Willow Song" is followed by the equally famous Ave Maria. The prayer is set in three sections. The first is an Italian translation of the traditional text, "Hail Mary, full of grace, blessed are you among women and blessed is the fruit of your womb, Jesus." Desdemona intones each syllable on a single repeated note, as a prayer would have been sung in the traditional liturgy, with the addition of an accompaniment of sustained chords. She then moves to a personal prayer for the sinner, the innocent, the oppressed, and finally for herself. In this very intimate passage she moves to a more melodic style.

Returning to the liturgical text, "Pray for us in the hour of death," she again sings on the single pitch, but becomes so emotional that she can only utter a few syllables at a time. On the final "Ave," she ascends an octave to a sustained high A-flat and then sinks back to the pitch of her recitation for a final, unaccompanied "Amen."

An ominous passage on muted double basses coincides with the appearance of Otello on the threshold of a secret door to the bedroom. He walks into the room, lays a sword on the table, blows out a candle, and moves to the bed. As he walks toward his sleeping wife, there is a crescendo that leads to two forceful chords as he stops. All becomes extremely quiet again as he looks down at Desdemona.

Like a long-held memory, the "kiss music" from the Act One love duet is heard as he kisses her three times. She awakens and calls his name. In a monotone that recalls Desdemona's Ave Maria, he asks her if she has prayed that evening, advising her that she needs heaven's forgiveness for her sins. He makes it clear that he plans to kill her and that her sin is her love for Cassio. When she denies it, he brings up the fateful issue of the handkerchief. She asks him to call in Cassio to vindicate her, and he announces coldly that Cassio is dead. As she senses his rising fury she begs him not to kill her, but with his anger increasing, he calls her a prostitute. As rapidly moving notes evolve into perpetual motion, he strangles her and she screams.

As Otello gazes at Desdemona's motionless body, there is a knock at the door and Emilia cries out to be admitted. He opens the door and she announces that Cassio has killed Roderigo and is alive. From her bed the dying Desdemona whispers with great difficulty that she has been killed unjustly. Emilia runs to her side and asks who has committed the crime. In a simple lyrical passage that resembles her Ave Maria she responds "No one . . . only I." She commends herself to God, proclaims her innocence, and says a final farewell as she dies.

Otello confesses that he has done the deed because Iago has told him of her infidelity. Emilia calls him a fool for believing her husband and runs to the door crying for help. Immediately Lodovico, Cassio, and

Iago arrive, followed by Montano and soldiers. The fury of this final confrontation is mirrored in the chromaticism of the orchestral music that moves rapidly through multiple keys. Courageously Emilia confronts her husband and reveals the truth about the handkerchief. Realizing that he has been trapped in his own plot, Iago runs out, pursued by the soldiers.

Lodovico tries to take away Otello's sword, and he responds with a brief soliloquy. Against the softest of sustained chords he declares that they have nothing to fear from him, for his road has come to an end. He goes to the bed, looks down at Desdemona, and utters an unaccompanied line that is a dramatic masterpiece of both Boito and Verdi: "E tu . . . come sei pallida! E stanca, e muta, e bella" ("How pale you are . . . and tired, and silent, and beautiful"). Each of the four adjectives is sung on a descending, stepwise sobbing figure. As he continues, the orchestra joins in with a repeated death motive.

Otello pulls a dagger from his clothing and, before anyone can restrain him, stabs himself. After an act that is replete with so many powerful moments and exquisite music, Verdi has reserved his *coup de théâtre* for the end. Gazing at Desdemona's body, he whispers "Before I killed you, my bride, I kissed you." For the third and final time the "kiss music" from the love duet is heard, and he kisses her twice. On the third statement of the word "kiss," the final syllable is cut off as he falls dead. The orchestra descends through a series of distantly related harmonies in hushed tones as the curtain falls.

o o o

Predictably, the premiere of Verdi's first opera in more than fifteen years was received with tremendous fanfare. *Otello* soon became an international success, and its stature within the operatic canon has continued to grow. By 1886 Boito had begun to collaborate with du Locle on a French translation for the Opéra and Verdi was composing the requisite ballet music. The French *Otello* premiered in 1894.

Otello was produced in London in 1889 and at the Metropolitan Opera in 1891. Beginning in 1909 Toscanini conducted twenty-nine performances of it in New York. The distinguished Italian soprano and Toscanini protégée Renata Tebaldi (1922–2004) made her Metropolitan debut as Desdemona in 1955. Most of the greatest tenors of the twentieth and twenty-first centuries have sung the part of Otello. Placido Domingo (b. 1941) has been especially associated with the role.

After *Otello*'s triumph both the management of La Scala and Verdi's close friends urged him to begin another opera, but he went back to Sant'Agata, protesting that he had nothing left to say. He spent time supervising the construction of a small hospital that he had financed at Villanova, near his estate, for those who could not afford to travel the thirty kilometers to Piacenza for medical care. The hospital, which Verdi refused to have named for him, opened in November of 1887. Verdi was easily irritated when he was expected, because of his celebrity, to contribute to causes that did not interest him, but was a generous philanthropist when he was confronted by human need.

More than once Giuseppina, Giulio Ricordi, Teresa Stolz, and others in Verdi's intimate circle had heard him announce that his career was finished. They knew from experience that the right libretto could make him change his mind and that in Boito he had found his greatest collaborator. They merely had to bide their time.

The wait extended for more than two years. In 1889 Verdi was taking the waters at the Tuscan spa of Montecatini when Boito sent him the outline of a libretto based on the Shakespearean character of Falstaff. He liked it immediately and the letter he wrote to Boito two days later betrayed his enthusiasm. He protested somewhat unconvincingly, however, that because of his age he might not be able to finish it.

Boito replied that working on a comic opera should be invigorating rather than emotionally draining like the composition of a tragedy. Verdi responded immediately: "Amen: and so be it! Let us then do *Falstaff*!"[10] For two years they kept their plans secret from everyone except Giuseppina.

Verdi worked steadily, finding, as he had with *Otello*, that Boito's poetry lent itself well to musical setting. The correspondence between the two was genial and filled with banter. Only a month after they had agreed to undertake the work Verdi wrote that he was experimenting with the idea of a "comic **fugue**" for the opera. Although the use of that traditionally serious and cerebral musical genre in a comedy seemed like a contradiction in terms, Boito cheerfully agreed that it would be perfect for *Falstaff*.[11]

By the time the last act of the libretto was delivered, Verdi had finished composing the first. By September of 1892 the opera was finished. Almost as difficult as the composition of *Falstaff* was its casting, and Verdi became involved with these decisions while he was still working on the music. Since the time of *Macbeth* he had demanded that his singers be able to act convincingly, and he believed this was even more crucial for a comedy. After some financial negotiation, Victor Maurel (1848–1923), the French baritone who had created the role of Iago, was signed as Falstaff.

By the beginning of 1893 the cast had been assembled and the Verdis had arrived in Milan. He presided over long exhausting rehearsals and his energy at almost eighty was a source of amazement. The premiere, on February 9, 1893, was, as expected, a major musical and social event, and two of most prominent young Italian composers, Giacomo Puccini and Pietro Mascagni (1863–1945), were in the audience.

FALSTAFF: SYNOPSIS

Boito's libretto is based on Shakespeare's comedy *The Merry Wives of Windsor* and portions of *King Henry IV*. The action, set in three acts of two scenes each, all occurs in and around the city of Windsor on a single day and evening in the fifteenth century.

The portly Sir John Falstaff is drinking at the Garter Inn with his friends Bardolph and Pistol. Old Dr. Caius enters and angrily accuses Falstaff of breaking into his home, beating his servants, and stealing a horse. Making light of the charges, but not denying them, Falstaff has Caius thrown out. Unable to pay his bill for food and drink, he complains that his companions are costing him too much. Hoping to improve his financial condition, he plans to court the wealthy married women Alice Ford and Meg Page, and he asks his friends to deliver a letter to each of them. When they refuse, he launches into a tirade on the subject of honor.

Later, in the garden of the Ford home, Meg and Mistress Quickly talk with Alice and her daughter Nannetta. They soon realize that Falstaff has sent identical letters to Meg and Alice, and they resolve to teach him a lesson for his dishonesty. They withdraw when Alice's husband arrives with Caius, Bardolph, Pistol, and Fenton, a young man who is in love with Nannetta. Falstaff's two cronies warn Ford of Falstaff's scheme.

The women plot to send Quickly to Falstaff with an invitation from Alice for him to come to her home. All the women plan to be there to deal with him. In the meantime the men make a plan that Ford will visit Falstaff in disguise.

Back at the inn, Falstaff is drinking when Bardolph and Pistol enter and pretend to apologize for their disloyalty. They announce the arrival of Mistress Quickly, who issues the invitation from Alice, advising him that her jealous husband is away between two and three every afternoon. She assures him that Meg also returns his affections.

After she leaves, Ford, disguised as "Master Fontana," arrives to tell Falstaff that he is unsuccessfully trying to woo Alice Ford. He offers him a reward if he will help him by pretending to court her himself. Falstaff happily agrees and boasts that he already plans to meet her while her husband is out of the house. He leaves to go dress himself, and the angry Ford makes a plan to catch the two in the act. Falstaff returns in fine clothes and the two exit together.

Quickly arrives at Alice's house to report to her and Meg that Falstaff has taken the bait and is already on his way. Nannetta complains because her father has betrothed her to the unattractive Dr. Caius. Two servants come in carrying a large linen basket. Alice instructs them to set it down in the room, but at her signal they are to dump its contents into the river.

The other women hide and Alice receives Falstaff. He brags that in his youth he was slender as a page. His speech is cut short by the arrival of Quickly, followed by Meg. He hides behind a screen as they tell Alice that her husband has learned that she has a lover in the house and is on his way there. Ford and his men search the house and, spying the basket, fling dirty laundry out of it to try to find their prey. They move on to another room and the women help Falstaff get into the basket. Nannetta and Fenton hide behind the screen, and their kissing can be heard throughout the room.

Ford finds the young lovers behind the screen and orders Fenton out of the house. Alice directs four servants to throw the basket into the river and calls her husband to see the basket, with Falstaff in it, plunge into the water.

Outside the inn that evening at sunset Falstaff, still cold and damp, orders a hot drink and bemoans his fate. Quickly arrives with a note from Alice asking him to meet her at midnight in Windsor Great Park.

The two enter the inn and Quickly tells him the frightening story of the ghost of the Black Huntsman, who sometimes appears in the park at midnight. She instructs him to come to the park dressed as the Huntsman. Alice, Ford, Meg, Caius, and Fenton overhear all of this and decide to converge on the park at midnight dressed as various forest creatures to frighten Falstaff.

Everyone exits except Ford and Caius. Ford tells the doctor that if he will dress in monk's robes that evening and present himself with Nannetta, who will be dressed in white, he will give their marriage his blessing. Quickly overhears this conversation and hurries to tell Alice and Nannetta.

That evening around midnight Fenton approaches Herne's Oak in the park singing a love song. Nannetta arrives and they embrace. Quickly appears and instructs Fenton to disguise himself as a monk. Falstaff appears wearing two stag horns on his head, followed soon by Alice. He tries to embrace her, but is interrupted by Meg, who cries in the distance that she is being chased by witches. All of the costumed creatures appear and dance around the terrified Falstaff. In the confusion Bardolph loses his mask and Falstaff recognizes him. All unmask and Falstaff is good-humored about their ruse.

Quickly has dressed Bardolph in the veil of the fairy queen. Caius, mistaking him for Nannetta, brings him to Ford. Quickly enters with another couple, and Alice asks Ford to bless the marriages of both pairs. He does this and then finds that he has betrothed Nannetta to Fenton and Caius to Bardolph. Falstaff revels in the fact that, like he, Ford has been duped, and he leads the entire group in proclaiming that all the world is a joke.

FALSTAFF: THE MUSIC

The formal opera overture or prelude had been of little interest to Verdi for some time, and here it is almost completely nonexistent. The curtain rises at the fourth measure of music and the dialogue begins in the eighth. The principal musical idea consists of a heavily accented chord on what is normally a weak beat followed by a group of four descending quick notes. This continues as the accompaniment for the opening dialogue and seems to represent the angry accusations of Dr.

Caius. Both its melodic outline and its propulsive rhythm recur throughout this remarkably cohesive opera.

Falstaff makes light of Caius's charges and boasts that he has done all of it on purpose. With this the orchestra introduces a second musical idea: a variant of the earlier descending figure, played first by clarinet and then imitated, an octave higher each time, by oboe, flute, and piccolo. This is in counterpoint to the rising line sung by Falstaff and doubled by the strings. The music moves to C-sharp minor. The opening theme returns in a new key as Caius turns his anger toward Bardolph, accusing him of getting him drunk and then picking his pocket. Bardolph denies it and the orchestra backs him up with resolute chords.

Falstaff suggests that it was Pistol who robbed the doctor, but he, seizing a broom and threatening Caius with it, declares his innocence. At this moment the orchestra reprises the opening music in the original key. When Falstaff reprimands Pistol for his temper, the rising melody of the second idea returns, also in the home key. The resulting scheme of statement-development-return gives the entire scene the basic outline of the classic **sonata form**.

Caius declares that if he becomes inebriated again, it will be in the company of honest gentlemen. The musical setting of this pronouncement resembles the decorous and emphatic ending of an old-fashioned aria and is accompanied by the doctor's "anger theme." Bardolph and Pistol mockingly sing "amen" in a parody of Renaissance ecclesiastical counterpoint. Making light of their musical display, Falstaff, in the foreign key of A-flat, suavely suggests that if they are to rob, it should be done with grace and timing. They begin to repeat the "amen," but Falstaff cuts them off, officially ending this segment of the scene.

The innkeeper brings Falstaff the bill for a huge amount of food and drink, and he complains that both of his companions are bringing him to financial ruin. With gross hyperbole he suggests that they will cause him to become thin. His line is doubled by piccolo and cello four octaves apart in a conspicuously thin-sounding texture. He notes that his fame is based on the size of his paunch. His companions sarcastically chant his praises: "Immense Falstaff! Enormous Falstaff!"

An abrupt change of key and mood accompany Falstaff's change of subject to a possible solution for his financial troubles. With a cheerful melody he speaks of Alice Ford, who holds the purse strings of her wealthy husband. As he goes on to describe her beauty, the musical texture becomes more subtle with increasing interchange of melodic material between voice and orchestra.

Falstaff grows more excited as he thinks of Alice's beauty. He declares that "love's inspiration flamed in my heart" in a grandiose mock-dramatic line in unison with the orchestra. He fantasizes that she admires all of his features and then, imitating Alice's soprano voice, he declares "I am yours, Sir John Falstaff!"

He goes on to explain that another wealthy matron, Mistress Page, is equally attracted to him. He hands Pistol and Bardolph each a letter and asks them to deliver them to the ladies, but both men, as a matter of honor, refuse. The page Robin walks in at that moment, accompanied by scurrying violins, and Falstaff assigns the delivery to him.

The remainder of the scene is a long solo for Falstaff, "L'onore! Ladri!" ("Honor! Thieves!"), in which he berates his companions for their disloyalty and soliloquizes on the futility of honor. For this remarkable **scena** Verdi utilizes virtually all of the vocal styles at his command, from the sophisticated recitative so characteristic of *Otello* to the distinctly old-fashioned rapid-fire patter of the opera buffa.

Falstaff picks up the broom and chases the others around the room and finally out the door. The orchestra races to a grandiloquent close, rounding out the scene in the brilliant C major in which it began.

Act One, Scene Two is set in the garden of the Ford home. The delicate perpetual-motion theme in the winds anticipates the light, humorous banter that pervades most of the scene. Meg and Mistress Quickly arrive to find Alice and Nannetta Ford emerging from their house. As in the previous scene, the introductory orchestral passage returns regularly as underpinning for the dialogue. Both Meg and Alice produce letters from Falstaff and are shocked to find that the two are identical. The inherent comedy is highlighted by the reading of portions of the two letters in alternation with their surprised commentary interspersed.

The letters become increasingly ardent. Reading "Facciamo il paio in un amor ridente di donna bella e d'uom appariscente" ("In smiling love let us form a couple, beautiful lady and striking man"), Alice's melody takes flight in a line that could have come from *La traviata*. All the women join in unison on "appariscente" ("striking"). The next line, "e il viso tuo su me risplenderà come una stella sull'immensità" ("and your face will shine on me like a star upon immensity"), inspires a passage of such overwrought chromaticism that it resembles a parody of Wagner. Falstaff's florid prose provokes two full measures of laughter from the women.

Alice speaks the last line of the letter, which requests a reply, and they all begin to hurl insults at Falstaff. This is set as an unaccompanied quartet in which each woman begins to hatch her own plans for his punishment. Like a traditional operatic ensemble, four separate texts are being sung, but in this case all sing the same rhythm so that each syllable is delivered simultaneously with three others.

As they sing the final notes of their quartet, the women exit and are replaced onstage by Ford, Caius, Bardolph, Pistol, and Fenton. The men begin their own ensemble, similarly disparaging Falstaff. Unlike the women, they sing in counterpoint, but each man enters with a variant of the preceding phrase, resulting in **imitation** that is mildly out of kilter. In the background the women are still enumerating their insults.

After the four men have poured out their complaints about Falstaff to Ford, Pistol arrives at the central issue. He tells Ford of the rogue's plan to court his wife and acquire some of his fortune. Bardolph encourages him, first by reminding him of Falstaff's letter to Alice and then by suggesting to Ford that he will soon wear the horns of a cuckold.

The four women come back into the garden. The men and women see each other, but each group believes that they have not been seen. All exit except Nannetta and Fenton. The two young lovers take this opportunity to steal some kisses and to sing a short duet, "Labbra di foco" ("Lips of Fire"). Fenton's demand for more kisses is reminiscent of the love duet in Otello, but the simplicity of both his melody and rhythm emphasizes this couple's youth and innocence. The late Verdi style reveals itself only near the end, when almost the entire spectrum of flat keys is explored. As the other women return and the couple hides behind the bushes, the music pauses briefly in the exotic realm of F-flat major.

The women now begin to plot in earnest. Alice takes the lead by proposing to write Falstaff a letter. Accompanied by a graceful melody in the violins, she proposes to invite him to meet her and decides that Quickly should be the messenger. In the midst of this plotting Quickly notices someone in hiding, and all the women exit except Nannetta.

Fenton emerges from hiding and the two resume their duet, now extended with playful banter.

The men return and Ford relates his plan to visit Falstaff in disguise. They resume their ensemble, with Fenton apart, first commenting to himself on the futility of their scheming and then turning, in an arching melody, to his love for Nannetta. The women appear and reprise their quartet along with the men so that all nine different texts are being sung simultaneously. To add to the musical chaos, the women's ensemble is in a different **meter** from the men's.

The men exit and the women continue their plotting in graphic terms. Led by Alice, they envision Falstaff's belly expanding and then splitting. At this image bassoons and trombones make a precipitous chromatic descent. One final reading of the last lines of Falstaff's letter provokes more laughter, and the hilarity continues through the orchestral passage that closes the act.

Introduced by a jovial orchestral passage, Act Two returns to the Garter Inn, where Falstaff is drinking his sherry with Bardolph and Pistol in attendance. The two offer exaggerated apologies and pledge their loyal service. Bardolph announces the arrival of Quickly, who enters to the accompaniment of a very proper minuet. Curtsying and addressing Falstaff as "Reverenza," she confides that Alice is smitten with him. She has proposed that he visit her between two and three o'clock while her jealous husband is away.

After Falstaff enthusiastically accepts the invitation, Quickly proceeds to reveal that Meg Page is similarly attracted to him. As she characterizes Meg as an angel, the music takes on a somewhat exaggerated romanticism that contrasts with the prevailing lightness. Reveling in this vision of himself as a great seducer, Falstaff gives Quickly a coin for her trouble, and she exits to the strains of the minuet.

Crying "Alice is mine!" he begins a short aria, "Va, vecchio John" ("Go Old John"), which is a musical depiction of pure hubris. The somewhat crass march figure in the bass instruments emphasizes Falstaff's pomposity.

Bardolph now announces the arrival of "Mastro Fontana," who is, of course, Ford in disguise. He carries a bag and is followed by Pistol with a bottle of Cyprus wine that he is bringing as a gift. He comports himself with the same feigned respect that Quickly had displayed. In this duet for two baritones, as in most of *Falstaff*, the orchestra is at least an equal participant, at times doubling one of the vocal lines and at others playing in counterpoint.

With Bardolph and Pistol in the background marveling at his slyness, Fontana begins with gallant pleasantries. He speaks of his wealth and hints that his bag is filled with gold, a fact that is confirmed by the jingling of the triangle as he sets it on the table.

In more lyrical style he tells Falstaff the woeful story of his futile pursuit of Alice Ford. He grows increasingly emotional, reaching toward the top of his vocal range as the chromaticism increases in the orchestra.

Falstaff shifts the key and the mood as he questions why his guest is telling him all of this. Fontana explains that Alice claims to be a paragon of virtue. Imitating her voice, he mocks her warning: "Woe to him who touches me!" With great suavity he makes the unlikely proposal that Falstaff will seduce Alice, assuming that once her false primness has been exposed Fontana will be successful with his own pursuit.

Naturally Falstaff accepts immediately and in his enthusiasm reveals that he already has an invitation to visit Alice between two and three. He goes on to denigrate Alice's husband, calling him a boor and boasting at length that he will make him a cuckold. Taking the gold, he leaves to prepare for his visit, instructing Fontana to wait for him.

Left alone, Ford begins a monologue that rivals any of Verdi's great arias for baritone. Though his tragedy is totally contrived and imagined, Verdi's music suggests that it is no less real to him. "Mastro Ford, Mastro Ford, dormi?" ("Master Ford, Are You Asleep?") is an explosion of fury accompanied by tremolo strings and outbursts in the lower instruments.

Throughout this solo scene the coordination between librettist and composer never falters. Boito captures the kaleidoscopic thoughts of one in a jealous rage, and Verdi's music moves fluidly from fury to cynical humor. He remembers the humiliating reference to the *corna*, the horns of the cuckold, the image of which has now been suggested to him twice. As Ford repeats the word, Verdi, taking advantage of the fact that the orchestral horns are called by the same name, adds a brass fanfare.

As though telling a secret, Ford begins to hatch his plan to trap Falstaff and Alice in the act. As he warms to the idea of such vengeance, he repeats his words again and again in a long **crescendo** reminiscent of Rossini. He reaches a grand climax as he declares "From the bottom of my heart may my jealousy always be praised."

The orchestra extends the triumphant ending, but abruptly dissolves into a dainty little tune as Falstaff, now dapper with hat and cane, walks in and asks Fontana to come with him. The scene ends with a joke as, with false politeness, each insists that the other go through the door first. Finally they compromise and exit together arm in arm as the orchestra "laughs."

Scene Two takes place in a room in the Ford home. A delicate, rapidly moving theme both introduces the scene and propels it forward. Alice, with an acerbic wit that by now has become obvious, proposes to introduce a bill in Parliament that will put a tax on fat people. The other three women come into the room, but Nannetta stands apart. Quickly announces gleefully that their plan is working. She relates what happened when she visited Falstaff in a solo section that approaches the style of an aria with its gracious melodies. She surprises them when she reveals that he will come between two and three. They all repeat her words "dalle due alle tre" in the same rhythm in which she first spoke them to Falstaff.

Laughingly Alice instructs the servants to bring in the laundry basket. Suddenly she notices that Nannetta is not laughing but weeping and asks her the reason for such sadness. The music darkens with gentle, but affecting, chromaticism. She starts three times before she can finish the statement that her father wants her to marry Dr. Caius. The others react with horror and utter as many derogatory descriptions of Caius as they had earlier found for Falstaff. Alice puts an end to the issue by telling her daughter not to worry. Nannetta's joyful reaction clearly implies that she knows who will make the final decision. Simultaneously the orchestra makes a subtle reference to Dr. Caius's "anger theme," which dominated the first scene of the opera.

The basket is placed in the room and, inferring Alice's plan, they all laugh at what a mighty "bombardment" will result when Falstaff is thrown into the river. Hilariously the orchestra depicts the great fall. Now the atmosphere grows more festive as they choreograph their jest. When Alice sings of a "spark of joy in the air," her voice takes flight all the way to a high C.

They hear Falstaff's arrival and all but Alice take their hiding places. She sits at a table and begins to play her lute, whose sound is provided by an offstage guitar. Falstaff walks in and begins to sing to her accompaniment. When he tries to embrace her, she stops playing. He continues his ardent wooing in accompanied recitative, suggesting that it would be good if her husband died so that they could wed.

Now Falstaff begins a short aria, declaring that her beauty, enhanced by his noble title, would be a winning combination. The doubling of his melody by bassoons emphasizes the inherent humor of this pseudoserious song.

They continue their banter with his ardor and her protestations increasing proportionately. When she mentions his plumpness, he responds with a simple aria that resembles a number from a Gilbert and Sullivan operetta. He assures her that when he was in the service of the Duke of Norfolk he was as light, slender, and lithe as a young page.

Falstaff now begins to pursue Alice, but the chase is interrupted by the entrance of Quickly, who announces that Meg has arrived and is in great distress. Falstaff hides behind a screen and Meg enters, her feigned agitation reflected by the turbulent music. She breathlessly reports that Ford, convinced that Alice is entertaining a lover, is on his way to exact revenge.

To this point everything is part of the women's plan, but then Quickly rushes in, almost hysterical, to warn that the furious Ford is actually on the premises. Alice, who has been in total control of the situation, now begins to wonder if their plot has gone awry. Ford, still offstage, cries "Rogue!" and Falstaff, in a shameless pun, responds to the racing violin line by singing "The devil rides on the bow of a violin!"

Ford gives instructions to Fenton, Caius, Bardolph, and Pistol to lock the doors and comb the house. Seeing the basket, Ford assumes his prey is hiding there and begins to throw the laundry on the floor. Throughout all of this the violins maintain their momentum, matching the pace of the action onstage.

Ford runs out of the room and, frantically trying to avoid mayhem, Meg suggests that Falstaff should hide in the basket. Alice responds that he is too large to fit, but he manages to squeeze into it. Meg pretends to be surprised to see him in Alice's room and, desperately needing her help, he declares that it is really she whom he loves.

As Falstaff finally makes it all the way into the basket, the two young lovers enter the room singing a waltz-like duet similar in style to their earlier one. They compare the madness of their love to the insane fury of their elders. Then, as Ford and his companions rush back in, they hide behind the screen and the frantic music resumes.

The men rush around madly without finding their quarry. Suddenly everything comes to a halt as the sound of a kiss is heard from behind the screen. Ford and Caius are sure they have found the offending couple, and as they slowly approach the screen they compete to see who can make the most violent threat to Falstaff.

This unlikely passage is the beginning of one of Verdi's most complex ensembles and a masterpiece of classic opera buffa. Action comes to a halt as Ford and Caius, joined by Pistol and Bardolph, continue to fantasize about Falstaff's punishment; Falstaff tries to escape from the confines of the basket; Quickly and Meg work to keep him there; and Fenton and Nannetta continue to sing of their love. These nine are eventually joined by a chorus of male neighbors who naturally support Ford and moralize about the alleged promiscuity.

Finally Ford decides that the time has arrived to pull back the screen. The whole company is amazed when they see who is behind it, and the orchestra lurches into a foreign key. Momentarily Ford directs his fury on Nannetta and Fenton, warning him to stay away from his daughter.

Bardolph and Pistol now exclaim that they see Falstaff running down the stairs and, as the perpetual motion recommences, all the men rush out in pursuit. Alice takes this opportunity to call the servants to fling the basket into the river. She also directs a page to bring her husband to the window to watch his rival's comeuppance.

After considerable joking about the excessive weight in the basket and encouragement for the servants, the basket is hurled through the window. Everyone cries "Patatrac!" ("Crash!") as the basket with its heavy load hits the river with a great splash, and the orchestra ends the act with triumphant fanfares.

Act Three begins at dusk on a square outside the Garter Inn. This is the only place in *Falstaff* with an extended movement for orchestra. Like so much of the music that precedes it, it is almost totally constructed from a light, rapid passage in perpetual motion. It builds from the bottom, beginning with the basses, and little by little harmony is added and the texture thickens. After a long crescendo the opening gesture returns powerfully, harmonized by full chords.

The curtain opens to reveal Falstaff sitting on a bench in deep thought. He rouses himself, angrily calls the innkeeper, and orders hot wine. In a long-winded recitative he mourns his undeserved fate. He theorizes that if his puffed-up paunch had not buoyed him, he would have drowned and would have died bloated with water. At the word "gonfia" ("bloated") the orchestra illustrates the idea with rapid step-wise passages moving up and down like floods of water.

In this monologue bits of motives that have already been associated with Falstaff appear briefly, paralleling his wandering thoughts. When the wine arrives and he begins to drink, his spirits improve quickly. Describing the effects of drink, he envisions a cricket (*grillo*) that vibrates inside a man who is drunk (*brillo*). The cheerful sky flashes with a trill (*trillo*) and the trill invades the world. Here Boito has provided Verdi with the opportunity for another musical pun. Beginning with a single flute he writes a trill that eventually spreads to every section of the orchestra over the span of thirteen full measures.

Falstaff's reverie is interrupted by the arrival of Quickly who, once again, addresses him as "Reverenza." She begins to speak of "the beautiful Alice" and he interrupts, grumbling "To the devil with the beautiful Alice!" He dramatically recites the miseries he has suffered at her hands, but the persuasive Quickly soon convinces him that everything was the fault of others in the household. As she speaks, the other women, along with Ford, Fenton, and Caius, are hiding and listening to the conversation.

Quickly gives him a letter from Alice and he reads it silently, then aloud: "I shall await you in the Royal Park at midnight. You will come disguised as the Black Huntsman to the Oak of Herne." Quickly then recounts the legend of Herne, a hunter who hanged himself in the oak. Now at night his ghost sometimes returns to the park.

At this point Falstaff wants to speak privately and leads Quickly into the inn. She continues her tale, and outside Alice repeats what Quickly is singing. Eventually Quickly's voice trails off, leaving Alice to finish the story alone. She says that at midnight spirits come to the oak, followed by the Black Huntsman. This portion is accompanied by an eerie funeral march that is interrupted when Nannetta becomes frightened. Alice then comforts her with a suave, but rhythmically off-kilter, waltz assuring her that this is only a fairy tale for children.

She resumes the story, finally arriving at the climax of this black comedy. The hunter has horns growing from his forehead that are getting longer and longer. This line, naturally accompanied by orchestral horns, elicits an outburst from Ford, who cannot contain his glee at the thought of the dreaded symbol of the cuckold on the head of Falstaff.

Alice now begins to make plans for the night's masquerade. Nannetta, dressed in white with a veil and wreath of roses, will play the queen of the fairies. Meg will portray a wood nymph and Quickly, a witch. Alice will bring children dressed as little goblins and devils. Together they will taunt and frighten Falstaff.

They all bid each other farewell and eagerly anticipate their nocturnal escapade. In the meantime Quickly notices that Ford and Caius are engaged in serious conversation, and she stops to listen. Ford is giving the doctor his instructions for the evening. He will dress as a monk and, identifying Nannetta by her white dress, veil, and roses, will bring her to Ford for his blessing of their marriage. Having heard Ford's plan, Quickly hurries away and a shimmering orchestral passage that moves rapidly through a half dozen keys in as many measures anticipates the fantasy of the final scene.

Scene Two is set in Windsor Park around midnight. The Oak of Herne is in the center. Horn calls of foresters sound in the distance, answered by bits of the young lovers' duet "Labro di foco." This signals the entrance of Fenton, who now sings the sonnet "Dal labbro il canto estasïato vola" ("From My Lips the Ecstatic Song Flies"), one of the few true arias of the opera.

Introduced by a short motive played by English horn, Fenton's sonnet elevates the vision of night from its role as the stage for the older characters' bizarre game to the setting for the blossoming of his love. This dual nature of night is expressed by a slight ambiguity between major and minor. At the beginning of the third stanza Fenton sings in declamatory style against a solo English horn that plays the sonnet's opening melody. In the third stanza Nannetta joins in from offstage and the couple reprise two lines from their first-act duet: "A mouth once kissed does not lose its future. Instead it renews itself like the moon." What was originally a minimal accompaniment is now enriched by broken chords on the harp.

This ecstatic passage is interrupted at its climax by the entrance of Alice, who gives Fenton a monk's robe and a mask. He questions her motivation, but she tells him to trust her plan. Now all the participants in the farce take their places in anticipation of Falstaff's arrival. This action is all accompanied by the now-familiar scampering orchestral music.

A solemn passage of ambiguous key and marked by the offbeat accents from the first act's opening gesture announce the approach of Falstaff, dressed ridiculously in cloak and antlers. Bells toll in the distance and he counts twelve chimes. The remarkable accompaniment to his brief soliloquy exemplifies how far Verdi's chromatic musical language had evolved by the end of his career.

A surprising shift to the simplicity of C major announces Alice's arrival. As in their earlier scene, Falstaff pursues her lustily and she resists primly. When Meg appears, he is delighted with the prospect of a "double adventure," but she has come to warn that something frightening is taking place. Alice flees, praying for forgiveness for her sins.

As queen of the fairies, Nannetta appears to gather her tiny charges. Her summons is echoed by a women's chorus from afar. Horrified, Falstaff observes that "These are the fairies. Whoever sees them will die."

The fairies enter to an appropriately dainty accompaniment and form a circle around Nannetta. She sings a charming "fairy song" in two stanzas, each of which is followed by a graceful chorus for the children. The two choral passages contain identical music, but during the first the fairies dance, and in the second they pick flowers.

The musical motion accelerates as all of the principal characters appear in their various disguises. Bardolph and Pistol spy Falstaff lying on the ground and they all feign surprise. Ford cannot resist the insult that he looks like an ox. They all follow his lead and begin to hurl cruel epithets at the unfortunate old man. While this is taking place, Alice warns Nannetta that Caius is looking for her and moves both her and Fenton out of sight.

Now the torture of Falstaff becomes physical. A group of boys dressed as goblins and devils pounces on him singing "Ruzzola" ("Tumble"), "Pizzica" ("Pinch"), "Stuzzica" ("Poke"), "Spizzica!" ("Pick"), "Pungi" ("Prick"), and "Spilluzica" ("Nip") as they perform each of these tortures. There is a momentary silence, and the three wives of Windsor repeat the miniature devils' sadistic chorus.

The four men lift Falstaff to his knees, and they are joined by the women in another chorus of insults. They all demand that he repent for his sins. This leads to a mock liturgical passage in which the three wives pray "Lord, make him chaste" and he responds "but save his abdomen." Their petition changes, but his response remains the same. Virtually every commentary on *Falstaff* points out the obvious similarity between this passage and the *Hostias* section of the *Requiem*.[12] To further secularize this remarkable passage, the men continue their insults and the fairies repeat their "Pizzica" chorus.

Finally the four men, accompanied by brass fanfare, demand that Falstaff agree to repent and he assents. With the overly enthusiastic Bardolph taking the lead, they all continue to taunt him. In his fervor Bardolph loses his hood, and when Falstaff recognizes him, he takes the chance to hurl insults of his own. True to her name, Quickly rapidly pulls Bardolph into the bushes, where she dresses him in a white veil.

One by one, Falstaff recognizes the demonic presences. When he greets "Signor Fontana," Alice formally presents him to her husband, and Quickly addresses him as "Cavaliere" ("Knight") with the same melody as her earlier "Reverenza" greeting. They all now join in a chorus of laughter at Falstaff's expense. In typical fashion he responds that although they may deride him, his wit adds spice to everyone's life.

Changing the subject, Ford announces grandly that there will now be a wedding for the Queen of the Fairies. Another elegant minuet accompanies the entrance of the masked Caius, holding the hand of Bardolph, who is wearing a veil. Everyone admires the handsome couple. Ford is so pleased with his matchmaking that when Alice announces that another couple desires his blessing, he quickly agrees. After he has sanctioned the union of the second pair, he instructs all to remove their masks. Everyone finds the surprising revelations hilarious except Caius, who exclaims "Fright!" and Ford who cries "Betrayal."

Turning to Ford, Falstaff asks "Now who is the humiliated one?" Ford points to Caius and he points back. There is general agreement that it is the two of them, but Alice, adding Falstaff to the group, exclaims "No! It is three."

Nannetta asks her father for forgiveness, while hints of the first-act duet and the "wedding minuet" are heard in the orchestra. Ford blesses her union with Fenton, and the company responds with a hearty hurrah. He then graciously asks everyone, including Falstaff, to dinner.

The culmination of this great work has now arrived. Begun by Falstaff, the characters all join in a brilliant fugue on "Tutto il mondo è burla" ("All the World's a Joke") that, despite certain liberties, contains all of the cerebral musical manipulations that are associated with the genre. In his letter to Boito before he even had the text, Verdi had described it as a "comic fugue." The humor is most clearly heard in the rhythm of the subject, which is related in its abruptness to the first orchestral statement of the opera. Exploring numerous keys and with the principals' parts eventually reinforced by the chorus, the piece comes to a triumphant end, and the orchestra makes a further musical joke with the fugue's subject as the curtain falls.

❊ ❊ ❊

The premiere of *Falstaff* was not perfect. Afterward Verdi made some suggestions to the performers, but soon he came to believe that there were weaknesses in his music. He revised portions of the second and third acts, and the revisions have been performed ever since.

As usual with a new Verdi work, *Falstaff* was soon produced in the major musical capitals, including Vienna, London, and New York. A French version premiered in Paris in May of 1894.

Some traditionalists have always decried the almost total lack of arias in *Falstaff*, and it has never enjoyed the popularity among the general public that many of Verdi's tragedies have. But its subtlety and its brilliant marriage of text and music have become increasingly admired in recent years. Moreover it stands as an example of the ability of a great creative mind to explore new directions even at the beginning of his ninth decade.

8

DEATH OF THE MAESTRO

At the Milan premiere of *Falstaff* and its Rome performances a few months later, Verdi exhibited remarkable vigor and enthusiasm for a man of eighty. Inevitably there was speculation that he might be convinced to compose still another opera, and Boito even broached the subjects of both Antony and Cleopatra and King Lear. Although he never officially closed the door on the possibility, he hinted to friends and associates that he was too old to consider another major project.

Through most of his career Verdi had avoided occasions of public acclaim whenever possible, but now he was more willing to be honored for his remarkable life's work. In 1894 he, Giuseppina, and Boito attended the Paris premiere of *Otello* at the magnificent Palais Garnier. The president of the republic was in attendance and presented him with the Grand Cross of the Legion of Honor. Later Verdi and Giuseppina were guests at a state dinner at the Elysée Palace.

Although he was unwilling to undertake an opera, Verdi continued to compose. In February of 1896 he began to work on a large-scale setting of the Te Deum and then a Stabat Mater. Both of them utilize a large orchestra, and the Te Deum features the massive sonority of a double chorus. The following year they were published by Ricordi, along with the previously composed unaccompanied Laudi and Ave Maria, as the *Quattro pezzi sacri (Four Sacred Pieces)*.

In January of 1896 Verdi had suffered what seemed to be a serious stroke. His hearty constitution prevailed, however, and he recovered within a few days. Sadly, Giuseppina was not so strong. For several years she had suffered with arthritis and gastric discomfort and had gradually lost her appetite. On November 14, 1897, she died of pneumonia at the age of eighty-two.

She had left specific instructions for a simple funeral without music or flowers. The service was held in the Busseto Cathedral with friends like Teresa Stolz and Giulio Ricordi in attendance, and the burial was in the Cimitero Monumentale in Milan. Verdi returned to Sant'Agata, devastated but stoic. He wrote to a friend: "Great grief does not demand great expression; it asks for silence, isolation, I would even say the torture of reflection."[1]

His spirits were boosted by the reception of the *Pezzi sacri*. In the spring of 1898 they were performed (without the Ave Maria) with great success at Paris, and soon afterward Toscanini conducted the three during the International Exhibition at Turin.

Depressed by the loneliness of Sant'Agata, Verdi began to spend more time at his hotel suite in Milan where he could be near his closest friends. He was also actively involved there in his last important act of philanthropy. In 1889, at about the time that he agreed to compose *Falstaff*, he determined to build a retirement home for musicians. He purchased the land on the outskirts of central Milan and began to plan the building with the architect Camillo Boito, the older brother of Arrigo.

In 1896 construction began on the Casa di Riposo per Musicisti (Rest Home for Musicians). It was planned to accommodate one hundred residents in double rooms. Verdi specified that these would be Italian musicians who were sixty-five or older and who found themselves in poverty. The neo-Gothic structure was large and austerely elegant and construction costs were high. As he had done with projects at Sant'Agata, he kept his eye on every aspect of the work, consulting with Boito and visiting the construction site regularly. He also planned for the institution's continuing operation by setting up a foundation with a large sum of cash and the pledge of income from his copyrights.[2]

The Casa di Riposo was formally instituted in December of 1899, but Verdi stipulated that it was not to be occupied until after his death. Consequently, the first residents did not arrive until 1902. He also expressed the wish that he and Giuseppina were to be entombed in the building's courtyard. The rest home, now popularly known as Casa Verdi, still functions as he conceived it. Residents continue to perform in recitals and to coach young musicians.

The Casa di Riposo has inspired two motion pictures. In 1984 the Swiss filmmaker Daniel Schmid produced a documentary, *Il bacio di Tosca* (*Tosca's Kiss*), about the lives of some of the residents. The 2012 film *Quartet*, directed by Dustin Hoffman, depicts life at a fictional retirement home in rural England that is modeled on Casa Verdi.

By the autumn of 1900 Verdi complained of constant fatigue and submitted to being pushed around Sant'Agata in a wheelchair. In December, however, he traveled to Milan and spent Christmas with his intimate friends and his adopted daughter Maria Carrara-Verdi. On January 21, 1901, he suffered a stroke in his suite and survived unconscious for more than five days.

The public reaction to the maestro's final illness resembled that for a head of state. The hotel was draped in black and large crowds gathered outside, awaiting news of his condition. Straw was spread on the street outside to quiet the sound of horses' hooves and carriage wheels. Boito lamented that in his dying Verdi "carried away with him a great quantity of light and vital warmth."

In the early morning of January 27 the great man died quietly. His instructions, like Giuseppina's, specified a simple funeral without music, but with "one priest, one candle, one cross."[3] Because burial at the Casa di Riposo required official permission, he was temporarily laid to rest beside Giuseppina at the Cimitero Monumentale until the move could be made.

The transfer of both bodies on February 28 provided the Milanese with the opportunity for a grand state funeral that Verdi had tried to avoid. Toscanini led a mass choir in the singing of "Va pensiero." A great procession, with various state officials and ordinary citizens walking behind the two coffins, moved from the cemetery to the Casa di Riposo. Thousands lined the streets to watch the cortege pass.

More than just Italy's most important composer, Verdi was the last of the great heroes of the Risorgimento. Ironically Cavour and Manzoni, the two members of that group whom he had most revered, are not generally so well known today outside Italy as he is.

In the long and proud history of Italian music, Verdi's position is unparalleled. He was born into a musical environment whose traditions were venerable, but tired and ossified. Although his immediate predecessors, Rossini, Donizetti, and Bellini, were gifted and eminently successful, Italy was no longer in the mainstream of European music.

Verdi's unique strength lay in his ability to absorb the influence of French and German orchestral richness, harmonic boldness, and formal flexibility without sacrificing the native Italian proclivity for lyrical melody. This is true even in an opera so nearly devoid of traditional arias as *Falstaff*. Thanks to Verdi, Italian opera in the late nineteenth century returned to its seventeenth-century origins as heard in the flowing, dramatically natural style of Monteverdi.

Verdi's most significant successors were the *verismo* composers Ruggero Leoncavallo (1858–1919), Pietro Mascagni (1863–1945), Umberto Giordano (1867–1948), and the immensely popular Giacomo Puccini. Verismo operas dealt with subjects from the everyday life of common people rather than traditional mythological or historical ones. Leoncavallo's *I Pagliacci* (1892) and Mascagni's *Cavalleria rusticana* (1890), with their essentially continuous music and declamatory singing style, owe much to the musical language of Verdi in his late works such as *Aida* and *Otello*. Giordano's *Andrea Chénier* (1896) and such iconic works of Puccini as *La Bohème* (1896), *Tosca* (1900), *Madama Butterfly* (1904), and *Turandot* (1926) embody Verdi's musical credo of combining dramatic realism with Italian lyricism.

One of the most memorable moments in Puccini occurs in the last act of *Turandot* when Calaf finishes the rousing aria "Nessun dorma" and the orchestra surges ahead into the next scene, discouraging applause in order to maintain a realistic dramatic flow. This moment is reminiscent of Aida's "O patria mia," where after a climactic high C the sudden entrance of her father drives the action forward.

On the rare occasions when Verdi offered advice to younger composers, he urged them to remain true to their roots and to emphasize melody. In November of 1900 Giovanni Tebaldini (1864–1952), director of the Parma Conservatory, visited with Verdi during his final month at Sant'Agata. When Verdi asked him if there were any students of great promise at the conservatory, he mentioned the name of Ildebrando Pizzetti (1880–1968), who was to become a successful teacher and composer of both opera and instrumental music. With this the maestro, in what was both credo and valedictory, declared, "Well then, tell him to hold his head high and set himself ever higher goals, and above all remember to be Italian."[4]

NOTES

1. ITALIAN OPERA BEFORE VERDI

1. H. C. Robbins Landon and John Julius Norwich, *Five Centuries of Music in Venice* (London: Thames and Hudson, 1991), 79.

2. Damien Colas, "Melody and Ornamentation," in *The Cambridge Companion to Rossini*, ed. Emanuele Senici (Cambridge: Cambridge University Press, 2004), 120.

3. Stelios Galatopoulos, *Vincenzo Bellini: Life, Times, Music, 1801–1835* (London: Sanctuary Publishing Ltd., 2002), 35.

4. Galatopoulos, 38.

5. Vincenzo Bellini to Carlo Pepoli, 1834, in *Lettere di Vincenzo Bellini*, vol. 2 of *Ricordanze biografiche: Corrispondenze epistolari* (Bologna: Fava e Garagnani, 1881), 30.

2. THE EARLY YEARS

1. The adult Verdi is said to have related the story himself. It is recounted in George Martin, *Verdi: His Music, Life and Times* (New York: Dodd, Mead & Co., 1963), 7–8 and Julian Budden, *Verdi* (London: J. M. Dent & Sons, 1985), 2–3.

2. The instrument is now in the museum of the Teatro alla Scala.

3. Most contemporary reports speculated that her illness was meningitis.

4. Letter to Tito Ricordi, Feb. 4, 1859, in Gaetano Cesari and Alessandro Luzio, eds., *I copialettere di Giuseppe Verdi* (Milan: Forni Editore, 1913), 556–57.

3. CHANGE OF FORTUNE AND "YEARS IN THE GALLEYS"

1. The opera premiered in March of 1842 with Solera's original spelling, but the title was eventually changed to the simpler and more euphonious *Nabucco*.

2. Nicolai's last and best-known opera, *Die lustigen Weiber von Windsor* (*The Merry Wives of Windsor*) (Berlin, 1849), was based on Shakespeare's comedy. Forty-four years later Verdi's last work for the stage was *Falstaff* (La Scala, 1893), whose libretto was adapted from the same work.

3. For a slightly differing account, see Julian Budden, *The Operas of Verdi*, rev. ed., vol. 2 (New York: Oxford University Press, 1992), 91–92.

4. See George Martin, *Verdi: His Music, Life and Times* (New York: Dodd, Mead & Co., 1963), 101–2.

5. Some favor the interpretation that Abigaille is the illegitimate daughter of Nabucco and a slave woman.

6. William Ashbrook, "The Nineteenth Century: Italy," in *The Oxford Illustrated History of Opera*, ed. Roger Parker (New York: Oxford University Press, 1994), 190.

7. Charles Osborne, *The Complete Operas of Verdi* (New York: Alfred A. Knopf, 1969), 50. See also Martin, 103.

8. For a more recent view see Roger Parker's introduction to his edition of *Nabucco* (Milan: Ricordi, 1987), xvi. See also Mary Ann Smart, "Verdi, Italian Romanticism, and the Risorgimento," in *The Oxford Illustrated History of Opera*, 33–39.

9. Since the early Renaissance the intervals of thirds (e.g., C to E), sixths (e.g., C to A), and tenths (an octave plus a third) have been considered to be the most harmonious and sweet sounding.

10. Gaetano Cesari and Alessandro Luzio, eds., *I copialettere di Giuseppe Verdi* (Milan: Forni Editore, 1913), 431.

11. Franco Abbiati, *Giuseppe Verdi*, vol. 1 (Milan: Ricordi, 1959), 643.

12. See Andreas Giger, "French Influences," in *The Cambridge Companion to Verdi*, ed. Scott L. Balthazar (Cambridge: Cambridge University Press, 2004), 121–22.

13. *Copialettere*, 451.

14. *Copialettere*, 62.

4. "SIGNORA VERDI," NEW HOPES FOR ITALY, AND THREE ICONIC OPERAS

1. See Abbiati, 1:732–33.
2. Abbiati, 1:744.
3. Martin, 220, and A. Bonaventura, ed., *Una lettera di Giuseppe Verdi finora non pubblicata* (Florence, 1948).
4. *Copialettere*, 86.
5. *Copialettere*, 55–56.
6. See *Copialettere*, 109.
7. See Abbiati, 2:62.
8. *Copialettere*, 110–11.
9. In Shakespeare, Romeo fled Verona to seek refuge in Mantua, less than thirty miles away.
10. *Copialettere*, 497.
11. A. Luzio, ed., *Carteggi Verdiani*, 4 vols. (Rome: 1935–1947), 1:26.
12. Abbiati, 2:122–23.
13. Letter to Count Opprandino Arrivabene, May 5, 1862, quoted in Abbiati, 15–17.
14. In Piave's libretto, as in the stage version of Dumas, the full contents of the letter are not revealed. In the original novel, however, Marguerite lies, asserting that she is now already involved with another man.
15. Budden, 2:137–38.
16. *Copialettere*, 533.

5. VERDI THE STATESMAN

1. An excellent English history of these events is Steven Runciman, *The Sicilian Vespers* (Cambridge: Cambridge University Press, 1958).
2. See *Copialettere*, 157–59.
3. Translated in Julian Budden, *The Operas of Verdi*, rev. ed., vol. 2 (Oxford: Oxford University Press, 1992), 187.
4. The French text is "Et toi, Palerme," but the Italian version is performed much more often.
5. *Le trouvère*, with a ballet added to the third act of the original, premiered at the Opéra in January 1857.
6. *Copialettere*, 553.

7. See Andreas Giger, "French Influences," in *The Cambridge Companion to Verdi*, ed. Scott L. Balthazar (Cambridge: Cambridge University Press, 2004), 111–38.

8. Julian Budden, *The Operas of Verdi*, rev. ed., vol. 2 (Oxford: Clarendon Press, 1992), 393. As Budden points out, productions that restore the Swedish setting usually substitute "della patria" ("of the homeland") for "d'Inghilterra."

9. Somma's original text indicates that he will send them back to England. In recent productions in which the Swedish setting is restored he makes Anckarström ambassador to Norway.

10. David Patrick Stearns, "Metropolitan Opera's *Un ballo in maschera* a Solid Four-Star Verdi," *Philadelphia Inquirer*, Friday, December 7, 2012.

11. George Martin, "La prima rappresentazione di *Un ballo in maschera* a Boston, 15 marzo 1861," in *Acts of the International Congress of Verdi Studies* (Venice, 1966).

12. Quoted in Budden, 2:427.

13. Abbiati, 2:762.

14. Martin, *Verdi*, 439.

15. *Verdi intimo*, 75. Quoted in Charles Osborne, *The Complete Operas of Verdi* (New York: Alfred A. Knopf, 1970), 351–52.

16. A complete but concise enumeration of the early revisions can be found in Harold Powers, "Verdi's *Don Carlos*: An Overview of the Opera," in *The Cambridge Companion to Verdi*.

17. Martin, 423.

18. Ursula Günther, "La genèse de *Don Carlos*, opera en 5 actes de Giuseppe Verdi, représenté pour la premiere fois à Paris le 11 mars 1867," in *Revue de la Musicologie* 58 (1972), 30.

19. Rudolf Bing, *5000 Nights at the Opera* (New York: Doubleday and Co., 1972), 148–49.

20. Giuseppe Verdi, *Don Carlos, opera in 5 (4) atti*, ed. Ursula Günther (Milan: Ricordi, 1977). This remarkable achievement by Ursula Günther contains text in both languages and all of the music, which has been reassembled from the various versions. The prefatory material provides a complete account of the work's genesis as well as a detailed comparison of the contents of the several versions.

6. RETURN TO MILAN

1. Martin, 429.

2. Abbiati, AGV, 3:142, and Budden, 97.

3. Osborne, 388.

4. There are conflicting versions of the instructions for timing of the entrances of both the large chorus and the principal characters.

5. *Copialettere*, 283.

7. THE FINAL MASTERWORKS

1. James A. Hepokoski, *Giuseppe Verdi, Otello* (Cambridge: Cambridge University Press, 1987), 22.

2. Abbiati, 3:789.

3. Martin, 509.

4. The hotel still operates as the Grand Hotel et de Milan on the Via Alessandro Manzoni.

5. Martin, 509–10.

6. *Copialettere*, 311.

7. *Copialettere*, 323.

8. *Copialettere*, 700.

9. Spike Hughes, *Famous Verdi Operas* (London: Robert Hale, Ltd., 1968), 440.

10. Martin, 537.

11. Abbiati, 4:388.

12. See Osborne, 448, and Budden, *The Operas of Verdi*, 523.

8. DEATH OF THE MAESTRO

1. Quoted in Martin, 558.

2. Rosselli, 186.

3. Frank Walker, *The Man Verdi* (London: Dent, 1962; Chicago: University of Chicago Press, 1982), 509.

4. Marcello Conati, ed., *Encounters with Verdi*, trans. Richard Stokes (Ithaca, NY: Cornell University Press, 1984), 370.

GLOSSARY

aria. A section of an opera in which the action stops and the character reflects on the situation; traditionally in a standard form, arias are the most melodic sections in opera and the most likely to feature vocal display.

arioso. A short vocal passage that has some of the melodic style of an aria but whose rhythm is freer and more speech-like.

banda. A band of wind, percussion, and occasionally strings that was common in certain scenes of nineteenth-century Italian operas. It was separate from the orchestra and was usually onstage.

basso continuo. Accompaniment style that evolved with the beginnings of opera. It usually involved a keyboard instrument or a lute playing chords and a low string instrument doubling the bass line.

bel canto. Style of opera in the early nineteenth century, particularly associated with Rossini, Donizetti, and Bellini; as the term implies, it emphasized beauty of sound and great vocal flexibility.

cantabile. Literally "singable"; normally the first section of a standard two- or three-part aria or ensemble in bel canto opera, it was in a moderate to slow tempo (often andante) and highlighted sensitive phrasing and beautiful vocal sound.

cabaletta. The final section of a bel canto aria or ensemble, livelier than a cantabile. It displayed the singer's vocal agility and usually portrayed a sudden emotional shift to a more agitated, excited, or angry state.

cadence. A progression of harmonies that leads to a temporary final place of repose.

cadenza. An improvisatory passage in a vocal or instrumental composition, usually in virtuosic style.

canon. A composition in which one or more new voices are derived from a single one; most often the original voice begins, followed at regular intervals by the others, each of which sings or plays the same melody.

cavatina. An "entrance aria" in bel canto opera. Normally in two or three contrasting sections, a cavatina was sung when a principal character first appeared on the stage.

chromatic, chromaticism. Containing numerous pitches outside the prevailing key; since the late sixteenth century it has been one of the principal means of expressing strong emotion in music.

coda. An ending section of a vocal or instrumental composition; often in a different tempo from what precedes it.

coloratura. Vocal style characterized by rapid passagework and ornamentation.

consonance, consonant. Two or more pitches sounding together to produce a sense of stability or repose.

counterpoint, contrapuntal. The interaction of two or more individual vocal and/or instrumental parts in a musical texture in which each moves independently.

crescendo. A gradual increasing in the volume of sound; the opposite is decrescendo or diminuendo.

da capo aria. Three-part aria prevalent in the late seventeenth and eighteenth centuries in which an opening section (A) is followed by another (B) that usually contrasts in mood and key. At the end of B, A is repeated, providing the opportunity for the singer to improvise embellishments.

dissonance, dissonant. Two or more pitches sounding together to produce a sense of tension; for centuries a dissonant harmony demanded resolution to a consonant one.

dynamics. The volume of musical sound. Often designated by the composer using standard Italian terms: piano (p) for soft and forte (f) for loud. The abbreviations pp, ppp, etc. and ff, fff, and so on, are used for more extreme degrees of each.

florid. Description of a melodic line, usually in vocal music, that is highly ornamented and contains long passages of rapidly moving notes.

fugue. A contrapuntal, imitative musical genre that evolved in the seventeenth century and reached a high point in the works of J. S. Bach. It typically follows strict structural principles with a principal subject that recurs throughout at different pitch levels.

grand opera. A genre that was extremely popular in Paris during the first half of the nineteenth century. Grand operas were usually based on historical subjects, were in four or five acts, and contained grandiose scenes with a large chorus, orchestra, and ballet.

harmonium. A small reed organ with wind supplied by a bellows controlled by the player's feet.

homophony, homophonic. Musical texture with a single melody accompanied by chords.

imitation, imitative. A contrapuntal technique in which a melody is stated in one part and imitated in one or more others, often at different pitch levels.

intermezzo. One-act comic theater piece that was performed between the acts of a serious opera or spoken drama in the early eighteenth century; precursor to opera buffa.

madrigal. An Italian secular song of the sixteenth and early seventeenth centuries. Madrigals were composed by the greatest composers of the era and were often marked by a very sophisticated relationship between text and music.

meter. The organization of rhythm into recognizable groupings called measures. In traditional music the number of beats in each measure usually remained consistent throughout a passage.

opera buffa. Comic genre that evolved in the early eighteenth century that often featured stock characters and situations.

parlando. The most speech-like form of recitative, often with many syllables sung on a single pitch.

parlante. A passage of recitative in which the singer declaims the text in speech rhythm on one or a few pitches while the orchestra plays a melodic line.

pizzicato. The plucking of a string instrument rather than producing the sound with the bow (*arco*).

recitative (Italian *recitativo*). The narrative, conversational passages in opera, usually in free rhythm that imitates speech and with minimal melodic interest. Dry (*secco*) recitative was originally accompanied only by basso continuo. Accompanied (*accompagnato*) recitative featured orchestral accompaniment and the vocal line tended to be more melodic.

romanza. A short aria, usually in a slow tempo.

scena. A scene for a principal character that includes various types of recitative and arioso; usually precedes and instigates a formal aria.

sonata form (sonata-allegro). The standard classical structure used for the first movements of symphonies, string quartets, and other multimovement works. It was based on the presentation of at least two musical ideas, followed by their development and eventual return with adjustments of key.

sotto voce. Literally "under voice"; a sung whisper.

staccato. Performance style in which notes are shortened with spaces of silence between them.

stretta. A section added to the end of a bel canto opera ensemble in which the tempo becomes markedly faster.

syncopation. Rhythmic effect in which a relatively long note is written on a beat that is normally weak.

tempo. The speed of a musical passage.

tremolo, tremolando. The rapid alternation by an instrument between two pitches. Although many instruments can perform a tremolo, the technique became widely used in the string section to produce a romantic, shimmering effect.

trill. Vocal or instrumental ornament that involves a rapid alternation between two adjacent pitches.

virtuoso, virtuosity, virtuosic. A performer who displays consummate technical ability; the adjective may describe such a performance or the style of music that demands such prowess.

SELECTED READING

Balthazar, Scott L. *The Cambridge Companion to Verdi*. Cambridge: Cambridge University Press, 2004. Contains independent chapters by Verdi specialists on specific and diverse topics.

Budden, Julian. *The Operas of Verdi*. 3 vols. Oxford: Oxford University Press, 1992. The most thorough study in English of all of the operas; features detailed historical background and musical analysis.

———. *Verdi*. New York: Schirmer Books, 1985. A comprehensive one-volume study of life and works by an important Verdi scholar.

Conati, Marcello, ed. *Encounters with Verdi*. Translated by Richard Stokes. Ithaca, NY: Cornell University Press, 1984. A fascinating collection of first-person accounts of interaction with Verdi.

Grout, Donald J., and Hermine Weigel Williams. *A Short History of Opera*. 4th ed. New York: Columbia University Press, 2003. A classic 1947 general history of the genre that has been extensively updated.

Hughes, Spike. *Famous Verdi Operas*. London: Robert Hale, Ltd., 1968. A subjective guide for the amateur by a British jazz musician and polymath.

Kimbell, David. *Italian Opera*. New York: Cambridge University Press, 1994. A detailed history of Italian opera from its beginnings.

Martin, George. *Verdi: His Music, Life, and Times*. New York: Dodd, Mead & Co., 1963. One of the classic Verdi biographies; detailed but immensely readable.

Osborne, Charles. *The Complete Operas of Verdi*. New York: Alfred A. Knopf, 1970. This study provides background information on the operas and vividly describes the musical high points of each. Also includes the *Requiem* and other significant works.

Phillips-Matz, Mary Jane, and Andrew Porter. *Verdi: A Biography*. New York: Oxford University Press, 1993. A magisterial work that was the result of thirty years of research; as the title indicates, the focus is biography with little analysis of the music.

Pistone, Danièle. *Nineteenth-Century Italian Opera from Rossini to Puccini*. Translated by E. Thomas Glasow. Portland, OR: Amadeus Press, 1995. The detailed information in this small volume provides an interesting glimpse into Verdi's musical environment.

Rosselli, John. *The Life of Verdi*. Cambridge: Cambridge University Press, 2000. A brief work that manages to provide a vivid picture of the composer and to include some thought-provoking musical commentary.

Walker, Frank. *The Man Verdi*. New York: Knopf, 1962; Chicago: University of Chicago Press, 1982. A subjective and selective biography by a brilliant amateur scholar.

Weaver, William, and Martin Chusid, eds. *A Verdi Companion*. London: Gollancz, 1980. An appealing collection of essays by a wide variety of scholars, composers, and philosophers.

SELECTED LISTENING

For each work that is analyzed in the text an audio compact disc and a digital video disc (DVD) are recommended. For the most popular works there are numerous choices. The selection here covers a chronological span of more than fifty years and includes some of the major artists who have been associated with Verdi performance. The dates are those of the performances, not the release of the discs.

OPERAS

Tutto Verdi (suggested for *Oberto*) is a collection of all twenty-six of Verdi's operas and the *Requiem* on DVD (HD and Blu-ray formats). This enormous project was organized by the Fondazione Teatro Regio di Parma/Festival Verdi Parma to celebrate the composer's bicentennial. The most significant contribution of this *Tutto Verdi* is the provision of video recordings of the less-performed works such as *Oberto*.

Oberto, Conte di San Bonifacio (1839)
(DVD) Teatro Regio di Parma; Parodi, Pentcheva, Allemandi, cond.; Tutto Verdi 72014, 2006. Parma's Teatro Regio was the closest major opera house to Verdi's birthplace. The theater has historically prided itself on its performance of his works.
(CD) Academy of Saint Martin in the Fields, London Voices; Ramey, Guleghina, Urmana, Marriner, cond.; Decca 4784169, 1996. Bass Samuel Ramey, at the height of his career, is superb in the title role, and the two female leads are excellent.

Nabucco (1842)
(DVD) Metropolitan Opera; Guleghina, Pons, Ramey, Levine, cond.; Deutsche Grammophon (DG) 0730779, 2002. This is a visually stunning performance with a stellar cast. The highly dramatic Guleghina is well suited for the role of the half-crazed of Abigaille.
(CD) Deutsche Oper; Cappuccilli, Domingo, Dimitrova, Sinopoli, cond.; DG 4105122, 1983. This is a superior performance in every respect. Dimitrova is a particularly fiery Abigaille, and Domingo is superb as Ismaele.

Ernani (1844)
(DVD) La Scala; Domingo, Freni, Muti, cond.; Warner EMI 13192642, 1982. La Scala was Verdi's musical home at the beginning and end of his career, and performances of his works there are usually memorable. All of the principals are in superb voice, and Muti is a passionate Verdian maestro.
(CD) Metropolitan Opera; Bergonzi, Price, Schippers, cond.; Sony 88691909962, 1962. This is a release of a live broadcast. Bergonzi was among the greatest Italian tenors of the twentieth century, and Price was one of the supreme sopranos of any era.

Macbeth (1847, rev. 1865)
(DVD) Metropolitan Opera; Lučić, Guleghina, Pittas, Levine, cond.; EMI 2063049, 2008. An effective modern staging with solid singing and acting. As usual, Levine and the great Met orchestra and chorus are outstanding.
(CD) La Scala; Cappuccilli, Verrett, Ghiaruov, Domingo, Abbado, cond.; DG 4497322, 1976. A stellar cast and insightful conducting by Abbado.

Rigoletto (1851)
(DVD) Staatskapelle, Dresden; Lučić, Damrau, Florez, Luisi, cond.; EMI 418689, 2008. Magnificently sung by the three principals. The coloratura of Damrau and Florez is dazzling.
(CD) La Scala; Gobbi, Callas, di Stefano, Serafin, cond.; Regis RRC2076, 1955. A classic performance. The legendary Callas, at the height of her career, is vocally elegant as Gilda.

Il trovatore (1853)
(DVD) Metropolitan Opera; Pavarotti, Zajick, Marton, Milnes, Levine, cond.; DG 0730029, 1988. Along with Levine's excellent conducting, Pavarotti is in the prime of his career, and Zajick gives a riveting performance as Azucena.
(CD) Maggio musicale fiorentino; Pavarotti, Banaudi, Verrett, Nucci, Mehta, cond.; Decca 001652002, 1990. Mehta leads a commanding performance with a distinguished cast. Verdi considered Azucena to be the central character of *Il trovatore* and here Verrett makes her so.

La traviata (1853)
(DVD) Royal Opera; Fleming, Calleja, Hampson, Pappano, cond.; OpusArte OA1040D, 2009. A very strong cast led by Fleming. Although she has some slight technical problems, her voice is rich and beautiful, and she gives a nuanced account of the role.
(CD) La Scala; Callas, di Stefano, Bastianini, Giulini, cond.; EMI 5664502, 1955. Callas is in her prime in one of her most celebrated roles.

Un ballo in maschera (1859)
(DVD) Salzburg Festival; Barstow, Domingo, Nucci, Solti, cond.; Arthaus 107271, 1990. This is a dramatically powerful performance with the setting restored to Sweden. Barstow and Domingo own the roles of Gustav and Amelia. Solti conducts an energetic and gripping performance.

(CD) La Scala; Callas, di Stefano, Gobbi, Votto, cond.; EMI 3192752, 1956. This is a live performance and there is also a studio recording with the same cast. Each has its adherents. Callas is in excellent voice, and her superb acting comes across even without video.

Don Carlos (Don Carlo) (1867, revised in Italian 1884)

(DVD) (Italian) Metropolitan Opera; Domingo, Freni, Bumbry, Ghiaurov, Levine, cond.; DG 0734085, 1983. Levine's interpretation of the later works is always insightful and probing. The cast is superb in every respect.

(CD) (Italian) Metropolitan Opera; Corelli, Rysanek, Dalis, Tozzi, Herlea, Adler, cond.; Sony 88697910042, 1964. A live radio broadcast that features Franco Corelli in one of his favorite roles. He, Rysanek, and Herlea give particularly passionate performances.

(DVD) (French) Vienna Staatsoper; Vargas, Tamar, Michael, Miles, de Billy, cond.; Arthaus 107187, 2004. A historic performance of the original, unabridged 1867 version.

Aida (1871)

(DVD) Metropolitan Opera; Millo, Domingo, Zajick, Milnes, Levine, cond.; DG 0730019, 1989. A visually spectacular production with a stellar cast. Millo and Domingo shine as the tragic lovers.

(CD) Vienna Philharmonic and Singverein; Tebaldi, Bergonzi, Simionato, MacNeil, von Karajan, cond.; Alto ALC2009, 1959. A classic recording with magnificent orchestra, conductor, and singers. The great Tebaldi was a protégée of Toscanini and thus had impeccable Verdi credentials.

Otello (1887)

(DVD) La Scala; Domingo, Frittoli, Nucci, Muti, cond.; Arthaus 107090, 2001. Otello had its premiere at La Scala, and this performance does honor to the theater's heritage. The title role was a Domingo specialty, and Muti is masterful in this repertoire.

(CD) Vienna Philharmonic; Del Monaco, Tebaldi, Protti, Von Karajan, cond.; Decca 4759984, 1961. By the time of Otello Verdi had become a master of orchestration, and the Vienna Philharmonic performs it superbly. Desdemona was one of Tebaldi's signature roles, and her voice was still stunning in 1961.

Falstaff (1893)

(DVD) Metropolitan Opera; Plishka, Freni, Horne, Lopardo, Levine, cond.; DG 0734532, 1992. This Zeffirelli production features an excellent cast of singer/actors. Levine leads a brilliantly paced performance.

(CD) Berlin Philharmonic; Terfel, Pieczonka, Kotscherga, Hampson, Abbado, cond; DG 4711942, 2001. Terfel inhabits the title role with brio, and the Berlin Philharmonic plays beautifully under Abbado.

CHORAL WORKS

Messa di Requiem (1874)

(DVD) La Scala; Price, Cossotto, Pavarotti, Ghiaurov, Von Karajan, cond.; DG 0734055, 1967. This is a historic performance with the young Price and Pavarotti. The La Scala orchestra and chorus excel under Von Karajan.

(CD) NBC Symphony, Westminster Choir; Milanov, Castagna, Björling, Moscona, Toscanini, cond.; Music and Arts MACD1269, 1940. Toscanini played the cello at the La Scala premiere of Otello and eventually conducted numerous memorable Requiem performances. Milanov and Björling were among the greatest singers of the era. Remastered in 2012.

Quattro pezzi sacri (1898)
(CD) Philharmonia Chorus and Orchestra; Schwarzkopf, Ludwig, Gedda, Ghiaurov, Giulini, cond.; EMI 0852192, 1964. Contains the *Four Sacred Pieces* as well as the *Requiem*. All four soloists and Giulini are exceptional.

CHAMBER MUSIC

String Quartet in E Minor (1873)
(CD) Amadeus Quartet; DG E4775739, 2005. This is a creditable performance of this seldom-recorded work. Also includes quartets by Bruckner and Smetana.

INDEX

ABOUT THE AUTHOR

Donald Sanders is professor of music at Samford University in Birmingham, Alabama. He studied at the University of South Carolina, Michigan State University, and Northwestern University and holds a PhD in musicology from the University of Kansas. He has published articles in American and British journals on eighteenth-century Italian keyboard music and seventeenth-century solo song. He is a contributor to the *New Grove Dictionary of Music and Musicians*, second edition and the author of *Music at the Gonzaga Court in Mantua*. He has been the recipient of two teaching awards and has led several student tours of Italy.

CPSIA information can be obtained at www.ICGtesting.com
Printed in the USA
BVOW07*0941221113

336886BV00004B/9/P